I0820639

Pierre-Alain Croset

Corvino + Multari
Architecture in dialogue with the city

CORVINO + MULTARI

Marsilio Arte

ARCHITECTURE AS DIALOGUE

1 A. Isozaki, 'Corvino + Multari e Renato Sarno, Restauro del Grattacielo Pirelli–Premio Speciale per il Restauro', in F. Irace (ed.), *Medaglia d'Oro all'Architettura Italiana 2006* (Milan, 2006), 50.

With a design approach that is both pragmatic and experimental, always rigorous and moved by a strong ethical tension, over thirty years Vincenzo Corvino and Giovanni Multari have realised architectural work that is very consistent in terms of quantity and quality. Their precocious talent led to their soon winning important competitions in Cosenza and Milan, and to the opening of their associate studio in Naples in 1995, coincided with the opening of the first construction sites. As early as the realisation of Piazza dei Bruzi in Cosenza (1995–98), they invited Mimmo Paladino to collaborate, displaying a singular affinity with contemporary art, which has never been disavowed since then, while soon afterwards the exemplary restoration project on the Pirelli Skyscraper in Milan (1998–2005) was hailed internationally for the rigour and philological respect with which it returned the architecture of Gio Ponti and Pier Luigi Nervi to its original splendour. In this regard, it is interesting to reread the motivations with which Arata Isozaki, as president of the jury of the Gold Medal to Italian Architecture in 2006, defended the awarding of the Special Prize for Restoration to this 'perfectly executed' intervention, which revealed the astounding topicality of the Pirelli Skyscraper. In the words of Isozaki, the building, 'returned to the condition when it had just been built', must be appreciated as 'a historic and at the same time still wholly contemporary work', which continues to possess 'a superior architectural quality compared to all the new works presented today'.[1] Simi-

2 B. Gravagnuolo, 'Introduzione, Leggere geometrie', in V. Corvino, G. Multari, *I rivocati: programma integrato di interventi a Cosenza* (Castellammare di Stabia, 2002), 14.

3 A. Izzo, 'Prefazione', in V. Corvino, G. Multari, *I rivocati*, 13.

larly to what has been stated by Isozaki, subsequently Corvino and Multari did not want to separate their design activity in the field of restoration, the reuse and upgrading of the existing, representing the most consistent part of their production, from that involving new buildings, because for them every project is always born from the critical interpretation of the urban or landscaping context and from study of the history of locations, but at the same time it must respond to our contemporary condition, to the mutations of functional programmes and the emergence of new lifestyles.

A precocious maturity and a significant methodological consistency characterise Corvino and Multari's work. The first critical writings devoted to their work recognised these characteristics of maturity and consistency from the very start. In a small publication from 2002 devoted to the Integrated Intervention Plan in the Rivocati district of Cosenza, the Neapolitan historian Benedetto Gravagnuolo was the first to recognise Corvino and Multari as 'a sure point of reference, beyond their youthful age', highlighting how rare it was 'to find so much expressive maturity in the work of two architects aged under forty'.[2] In the same publication, Alberto Izzo, recognised by them as the most important figure in their years of training at the School of Architecture in Naples, commented on their 'consistent research around the themes of a minimalist figuration', underlining how their first architectures were the 'result of extensive reconnaissance in the various contemporary formal researches'. He too saw their precocious maturity reveal itself in overcoming 'the youthful enthusiasm [that] projected them into studying all the fixed stars in their architectural firmament,' including Herzog & De Meuron, Souto de Moura, Chipperfield and Byrne, to finally affirm that 'their intellectual vivacity has gradually led to their raising some doubts and employing more careful work of selection and research.' His concluding judgment was that of an authentic master who did not restrict himself to best wishes to suit the occasion, but rather affirmed 'with conviction' that the promises expressed by the first projects realised 'will be maintained, and the good star that has favoured their youthful debut will not abandon them, due to their constant desire to get to know, to assimilate and above all to continually question themselves.'[3]

A few years later, this promise was indeed maintained, and the *corpus* of the works realised or solely designed had already grown considerably, to the point of enabling the publication in 2005 of a monograph devoted to their first ten years of activity.[4] In a brief and equally pointed critical comment, Valerio Paolo Mosco used the expression 'strategy of order' to characterise Corvino and Multari's design method, an expression taken up subsequently by the architects themselves in numerous writings.[5] Mosco was the first to highlight the need to consider their architecture more in its strategic value that in its poetic dimension, defining this strategy as 'a disenchanted *modus operandi* that observes the environment surrounding us, distances itself from it and seeks to regulate it with calibrated moves, without falling into that moralistic detachment that has afflicted architecture around these parts for years.'[6] The critical reception of Corvino and Multari's work is essentially manifested in publications devoted to a single building, with only a limited number of texts seeking to record the individual works analyzed within a broader critical perspective. Among the few examples to be cited, in a publication on the pages of the magazine *The Plan* in 2011 devoted to the residences in Piazza Molino in Cosenza, Luigi Prestinenza Puglisi did not restrict himself to commenting on this specific work, but rather sought to characterise Corvino and Multari's entire production as 'refined and elegant research, cautiously experimental, but with a careful eye on the tradition and the context, pragmatic in its technological choices,' to conclude with the forecast that 'among the ten Italian professional studios that will be most under the spotlight in the next twenty years, in terms of the number and quality of their works, there will be Corvino and Multari.'[7] Indeed, the studio's production continued to grow in numbers and quality in the years that followed, leading to the publication of a second monograph in 2017, edited by Pino Scaglione,[8] with the exhaustive publication of six buildings realised at the centre of the attention. More recently, Marco Mulazzani, who already as editor of *Casabella* magazine since 2001 had devoted particular critical attention to the work of the Neapolitan duo,[9] dedicated a very detailed monograph[10] to one single important building: the new Public Prosecutor's Office of Catanzaro in the former convent of the Order of Observant

4 G. Bonelli, *Corvino + Multari 1995-2005* (Naples, 2005).

5 The small publication from 2018 that takes up the title of the essay by Valerio Mosco is to be considered a genuine theoretical manifesto of their positions: V. Corvino, G. Multari, *The Strategy of Order* (Divisare Books n. 149; Rome, 2018).

6 V. P. Mosco, 'La strategia dell'ordine di Corvino e Multari', in G. Bonelli, *Corvino + Multari 1995-2005*, 84.

7 L. Prestinenza Puglisi, 'Made in Italy: Corvino+Multari', *The Plan*, 49 (2011), 40.

8 G. P. Scaglione (ed.), *Corvino + Multari Esperienze dell'architettura / Architecture Experiences 2007-2017* (Milan, 2017). The six buildings realised that are illustrated in the monograph are the temporary schools in L'Aquila, the La Cartiera shopping centre and park in Pompeii, the restoration of the Covered Market in Reggio Emilia, the primary school in Carate Brianza, the PEEP dwellings in Naples-Quarto and the parish church complex in Dresano.

9 As editor-in-chief of the annual *Almanacco di Casabella* devoted to young Italian architects, M. Mulazzani published four of their buildings: 'Programma Integrato di Interventi' (2001), 63–7; 'Sistemazione di viale Omero e piazzale Gabrio Rosa, Milano' (2003), 54–9; 'Edificio per uffici a Casoria, Napoli' (2004), 42–7; 'Recupero del Quartiere Militare Borbonico' (2008), 60–5. In 2005 he published the restoration of the Pirelli Skyscraper on the pages of *Casabella*: M. Mulazzani, 'Il Pirelli ritrovato', in *Casabella*, 733 (2005), 78–87.

10 M. Mulazzani (ed.), *Costruire nella città / Building in the City. La Procura della Repubblica di Catanzaro / The Catanzaro Public Prosecutor's Office* (Milan, 2023).

11 M. Mulazzani, 'Progettare nella città / Designing in the city', *Casabella*, 944 (2023), 29.

12 The general manager of the state property agency Alessandra dal Verme, the public prosecutor of Catanzaro Nicola Gratteri, the director of the superintendence Stefania Argenti, the president of Rina S.p.A. Ugo Salerno, the head of the restoration project Fiammetta Adriani, the project manager of structures Gianluca Ciullo and the works manager Fabio De Falco all write in the monograph, as well of course as Mulazzani, Corvino and Multari.

13 V. Corvino, G. Multari, 'Imparare dalle città / Learning from Cities', in M. Mulazzani (ed.), *Costruire nella città / Building in the City*, 65 and 67.

14 Cf. the following quotation, in which they affirm that the project 'is process, which works with different programmes, on very different territories and cities, which is in dialogue every time with interlocutors who change and which must correspond to a response with respect to the needs, demands and aspirations both of those who commission the architecture and of an entire community to which the project will have to belong'. V. Corvino, G. Multari, *The Strategy of Order*, 6.

Friars Minor (2017–22), an exemplary public work the final quality was also made possible thanks to a virtuous procedure that avoided recourse to the integrated contract, as Mulazzani himself writes, 'enabling the group of professionals appointed to retain responsibility for all the phases of design and execution, that is, the works management as well as the artistic, structural and restoration work management.'[11] The interest of this publication lies in the choral form of the story, which involved all the protagonists of the endeavour: not only Corvino and Multari with their partners for all the specialist designs, but also the client, the user body, those with responsibility from the municipality and the superintendence, the works managers and the companies.[12] In the same volume, Corvino and Multari express how in recent years their work is 'increasingly freed from the condition of operating individually, in favour of a form of shared participation', deeming it necessary to consider 'the occasion of construction as a service to the community', but at the same time recognising how in this shared action 'one cannot avoid the architect's role in pursuing that "right to beauty" to which our communities must aspire.'[13]

To put together the critical story of their first thirty years of work, I proposed using the literary form of the dialogue to Corvino and Multari. There are several reasons to justify this choice. Firstly, it is their architecture itself that has always possessed a specific quality of dialogue: the architecture is in dialogue with the city, with the landscape and with all the pre-existing elements, the new is in dialogue with the old, the inside spaces with the outer skin of the façade, the traditional materials with the more innovative construction systems, the local culture with the international references. Secondly, their design method is based on a rare capacity for listening and dialogue with all the actors involved in the complex process of conception and realisation:[14] far removed from any demiurgic conception of the work of the architect, they practise the craft in continuous dialogue with clients, consultants and collaborators, with artists, historians and archaeologists, with the superintendences and the skilled workers at the construction site. Thirdly, I think that my role as a critic must also take on the dimension of a dialogue. More than imposing my own vision and my own interpretative reading, as happens in the dogmatic forms of criticism, I am interested in

15 These materials were gathered and made available by Marco Poerio, whom I wish to thank for his generous and precious collaboration during all the phases of the development of this book.

16 Conversations recorded on 29 July, 9 August, 18 September, 4 November, 13 November, 20 November, 25 November, 11 December, 23 December 2024 and on 7 January, 10 January, 18 January, 22 January and 29 January 2025.

a dialogue with the authors, posing questions, underlining contradictions and sometimes disagreements, attempting to tease out the reasons and the complex processes that are concealed behind the physical evidence of the constructed architecture. The construction of the story is therefore based on a double task, which is accomplished, on one hand, through the gaining of awareness and the systematic analysis of all the projects through the materials of the Corvino and Multari studio archive,[15] and on the other with the recording of twenty or so hours of conversations with the architects, in their studio or remotely.[16] In beginning these conversations in the summer of 2024, I did not yet have a clear idea of how to structure the book, and I therefore considered the first recordings as functional to an enrichment of my knowledge of their work, but also and above all to getting to know Corvino and Multari's thought and design method better. Even subsequently, when the concept for the book had become more defined, I continued to propose that these conversations, even though recorded, had to be evaluated as fragments of a future text, yet to be written, rather than as a document or an oral testimony to be transcribed literally, as may happen with journalistic interviews. Vincenzo Corvino and Giovanni Multari lent themselves with great enthusiasm, generosity and intellectual honesty to this delicate exercise of revisiting the thirty years of their professional and cultural path. From their past there re-emerged not only memories, but also conflicts and contradictions, and my role changed: as I gradually proceeded in deepening my knowledge, more than continuing to pose questions seeking explanations or simply information on the projects, I was interested in bringing into play my own general reflections on the architect's work and my interpretative hypotheses, to be confirmed or disproved.

The final story is not, therefore, a simple transcript of fragments of interviews, but rather the result of a complete rewriting, on the basis of a structure of six themed chapters, with a different form of assembly with respect to the original sequence of the recorded dialogues. Each chapter is composed of two parts: the text of the dialogue, illustrated with small images of reference, is followed by a portfolio of full-page photographs and drawings, to enrich the knowledge of the most important projects, accompanied by a brief descriptive note.

17 **The only exception is the Capodimonte Museum, of which only one completed part has been able to be photographed, while other parts that are still under construction are represented with drawings.**

Overall, fifty-four projects are discussed in the story, and only around half of these, twenty-six, are illustrated in the portfolio, of which sixteen realised and therefore represented with photographs,[17] and six currently under construction, described with only perspective views. The last four are projects in competitions not won, unjustly ignored by the critics but meriting attention for their great quality and importance within the work of Corvino and Multari as a whole: they are the projects for the Temple–Cathedral of Pozzuoli (2004), for the Polcevera Park in Genoa (2019), for the new headquarters of the Tuscany Regional Authority and the restructuring of the stadium designed by Pier Luigi Nervi in Florence, both from 2022. A significant part of the contents of the book are entirely previously unpublished, also due to a marked intensification in the studio's recent production: of the ninety-six projects listed in the register of the works, more than a quarter—twenty-five—have been developed in the last five years, while there are no less than twenty-one buildings currently under construction, which will be completed by 2028. Other monographs may therefore emerge in the near future.

The story in dialogue form delineates some paths of interpretation through thirty years of work, highlighting the conceptual relations between the various projects, the recurring themes, the methodological constants, the processes of development, but also the profound mutations in the architects' work. The organisation of the six chapters only partially follows a chronological order; it intersects with a thematic structure that is intended to transcend the traditional classifications of architecture in terms of types and programmes. In the first chapter ('Public spaces and urban connections'), the first works realised in Cosenza are discussed in relation to the theme of the university and professional training, but also to the particular political conditions of the 1990s, which in Italy had led to a season of competitions, which were fundamental in enabling a new generation of talented architects to emerge. The theme of urban connections is common to the projects for piazzas and for commercial spaces conceived as *passages*, standing out among which is the La Cartiera shopping centre in Pompeii, an important work yet barely considered by the critics, which is particularly interesting due to the fact that it relates together different scales of intervention, but also different project dimensions, being an intervention of restoration of the modern, of the architecture of interiors and architecture of the landscape, all at the same time. In the second chapter ('Monumental restorations'), the theme of the dialogue with artists, inaugurated with Piazza dei Bruzi in Cosenza and the participation of Mimmo Paladino, is considered together with a discussion of a series of significant monumental restoration projects in Naples (Torre delle Nazioni, Tempio della Scorziata, Aragonese Castle in Baia), while the two cornerstones of Corvino and Multari's work are compared in the middle of the story: the Pirelli Skyscraper and Capodimonte Museum. In both cases the complex process of development of the project and its realisation is analyzed, coming about from a competition in Milan, and from an innovative and virtuous project financing procedure in Naples, in relation to the very contemporary issue of ecological transition, while other general themes in the field of restoration are discussed, associated with the use of materials, the insertion of technological systems, philological reconstruction and anastylosis. In the third chapter ('Representation buildings') a large number of projects are discussed—no less than fourteen—starting with the theme of metamorphosis and the modification of the existing. Beginning with a series of small interventions on the façades or in the interiors of buildings without any monumental value, the dialogue proceeds with the examination of the important project for the Public Prosecutor's Office of Catanzaro, with reflections that associate the theme of the heritage values of historical architecture with that of the repurposing of institutional buildings. These reflections lead onto the theme of architectural language, and its values of representation in both the relationship between existing and new and the expression of contemporary forms of abstraction that characterise certain interesting recent projects, such as the headquarters of the Tuscany Regional Authority in Florence and the Italian Embassy in Nairobi. The fourth chapter ('The house inside the house') introduces a reflection on the ways in which Corvino and Multari intervene as contemporary architects inside historic buildings ruined by the ravages of time, first in the exemplary competition project for the Temple–Cathedral of Pozzuoli, and subsequently in the old Customs House in Avellino, currently in the construction phase, through the compositional instrument of the inclusion of autonomous volumes inside other volumes. This compositional theme transcends programmes and contexts, intersects with the theme of the dialogue between architecture and archaeology in the interventions in ancient buildings, while it takes on extraordinary expressive power in the project for the restructuring of the stadium in Florence, with the spectacular gesture of the new terraces that are raised up, like huge unfurled wings, above the line of height of the pre-existing stadium, enabling, thanks to the force and clarity of this gesture, the historical architecture of Nervi to be fully preserved. Finally, in kinship with these projects, the noteworthy church in Dresano is discussed, the spatial device of which recalls the theme of the 'house inside the house'. The fifth chapter ('The functions of inhabiting: residences and schools') is the only one in which buildings and projects are grouped together according to a classification by type. The theme of urban connections returns in the first residential projects; this theme was already discussed in the first chapter, not only in the realisation of the block in Piazza Molino in Cosenza, but also in the interesting 'I Portici' competition project in Frosinone, in which the volume of a single large building is folded up to create an urban system of courtyards, passages and crossings. The theme of the prefabricated construction as a strategic response to extreme conditions is discussed on the subject of the temporary residences and schools realised in 2009 following the earthquake in L'Aquila, while similar questions associated with the reduction of costs feed the research into other social housing projects in Naples and Cosenza. More recently, Corvino and Multari have associated the theme of residence with that of the reinstatement of the existing in two significant projects that are currently in the construction phase: the first, in Capua, concerns the very topical issue of the energy-saving and structural upgrading of the public housing neighbourhoods of the post-war period, while the second, for Palazzo Frisini in Taranto, proposes a significant synthesis between the research into residence and the theme of monumental restoration, with changes of intended use in historical contexts. In the sixth and final chapter ('De-

18 See B. Gravagnuolo, 'Un recupero esemplare. "L'AltraReggia": un centro di incontro tra culture diverse', Il giornale dell'architettura, 64 (2008), 16–8. The author states that this exemplary intervention has 'the added value of being emblematic of a new way of thinking about the protection of Italy's historical heritage'.

19 V. Corvino, G. Multari, 'I colori delle idee. Progetti come conoscenza di storie, contesti e luoghi', in M. Balzani, F. Maietti (editor), *Colore e materia*, Rimini 2010, p. 221.

commissioned locations'), finally, the discussion concerns the design strategies of the urban regeneration of abandoned buildings and sites, a theme that is increasingly central in the studio's recent activities, even though it had already been tackled more than twenty years ago with the restoration of the Bourbon military quarter in Casagiove.[18] Many projects concern state properties, once used as barracks, warehouses or workshops, brought back to life through complex competition procedures activated by the State Property Agency, which has taken on the role of a driving force in recent years. In the middle of the chapter, the dialogue considers the series of projects and buildings realised in Mantua—a school in a former factory, a new gymnasium and the conversion of a series of sheds connected by an organic system of spaces and public pathways—which in some ways represents the most complete synthesis between an intervention on the existing and new building, also considering the significant renewal of the public role of the architect.

To conclude, this story in dialogue form would like to contribute to a better understanding of the 'why' and 'how' of Corvino and Multari's architecture: not only the architecture that is embodied in the concrete materials of the constructed buildings, but also the architecture of the thought and ethics of making. What lessons are to be learned for the future? Beyond the specificity of the works and the contexts in which they operate, Corvino and Multari continue with great consistency to cultivate an open and anti-demiurgic conception of the role of the architect as interpreter, director and organiser of increasingly complex processes. There is still validity in their conception of architecture as 'an open process, where nothing is discounted or pre-established. Our projects are first and foremost knowledge of stories, contexts and locations. Locations are the soul of the project, a soul that thrills, that arouses curiosity, that causes to reflect, that instigates discussions until that moment when you feel that something is being created, that the solution becomes the synthesis of the entire creative process.'[19]

1
PUBLIC SPACES AND URBAN CONNECTIONS

Pierre-Alain Croset **I'd like to begin this dialogue with you by bringing up the years of your education and the circumstances in which you got to know each other and then decided to work together. There are often biographical reasons behind such decisions, and these reasons may be of various kinds. If we wish to consider two very famous examples, Le Corbusier and Pierre Jeanneret were cousins, whereas Jacques Herzog and Pierre de Meuron knew each other in Basel when they were children, at school and playing football, before continuing their friendship at the Polytechnic in Zurich, gaining their degrees and then opening their professional studio, which today is recognised as perhaps the most important in the world. I've read in your biographies that the Faculty of Architecture in Naples was where you met, with Giovanni a student away from his home in Cosenza, whereas Vincenzo was born in Naples, and that more precisely you met in the professorship of Professor Alberto Izzo, immediately after gaining your degrees. How important was this job as university assistants to Alberto Izzo?**

Giovanni Multari We had two different training paths, as I graduated in the 1991–92 academic year, whereas Vincenzo had already joined Alberto Izzo's staff a year earlier, just after graduating. Our role as assistants was the traditional one of helping the professor to develop the students' projects **[1]**, and the first student I supervised was the young Marco Poerio, who later joined and worked in our studio. This work as assistants was an extraordinary training ground for us, because Alberto Izzo was an all-round architect and professor, who had made the blending of his professional practice and teaching the distinguishing feature of his story, his research and his role as an architect. His own personal history was an amazing one, as a protagonist in Naples, but also outside Naples with some of the great masters. He had been in the United States for almost a year, also working in the studio of Marcel Breuer, and so for us he offered an extraordinary example that we could always view with interest, enthusiasm and curiosity. Talking and listening to the professor, having a moment to exchange ideas with him and with each other, always in an open dialogue, was an experience that in some ways, gradually, without realising it, actually made us what we are, undoubtedly creating the conditions that, over the period of a few years, led to us taking the decision to found the Corvino + Multari studio. The possibility of meeting at Alberto Izzo's department was decisive, because through this work what we shared above all were the methods, the culture, the approach to things, and also a certain humanity. With Vincenzo there's a beautiful relationship of friendship that has built up over time, very solid, but I don't know if all this would have happened if we had not had this common faith and the point of reference of the great person that was Alberto Izzo.

PAC **Alberto Izzo was the classic figure of an architect and a professor who associated professional practice and academic activity. What emerges from your account is the importance of having had this point of reference for the be-**

1 LEFT TO RIGHT: GIOVANNI MULTARI, VINCENZO CORVINO, FERRUCCIO IZZO, WIEL ARETS, ALBERTO IZZO.

2 ALBERTO IZZO SKETCHING.

3 VINCENZO CORVINO (LEFT) AND GIOVANNI MULTARI (RIGHT) WITH RICHARD MEIER AT THE INAUGURATION OF THE EXHIBITION IN NAPLES, 1991.

4 GIOVANNI MULTARI IN CONVERSATION WITH ALBERTO IZZO IN HIS STUDIO.

ginning of your professional career. As well as being his teaching assistants, did you have any practical experience in his studio? Did you develop projects together?

Vincenzo Corvino I never worked in Alberto Izzo's studio, whereas Giovanni did. But we did have some project experiences with him, also of competitions, and I have fond memories of Izzo's practice of sketching by hand, an intense practice that he passed on to us **[2]**. To this day we fill up entire notebooks of sketches every day, convinced as we are that hand drawing continues to be the best instrument of control compared to the many digital technologies with which it is necessary to represent architecture. As Giovanni was explaining earlier, for us Alberto Izzo was an example, more than a teacher, and with him we shared the idea that architecture always coexists in a relationship between theory and practice. He represented the figure of a militant architect who taught architecture and existed daily in this relationship of research and design, also in an international climate. Through Alberto Izzo we were able to get to know architects such as Richard Meier **[3]**, with whom we were called upon to collaborate in preparing the exhibition of his work in Naples in 1991. His lessons were also extraordinary on account of the fact that he used his own slides, so when he talked about Le Corbusier, Frank Lloyd Wright or Mies van der Rohe, he cited buildings that he himself had visited during his extensive travels. We were also interested in the fact that he worked together with Camillo Gubitosi, a possible model for our future architecture studio. At the end of his life, he wrote a beautiful dedication to us: 'To Vincenzo and Giovanni, my Dioscuri of architecture.' We felt a little like his right and left arms when we moved around in the corridors of the faculty; we liked to be beside him. We undoubtedly owe him a debt, but our gratitude is not only the traditional one between master and disciple, it's also that of having identified him as an example to feed upon to develop our work.

PAC **Are there other important figures from the Faculty of Architecture in Naples who made a mark on your training and development?**

VC The overall context of the Naples School was high quality and had recognised credibility, with excellent professors in all the disciplines, certainly as regards history of architecture, restoration and architectural design. Among others, I'd like to mention Michele Capobianco, Nicola Pagliara, Uberto Siola and Salvatore Bisogni, the latter more associated with the neo-rationalist *tendenza* and therefore keen to pass on a certain stylistic conception of architecture. I later graduated with Alfredo Sbriziolo, who, being particularly committed to research into the typological and morphological models of community housing, didn't have a dogmatic approach. This facilitated my initial contacts with Alberto Izzo, with whom I'd never studied before joining his staff as an assistant. The figure of Alberto Izzo was quite unique, due to his numerous international contacts and a conception of architecture that was not based on axioms and preconceptions. Another lesson was seeing him work together with structural engineer Pasquale Giancane and building services engineer Aniello Castaldo, strongly aware as he was that architecture is the art of building.

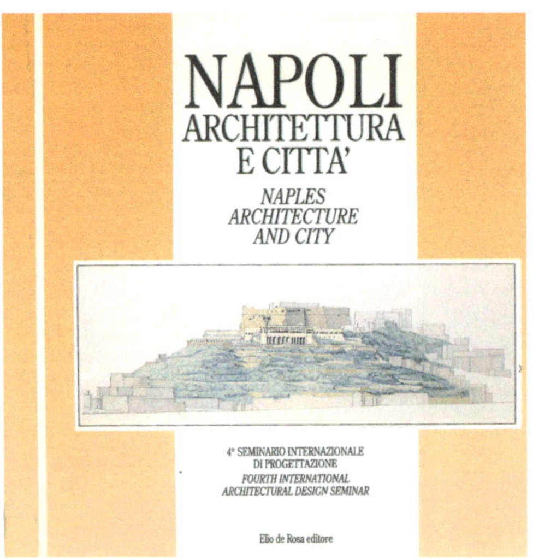

5 *NAPOLI ARCHITETTURA E CITTÀ, 4°SEMINARIO INTERNAZIONALE DI PROGETTAZIONE*, PUBLISHED BY ELIO DE ROSA, 1993.

6 EDUARDO SOUTO DE MOURA, VINCENZO CORVINO, GONÇALO BYRNE IN NAPLES, 1993.

7 THE FINAL MODEL OF THE PROJECT BY CORVINO AND MULTARI, TOGETHER WITH THE OTHER STUDENTS PARTICIPATING IN THE 4TH INTERNATIONAL DESIGN SEMINAR WITH GONÇALO BYRNE, 1993.

PAC **Were they engineers within the studio?**

GM No, they had their own engineering studio, but they'd formed a single design team with Izzo ever since the fundamental experience of the project for the Faculty of Theology in Naples, which was a 'first work' and at the same time a masterpiece by Alberto Izzo as an architect. As Vincenzo has recalled, immediately after my degree I worked for three years as a collaborator in Izzo's studio **[4]**, beginning a working experience in parallel between the profession and the academe that still continues today. There was no concern over doing too many things at the same time: we slept very little, and I still remember the real fatigue, but also the joy at being able to do that type of job in a context where you realised you were growing, gradually acquiring the capacity to form a relationship with this world of architecture that was so complex and difficult. Then at a certain point a season of competitions began, a point to which we will return, and so all these teachings, all these skills, all this enthusiasm and all this curiosity found a positive outlet, offering us the possibility of practising this craft autonomously.

PAC **And you Vincenzo, what professional experience did you have before opening the studio in partnership with Giovanni?**

VC After my degree I began with a few small experiences with interiors, developed independently, with the idea of forming a partnership with the classmate with whom I'd followed the entire degree course. I'd like to mention another important formative experience: our participation in the international design workshops 'Naples, Architecture and City' **[5]** in 1991 and 1992, which offered us the opportunity to get to know the most important European architects of that period, and in particular to gain a very intensive experience of post-degree urban design, the first year with Gonçalo Byrne **[6]**, the second with David Chipperfield: two opportunities that made a profound impression on our development **[7]**.

PAC **Returning to your relationship with Alberto Izzo, in an interview published in 2016, Giovanni stated that he considered him to be 'my teacher, in the noblest sense of the term',[1] while now Vincenzo has said that Izzo represented 'an example, more than a teacher'. I don't believe it's all that important to make a distinction, as the important thing is the way to highlight a sense of gratitude, and also of affection, in relation to a great architect and professor whom you chose as a guide and a model. I therefore don't particularly agree with the statement made by Valerio Mosco, in the first monograph on the first ten years of your studio, which recognised you as representatives of a generation 'without masters and without illusions, realistic and tenacious'.[2] I think in reality many architects of your generation were trained following the lessons of 'masters' who did not impose a precise stylistic code, as had happened previously with the followers of Aldo Rossi or Paolo Portoghesi, often looking for points of reference abroad, also thanks to the Erasmus programme, going to Spain, Portugal, the UK, France or Switzerland.**

GM This is a rather complex issue, as Alberto Izzo was also trained in a non-traditional way, with certain extraordinary architects such as Giulio De Luca or Francesco Di Salvo, who taught him the trade but also had the clever idea of allowing him the full freedom to express himself. What was ended was the relationship of dependence between masters and disciples, which often produced phenomena of foolish stylistic imitation, also in the academe. What we remember about Alberto Izzo is the extraordinary, very elegant way in which he stimulated reasoning in us youngsters, encouraging us to grow. And for us this is perhaps his true legacy, what we're attempting to do with our studio, which today is full of young people: to try to be people who are willing to help the younger ones, capable of making projects grow together with others.

THE BEGINNINGS: PIAZZA DEI BRUZI IN COSENZA

PAC **Now I'll ask you to tell about your beginnings, with the foundation of the Corvino + Multari studio in 1995. The early years are always difficult for young architects; you habitually try to have at least a few secure jobs, in order to pay the rent for premises and make a living. In your case, was the decision brought about by having won first prize in the competition for Piazza dei Bruzi in Cosenza, or did you already have some other jobs?**

VC We were actually able to begin our partnership with a few small interior design jobs for public offices and bank branches on behalf of Olivetti Engineering, working on design and building on specific occasions.

PAC **How did this relationship with Olivetti Engineering come about?**

GM Quite by chance, I remember when we began to visit the Olivetti offices in Naples, a very beautiful building by Luigi Cosenza, with the possibility of talking about architecture with our first clients. In reality, this happened before the foundation of our studio, which took place on 10 May 1995. We were working together without having a formal structure yet; we were hosted in spaces owned by Vincenzo's father, but from the beginning we'd decided to pay the rent, taking on a commitment to find out if we could actually overcome the first economic difficulties. But then we decided to formalise our partnership, investing equal stakes in the foundation of our studio, with an initial capital stock of fifteen million lire. Now thirty years have gone by, and we've not needed to interfere with this capital, because we've always reinvested everything we've earned in our firm.

PAC **Let's talk about the competition for Piazza dei Bruzi now, which was so important for the beginning of your career. What type of competition was it? How did you win? What happened after the victory?**

GM Before answering, I'd like to recall the Italian context of the 1990s, and certain decisive changes in the politics of that time. Firstly, the European Community required Italy to provide public evidence of the entrusting of professional appointments through competition procedures. Secondly, the politicians found themselves obliged to take a step back on all fronts, following the Tangentopoli scandal, losing control of the old procedures of distribution of professional appointments on the basis of party loyalties. Thirdly—and this was decisive—the new law on the direct election of mayors significantly changed the mayor's role. For the first time, the mayor could decide on the future of his city with a board appointed by him, and so consisting of people he trusted, no longer representatives organised according to party allegiances. So these new mayors proposed visions of the city and began to promote architecture competitions, as happened in Rome with Francesco Rutelli, in Naples with Antonio Bassolino, in Salerno with Vincenzo De Luca and in Cosenza with Giacomo Mancini. In this historical period, the South began to receive a series of significant financial packages for public works. A major space therefore opened up for architects to work, in which the juries in the competitions were also appointed on the basis of more serious criteria. The competition for Piazza dei Bruzi came about within this context.

PAC **You're quite right to remember this context of major changes; I could also cite my own experience as a member of the jury for the 'Centopiazze' (one hundred squares) competition in Rome, in 1995. An excellent and very innovative experience for Italy, inaugurated by Mayor Francesco Rutelli and coordinated by Francesco Ghio, who called me to take part in the jury: the model of competition was the Europan, with many competition sites but with a single jury, of which I remember that Francesco Cellini and Laura Thermes were members; this offered the participants numerous possibilities of receiving a public appointment after the outcome of the competition. It was no coincidence that the vast majority of the winners were young and very young architects, some of whom were really just starting out, and the competition was very important in underlining the importance of the theme of the designing and upgrading of open spaces. What was the theme of the competition in Cosenza?**

GM It was the upgrading of a very central space in the city of Cosenza, characterised by imposing modern buildings. Feeding on our enthusiasm and passion, we decided to participate with a group of youngsters, and to launch our design process based on listening and dialogue, encouraged by visits to the site, but also by talking to Salvatore Giuliani, who had designed the square at the time of the Post-War Reconstruction Plan for Cosenza. We therefore became aware of a powerful, important history, with respect to which, as very young men, we decided to attempt a few targeted moves, without allowing ourselves to be swayed by the earlier work, by the desire to leave our mark, by the idea of creating a project that was in some way able to go outside of this modern register that often characterises our work: a modernism that we learned from the locations, from this experience, from viewing the munici-

8 SALVATORE GIULIANI, SKETCH FOR THE MUNICIPAL BUILDING IN COSENZA IN PIAZZA DEI BRUZI.

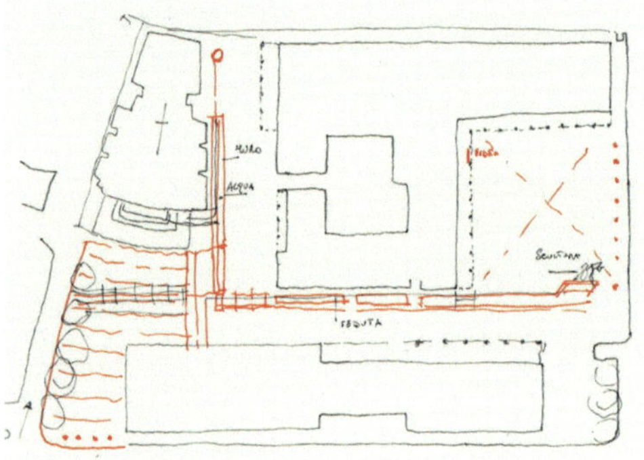

9 CORVINO AND MULTARI, SKETCH FOR THE COMPETITION PROJECT FOR PIAZZA DEI BRUZI AND THE SQUARE OF THE CHURCH OF SAN NICOLA IN COSENZA.

10 MEETING IN STUDIO FOR THE PROJECT FOR PIAZZA DEI BRUZI, LEFT TO RIGHT: CARMEN DEL GROSSO, MIMMO PALADINO, ROBERTO SERINO, VINCENZO CORVINO, GIOVANNI MULTARI.

11 MIMMO PALADINO, COMPETITION SKETCH FOR THE SCULPTURE *THE HELMET* IN PIAZZA DEI BRUZI.

pal buildings **[8]** designed by Giuliani, but also the Church of San Nicola, designed by Vittorio Morpurgo, the architect of Piazza Augusto Imperatore in Rome. Learning from places and from their history, and listening in order to design: that's something that we continue to do **[9]**, whether it concerns architects such as Salvatore Giuliani or Gio Ponti, a community, the head of a Superintendence, a person who has something to do with the design process, we continue to do this type of work, we're always listening, I believe this in some ways is a distinctive feature of our work.

PAC **Was it a competition that was open to everybody?**

VC Yes, with a good jury, and we wanted to deploy one of the teachings that Alberto Izzo passed on to us: to always fly high and think big and, since the notice of competition asked us to participate with an artist, we immediately thought of Mimmo Paladino **[10]**, who was Campania's greatest artist and already one of the greatest artists on the international scene. We contacted him thanks to Roberto Serino, who'd created the *Hortus Conclusus* with him in Benevento in 1992, and we went to see him at his studio in Paduli with a physical model of our project proposal. The night before delivery a fax arrived with the beautiful sketch of the large helmet **[11]**, with the black shadow that stands out from the waterline of the pool, just in time for us to be able to glue it onto the final project drawing.

PAC **And then, after winning the competition, did you receive the instruction to proceed towards the realisation immediately? Was the work already financed by the Municipality at the time of the opening of the competition?**

GM The competition had been decided on by the mayor in order to complete a restructuring of the square, which had been begun but never completed. It was a necessary project, therefore, but there was no financing yet. Luckily for us, Giacomo Mancini was a great mayor; we're talking about a protagonist of Italian politics, a socialist from the outset, a famous antagonist of Craxi. I remember that Vincenzo and I were on holiday on the Aeolian Islands, and we had one of the first mobile phones with us, with a telescopic antenna. The telephone rang, and it was him, Giacomo Mancini: 'It's the mayor here; I'd like to know how much your project for Piazza dei Bruzi costs.' And we replied: '900 million, almost a billion,' and he declares: 'Perfect! We're about to sell a building owned by the Municipal Authority, so we can recover this sum. So get ready because in September we start the project.' These were the mayors of that time.

PAC **Very fortunate, if we consider that even then many competition projects were to remain on paper afterwards.**

VC It's true, but we must remember that competitions became an indispensable tool in that particular political climate, because Italy had had to abandon the methodology of the fiduciary arrangement without an upper threshold amount. We therefore found ourselves, at the start of our career, in the position of investing almost all our energies in competitions, which were not a hobby, but the instrument to access an assignment and the best way to conduct research. Today we still continue to take part in many competitions and, even when we don't win, the competition remains our preferred instrument to proceed with experimentation and to grow. Returning to Piazza dei Bruzi, I'd advise youngsters to start their careers by first laying a stone horizontally rather than vertically; that is, before constructing a building, to attempt to create a public space, because this forces us to take on a very high level of civil responsibility. For us it represented an extraordinary experience in measuring everything, checking every thickness, verifying the laying of the materials. I remember when I was waiting for Giovanni to return from the worksite, my strongest desire was to see the slides he had made in Cosenza, to start to understand how the project had passed the construction trials.

GM These are the reasons why we stress the importance of the political-institutional changes of those years, which had opened up many opportunities for young architects. We must ensure that this vision is able to return in Italy, to give the younger generations who'll come after us the possibility of starting out in the various professions, not only in the field of architecture. It's the rules that make the game; if the rules are not the right ones, then the game can't be played.

PAC **It also appears fundamental to have complete faith in young people; in your case there was an enthusiastic mayor who'd found the financing and had entrusted you with the responsibility of going to the construction site. We know that acting upon the public space, not only in Italy, is often a very delicate issue, since construction sites halt the traffic, the citizens complain, the shopkeepers protest. How did you manage the executive development of the project, the contract, and subsequently the worksite and the relationship with the construction firms?**

GM Being originally from Cosenza, it was quite logical for me to be the one who would supervise the worksite, whereas Vincenzo has supervised many others. We divide up tasks; we've always had the idea of working for both and never each for himself, this is a very important fact that's part of our ethics. Piazza dei Bruzi was a formative experience from all perspectives, because we tackled the technical part, along with the economic part, with the preparation of the worksite in a very busy part of the city where the municipal hall is located, and so the mayor and the public offices as well. The checks were continual, and questions from citizens were very common. The first occasions of confrontation, quarrels and disagreements also occurred with the building company regarding certain choices of materials, always for economic reasons, and we understood that it's sometimes necessary to mediate, attempting to resolve problems.

PAC **Had you been appointed to manage the worksite?**

GM We fulfilled the artistic management role.

PAC **This too was an exception compared to current practices.**

VC Actually it wasn't, because in that period winning a competition guaranteed the appointment for the preliminary project and the executive project, as well as the construction management, or at least the artistic management, irrespective of the studio's technical-economic qualifications. If, as happens today, they had asked us to show that we'd previously realised three similar works, then we'd never have received that appointment.

THE SQUARES OF MILAN

PAC **After the realisation of Piazza dei Bruzi in Cosenza, in the years that followed you continued to devote significant attention to the theme of the upgrading of open spaces, participating in several national and international competitions. I'm interested in particular in discussing the projects for the squares of Milan, realised following your victory in two international competitions, in 1999 and 2001. The first was called 'Cinque piazze per Milano' (five squares for Milan), announced in 1999, and you received an award for three of them: Piazza Gabriele Rosa, which you won and then realised, Piazza Tirana with a second prize, and Piazza Costantino with a third prize.**

GM The first competition was interesting because altogether it involved five different sites, but it was also possible to choose to participate in just one or two; in reality we developed projects for all five sites, with the last two being Piazza Santa Giustina and Piazza Anita Garibaldi. It was a competition in two phases, and—as you quite rightly remember—we were selected for three squares. For the second phase it was necessary to further explore the choices concerning materials and costs. The project realised **[12, 13]** concerned not only Piazza Gabriele Rosa, with the large fountain oriented along the axis of the forecourt of the Church of San Michele Arcangelo and Santa Rita, but also the redesigning of the road section along Viale Omero, with the upgrading of the central strip as an urban walkway.

PAC **The second competition was announced in 2001 and concerned three other squares: Piazza Ohm, which you won and realised, Piazza Gambara and Piazza Rosario.**

VC We need to remember that these competitions were conducted in a very interesting season for the Municipal Authority of Milan, which in those years had created a specific office for design competitions, as had previously happened in Rome. This season enabled a number of Italian architects of various origins to contribute to the realisation of contemporary public spaces. Our idea for Piazza Ohm, which is situated along a major traffic axis, was to enhance the dynamic perception from cars for those entering Milan, arriving from Genoa and from the western bypass. The two large totems **[14]** on each side of the square form an entrance gate to the city. The other theme concerned the connection of this large traffic roundabout with the forecourt of the Church of Santa Rita, connecting up a series of small interstitial spaces between them.

12 AERIAL VIEW OF PIAZZA GABRIELE ROSA IN MILAN.

13 VIEW OF THE FOUNTAIN REALISED IN PIAZZA GABRIELE ROSA.

14 NIGHTTIME VIEW OF PIAZZA OHM IN MILANO WITH THE COLOURED TOTEM.

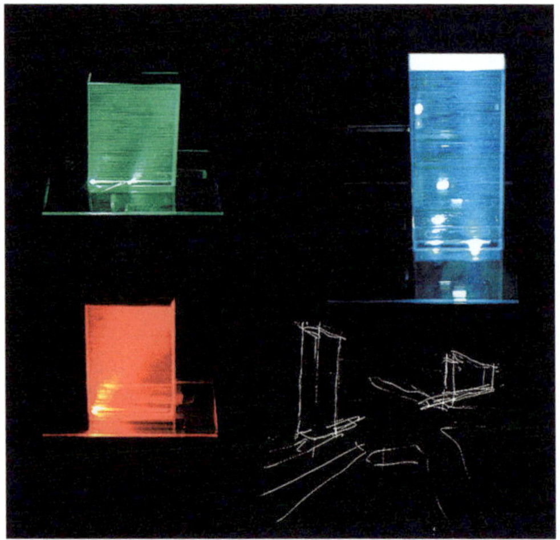

15 STUDIO MODELS FOR THE COLOURED GLASS FOUNTAINS IN PIAZZA OHM.

PAC **In nighttime views, the two totems become colourful lanterns. How did this idea of colour come about? Did you work with an artist?**

GM In an initial phase, we'd designed a series of fountains with coloured glass slabs **[15]**, because the public administration had given a precise indication regarding the theme of water, being close to the Naviglio Grande. We also prepared some samples of flooring, which we originally thought of realising with asphalt and inserts made of Montorfano white granite, a stone typically used for Milan's pavements. The themes were therefore water, colour, light and green space, but, after a few conversations with the administration, difficulties emerged concerning the construction and maintenance costs, particularly for the glass fountains. Subsequently we asked for some advice from Mario Nanni, the great 'master of light' and founder of the company Viabizzuno, discussing with him how to adapt his famous 'totems of light' to suit our project. It was from this meeting that the totems of Piazza Ohm came about, which change colour depending on the outdoor temperature: they're red in summer and blue during the winter, taking on intermediary colorations in the other seasons.

RETURN TO COSENZA: THE ISOLATO DEI RIVOCATI

PAC **Let's return for a moment to the city of Cosenza, to talk about the project for the Isolato dei Rivocati, a city block that represented another significant experience, offering you the possibility of realising the first buildings in a highly complex urban setting. I'm interested in discussing with you the project strategy that's based on the idea of urban connection, through a new structure of public buildings and spaces to replace the pre-existing fruit and vegetable market. How did the appointment for this project come about?**

GM The Municipal Authority had defined the urban planning rules for an Integrated Intervention Plan, subsequently announcing a competition in which construction companies were intended to participate in partnership with designers. We felt ready and well equipped to participate, also because in the meantime we'd enriched our baggage of experiences with the Europan competition, in which young architects aged under forty coming from Europe participated, gaining a second prize in Cagliari for the area of the Lazzaretto. So, having also demonstrated a certain expertise and reliability with the realisation of Piazza dei Bruzi, we decided to participate in this tendering for contracts with the same construction company, and our proposal won. The process was different, therefore, because for Piazza dei Bruzi we drafted the executive project, then joined the tendering process, and in the realisation we found ourselves having to deal with all the problems and difficulties involved in the choice of materials, the control of costs and the definition of the construction details, interacting with the building

16 THE WORK GROUP OF THE CORVINO-MULTARI STUDIO AT THE CONSTRUCTION SITE OF THE ISOLATO DEI RIVOCATI IN COSENZA, 2001.

17 THE OLD FRUIT AND VEGETABLE MARKET IN COSENZA BEFORE DEMOLITION.

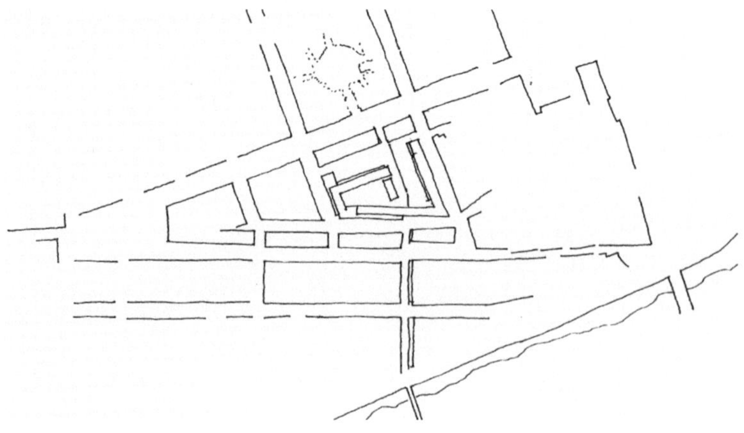

18 PROJECT SKETCH WITH THE ISOLATO DEI RIVOCATI AT THE CENTRE, THE VILLA COMUNALE ABOVE AND THE RIVER BUSENTO BELOW.

company, whereas in the project for Isolato dei Rivocati the work was carried out together with the construction company from the outset.

PAC **It seems to me to be a rather unusual fact that such young architects, barely thirty years old** [16], **could participate in a tendering for contracts like this. For this type of procedure, companies normally relied on the major engineering companies or else on already well-known architecture studios.**

GM It was indeed a rather unusual event, the result of our previous work, which had led to positive relations with the city: the square had been inaugurated, the square worked. A relationship of trust had come about, based on expertise and transparency, and the administration had been able to verify that our project group had worked well, proving to be reliable.

PAC **Your project has a significant urban value in defining a system of roads, squares and pedestrian crossings. Was this principle of the crossing and pedestrian permeability of the block already defined in the competition notice?**

GM No, it wasn't envisaged. The idea came about from observation of the old fruit and vegetable market **[17]**, which was a structure traversed by flows of people and goods; it was therefore quite logical to attempt to establish relationships between all the public spaces around it **[18]**. We wanted to enhance the value of Via San Martino, which connects the Villa Comunale, built during the fascist era, with the bank of the River Busento, and we would ideally have wanted to extend this route with a pedestrian walkway over the river to reach the historic centre.

PAC **I'm now interested in discussing the linguistic choices that characterise your architecture. With this being your first building, what were your points of reference at that time? It seems to me that we can quite clearly notice a reference to contemporary Spanish architecture—I'm thinking, for example, of certain brick and stone buildings by Pep Llinàs in Barcelona—and Portuguese architecture, remembering your experience with Gonçalo Byrne at the 'Naples, Architecture and City' seminar a few years earlier.**

VC I agree that these points of reference certainly influenced us, but our first experience was inspired above all by the lessons of the great masters of Italian Modernism, such as Figini and Pollini, Terragni or Libera: that influence can be recognised in certain elements such as the stone shading devices, the use of brick and the design of a plinth that's linked to the public space **[19]**. The proportional relationships between height, width and depth also recall these lessons; they feed that rooting in the urban context that is the point of departure of our work as architects.

PAC **On the subject of the relationship with the context, did you use a local stone?**

19 THE COMPLETED BUILDINGS IN THE ISOLATO DEI RIVOCATI: APRICENA STONE BASE AND RED BRICK CURTAIN WALL, SEPARATED BY A UPN STEEL BEAM.

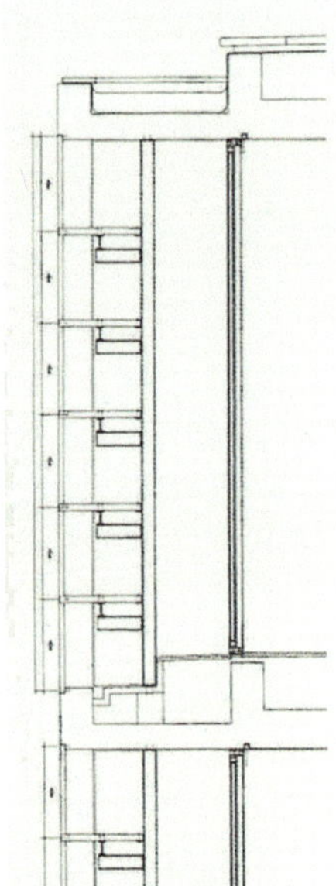

20 EDUARDO SOUTO DE MOURA, BUILDING OF THE FACULTY OF GEOLOGICAL SCIENCES, UNIVERSITY OF AVEIRO, 1989-1994, DETAIL IN SECTION OF THE SHADING DEVICE.

21 THE COMPLETED BUILDINGS IN THE ISOLATO DEI RIVOCATI: THE APRICENA STONE SHADING DEVICE.

GM We used Apricena stone, which was used by Renzo Piano in those years, for example in the Church of San Giovanni Rotondo, a beautiful and reasonably affordable stone. This enabled us to use it with significant thicknesses, whereas today it's become more expensive, on a par with travertine. With this being our very first building, it captured the enthusiasm of two young men who were tackling the theme of construction for the first time, in a very significant urban context: it was very important to reference the immediate context of the district, which had been built in the first half of the 20th century. Near to our site, for example, is the Banco di Napoli building, designed in the 1930s by the technical office of Cosenza and inspired by the architecture of Piacentini, with a travertine basement and a red brick curtain wall. As Vincenzo explained earlier, we've always paid great attention to the architects of Italian Modernism, but we were also influenced by Spanish and Portuguese architects such as Gonçalo Byrne, who often uses the colour palette of pale stone and brick.

PAC **Has Álvaro Siza also influenced you?**

GM Of course, if we think of the library in Aveiro, or, again in Aveiro, the building by Souto de Moura with its large stone shading device **[20, 21]**. As another example of an influence, I could cite the use of a UPN steel beam with a 'U' section, to create a continuous joint between the stone plinth and the red brick curtain, which we took directly from the large Illa Diagonal building realised in Barcelona by Rafael Moneo and Manuel de Solà-Morales, in which a similar UPN beam creates the connection between pale stone and dark stone.

SPACES OF COMMERCE AS URBAN EXPERIENCE

PAC **As we've seen above with the project for the Isolato dei Rivocati in Cosenza, the project for the former Mercato Coperto in Reggio Emilia is also based on a principle of crossing and connection between various public spaces. How did this project come about? Was it also from a competition opportunity in this case?**

VC The Municipal Authority had defined the competition brief for the designing, building and management of the regeneration of the old Covered Market **[22, 23]**. In those years it was Mayor Graziano Delrio, who with his council inaugurated a major season of tenders, competitions and openness towards the construction of contemporary architectures. In this case there was a project financing tendering procedure, in which we participated with the Coopsette cooperative of Reggio Emilia. The project financing envisaged a very limited public contribution and the inclusion of commercial functions, the reason why the promoter subsequently chose to involve the Coin chain in transforming the former market into a department store.

PAC **How had this relationship with Coopsette begun?**

22 THE RECENTLY INAUGURATED COVERED MARKET IN REGGIO EMILIA, 1927.

23 THE COVERED MARKET TRANSFORMED INTO A CLOTHING EMPORIUM, 1930S.

24 CONSTRUCTION SITE OF THE COVERED MARKET WITH THE NEW OPENING TOWARDS PIAZZA SCAPINELLI

25 THE CONSTRUCTION SITE OF THE NEW FAÇADE TOWARDS PIAZZA SCAPINELLI.

VC We were invited to participate in the competition in Reggio Emilia because we already had other jobs under way with Coopsette in Naples, in particular for an auditorium in Ponticelli. In Reggio they'd already drafted a proposal with other architects, but that project wasn't approved by the Municipal Authority, who asked for greater attention to be devoted to the history of the former Covered Market, and also a greater sensitivity as regards the relationship between historical context and contemporary architecture. So they invited us to participate in the tendering process as indicated architects and we immediately found an easy understanding with the Municipal Administration and with the Superintendence of Architectural Heritage of Reggio Emilia.

PAC **One of the major qualities of your project is having transformed the Covered Market, which was only accessed from Via Emilia San Pietro to the south, into a genuine 'passage', enhancing the value of the facing towards Piazza Scapinelli to the north. Where previously there was an almost totally blind façade, devoid of quality, how did you arrive at the solution of a new façade with a clearly defined contemporary language?**

VC Our basic idea, from the outset, was to bring the space of the Covered Market back to life by designing a genuine piece of the city, creating permeability on all sides **[24]**. The new façade looking onto Piazza Scapinelli was conceived as a kind of frame, connected with the ideal line of the forecourt of the original church. In agreement with the Superintendence, we therefore proposed vertical elements made of glued laminated timber, aligned with the neighbouring building, leaving exposed the original façade **[25]** that had been left incomplete. To complete the project, we demolished an old warehouse that occupied the 15th-century internal cloister, freeing it up and highlighting it as a further location for crossing and entry.

GM This new façade uses very simple geometries, recognisable *in situ* in the shape of the existing building, while the fact of being detached enables a cavity to be created, which is also useful to resolve a whole series of technical problems, such as the location of certain installations and the fire-escape.

PAC **How was the dialogue conducted with the Superintendence? Did you arrive with various proposals before reaching a synthesis?**

VC There are no particular recipes; dialogue with the Superintendence is a working method that characterises us. Initially we'd only imagined this new façade in terms of its upper part, whereas it was the head of the Superintendence herself who discussed the possibility of designing a continuous shape with us. Another important aspect of the restoration project was the reinstatement of the original skylights dating back to the project from 1927 by Prospero Sorgato, who was chief engineer of the Municipality of Reggio Emilia for a long time. All the skylights had been hidden by a series of successive interventions, and our intention was to rediscover the beautiful natural light that characterised the images of the building in the historical photographs. Once again we called upon Mario Nanni and his company Viabizzuno to collaborate with us, designing new lamps with him in the upper part of the main gallery **[26]**, which were later also used by David Chipperfield at the site of the Palace of Justice in Salerno. We also had to pay particular attention to the insertion of the installations **[27]**, which couldn't be in the ceiling due to the presence of the old skylight, as well as to selecting hexagonal tiles for the entire flooring, also a reference to the hexagonal *forma urbis* of the historic centre of Reggio Emilia. The design of the commercial layout, developed in collaboration with the Coin technical office, was devised with iron and glass elements positioned low down, and completely transparent, so as not to conceal the view of the ceiling of the gallery.

PAC **How did you redefine the other parts of the intervention?**

VC Apart from the space of the former students' hall of residence, which was left without being defined in the absence of a management company, we upgraded all the other spaces, also opening up a lateral path on the axis with Via dell'Abbadessa. Silvia Ghirelli, a landscape architect from Reggio Emilia, intervened here, designing a green wall to evoke Reggio's cloisters, which have always been characterised by an abundance of vegetation and decoration.

PAC **You explained earlier that your relationship with Coopsette began in Naples with other projects. What projects were these?**

VC The first project was for the Palaponticelli **[28]**, conceived as a structure for music and major events, with an annexed shopping centre; this was an amazing experience that, despite being approved by the Naples Municipal Authority, was unfortunately not able to be realised.

GM I may add that Coopsette was an important partner in that period, as it offered us the opportunity to work for private clients on very ambitious, but also very costly projects, in problematic areas. For example, in Ponticelli it was necessary to conduct reclamation work in areas very close to Vesuvius. Even though it wasn't implemented, it was a very formative project, because it enabled us to experiment with large dimensions.

PAC **And then what happened?**

VC We consolidated our relationship with Coopsette in the work on the former paper mill in Pompeii; they were promoting a public interest initiative, the result of a protocol of understanding with the Prime Minister's Office to rehire the workers or the relatives of skilled workers from the paper mill that had been decommissioned.

PAC **This project for the former paper mill in Pompeii is of interest to me for two reasons. On one hand, it places the conception of the shopping centre as a 'covered passage' at the centre of the intervention, and in this we find a certain**

26 THE RESTORATION OF THE ORIGINAL SKYLIGHT WINDOWS WITH THE INSERTION OF THE NEW LAMPS BY MARIO NANNI.

27 THE CONSTRUCTION SITE WITH THE INSERTION OF THE NEW UNDERFLOOR SYSTEMS.

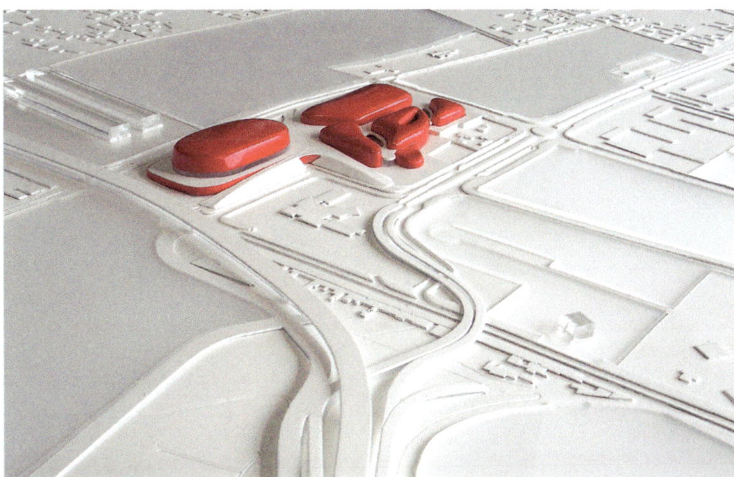

28 CORVINO + MULTARI, PROJECT FOR THE PALAZZO DELLA MUSICA AND SHOPPING CENTRE IN PONTICELLI, NAPLES, 2006.

analogy with the project for the Covered Market in Reggio Emilia. Secondly, it prioritises interventions in public spaces, with the creation of a park and a series of spaces with facilities for young people's leisure time.

GM The project for the former paper mill in Pompeii forced us to take on a number of very difficult challenges, in a delicate geographical area that was subject to the flooding of the Sarno River and the Bottaro Canal **[29]**, which delimit a full-blown river island. One of the difficulties concerned the obligation to talk to the many bodies responsible for different authorisations, from environmental safeguarding to traffic, to understand well how to transform the existing situation. On one hand there were a number of industrial buildings of notable architectural quality **[30]**, characterised by beautiful vaulted sheds, which we wanted to conserve and which were clearly at surface level. On the other hand, precisely due to the risks of flooding and the impossibility of excavating the terrain to locate the car parks, we proposed to free up the ground floor and to raise the new volumes **[31]**, creating an artificial level for the shopping mall, with parking at both the ground floor and the roof levels. This idea was the main innovation with respect to traditional shopping centres: an idea that could have been wholly rejected by the investor, because having a shopping mall on the first floor means modifying the road accesses for loading and unloading. The large prefabricated ramps running along the façade that characterise the building were created for these reasons. From this perspective, the project was a very important formative experience, because it enabled us to understand how important the issue of transport, accesses and logistics is in relation to the environmental issues. It was not only a question of architecture; there were many other implications involving industrial heritage, and therefore memory, but also social issues, because the programme didn't solely concern a shopping centre, but also a public park and facilities for leisure time. In my role as a university lecturer, I occasionally run into students from Pompeii who talk to me with pride about this project, completed more than ten years ago, because they remember the former paper mill area as a place of play and fun for the kids of Pompeii. To this day it's a very regularly visited place, but also very safe, due to the presence of the large public park. Of course, financial issues are very important for this type of programme, but I believe we've succeeded in finding an interesting relationship between the new commercial functions and what needed to be conserved. The memories of the old Aticarta factory, which produced paper for Monopolio di Stato cigarettes, are displayed in the huge steel skeleton of the old shed, but also in the undulating roof **[32]** that evokes the machines and the paper production process.

PAC **Did you work together with a landscape architect on the project for the park?**

VC Yes, we benefited from the contribution of a Neapolitan landscape architect, Bartolomeo Di Bartolomeo, also considering the various environmental restrictions affecting the area. As Giovanni said earlier, there were no less than thirty-two different bodies that had to express an opinion on the project, but we've long been used to looking at restrictions as a major opportunity, an occasion to define the idea. We conceive the project as a place of sharing,

29 AERIAL VIEW OF THE FORMER PAPER MILL IN POMPEII, WITH THE RIVER ABOVE AND THE BOTTARO CANAL BELOW.

30 THE FAÇADE OF THE FORMER PAPER MILL SEEN FROM THE BOTTARO CANAL.

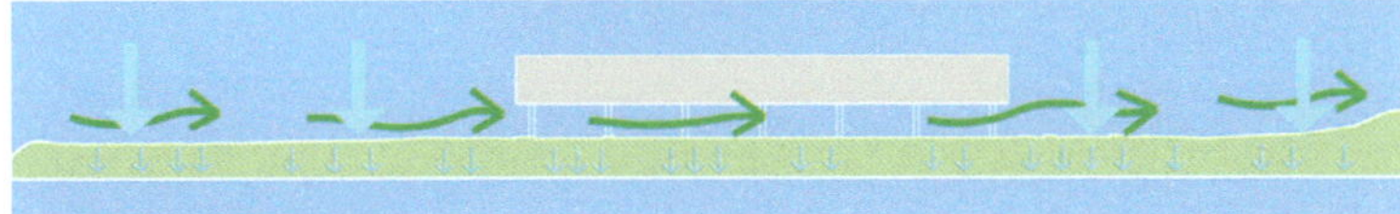

31 PROJECT SKETCH WITH THE RAISING OF THE LEVEL OF THE SHOPPING CENTRE.

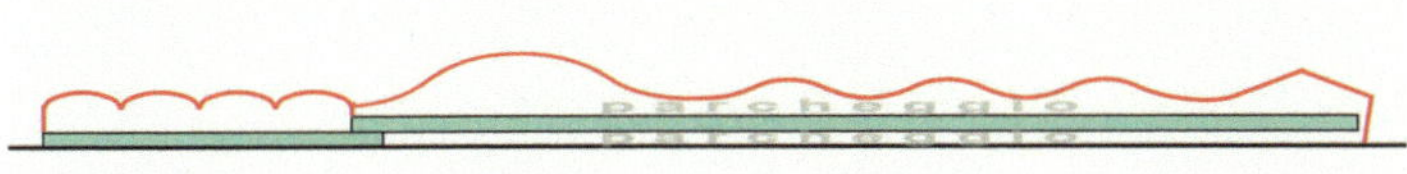

32 PROJECT SKETCH WITH THE PROFILE OF THE ROOF RECALLING THE CURVES OF PAPER BOBBINS.

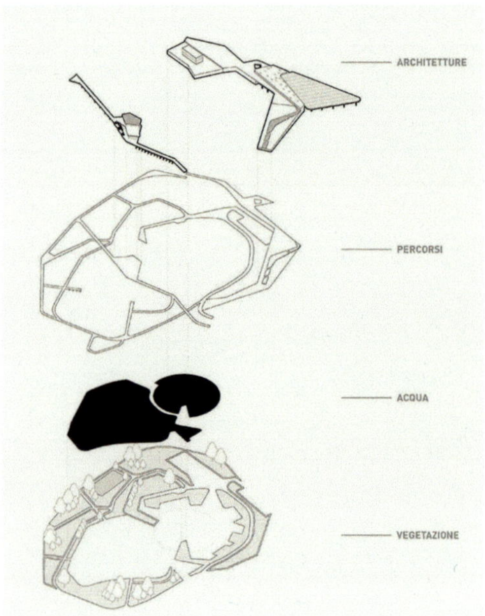

33 PROJECT DIAGRAMS FOR THE SANTA CHIARA WATER PARK IN RENDE.

34 LAYOUT PLAN OF THE SANTA CHIARA WATER PARK IN RENDE.

35 OVERALL VIEW OF THE PARK.

36 THE CENTRAL LAKE FOR BATHING.

and we do so in order that all the restrictions are acknowledged in an integrated manner, from the hydraulic restriction to the number of staff to be recruited, from the distance from the boundaries to the structural restrictions, to the conservation of the elements that deserve to be valued; everything must contribute to the designing of a contemporary form that must properly comply with all the regulatory instruments.

PAC **This project for the paper mill in Pompeii is interesting on account of the fact that it relates various scales of intervention together, but also various dimensions of the architectural project: it's an intervention of restoration of the modern, of the architecture of interiors, and of architecture of the landscape, all at the same time. The theme of the landscape has been tackled by your studio on various occasions, and you've often collaborated with landscape architects. In this regard, I'm interested in discussing the project for the Santa Chiara water park in Rende, perhaps your most directly 'landscaping' project.**

GM This was a very complex project **[33]**, developed with a group of experts including geologists, hydraulic engineers, agronomists and landscape architects on the basis of a landscaping scheme **[34]** curated by Fabio di Carlo, professor of landscape architecture at the 'La Sapienza' University in Rome. The orientations were clear and the landscaping goals to be achieved were interesting, with the large artificial lake **[35]** at the centre, the realisation of which represented the biggest challenge in project terms. The main issue concerned how to contain the energy consumption. We attempted to mitigate the intervention with the most logical solution, which consisted in diverting water from the Campagnano, a tributary of the River Crati, but this take-up appeared impossible for environmental reasons, so we had to opt for a more traditional solution, digging deep wells to fill the lake **[36]**. To achieve greater energy sustainability and reduce the running costs, we covered the roofs of the service buildings with solar panels. Ultimately, as well as possessing the necessary environmental features, the park is a place devoted to swimming and outdoor sporting activities, but it's also served by an auditorium and a restaurant. It's a location that's very busy in summer; it's not a traditional swimming pool, but rather offers the community of Cosenza the possibility of having 'the sea in the city'.

1 **Pino Scaglione, 'Conversazione', in *Esperienze dell'architettura. Corvino + Multari*, (Rovereto: ListLab, 2017), 148.**

2 **Valerio Paolo Mosco, 'La strategia dell'ordine di Corvino e Multari', in Giulia Bonelli, *Corvino + Multari 1995–2005* (Naples: Cronopio, 2005), 84.**

PIAZZA DEI BRUZI
COSENZA, 1995–98

The main aim of the project was to redefine the role of Piazza dei Bruzi inside the civic centre, conceived in its current configuration in the 1950s, and to establish a relationship between this and the historic city located over the river. They therefore sought to render visible the stratifications of the urban history of Cosenza through a spatial and material system capable of evoking the past and at the same time meeting contemporary needs.

One of the most significant aspects of the intervention was the redevelopment of the square of the Church of San Nicola, previously occupied by a car park. The elimination of cars enabled a balanced relationship to be re-established between the church and the square, giving the religious complex a representation space. The intervention is characterised by a clear architectural composition based on just a few geometrically and formally strong elements, which contribute to giving the space order and legibility. A fundamental role is played by the wall with amenities located along the east side of the church. This structure incorporates a ramp, a seat and a fountain, thus forming a boundary element for orientation purposes, which guides the pedestrian walkways and defines a new urban backdrop of access to the religious complex. Furthermore, the wall is delimited by two cypress trees, which contribute to underlining its verticality and to creating a dialogue with the church façade. Another central element of the project is the travertine pool-fountain, a long parallelepiped that establishes a visual and functional connection between the church square and Piazza dei Bruzi. As well as marking the main route of the piazza, this element has been designed to also have a double function: as a stretch of water and as continuous seating, thus enabling the usability of the space to be increased. The axis of the fountain guides the gaze and movement to the point of conclusion, marked by an imposing bronze sculpture by Mimmo Paladino: a huge helmet, a symbol of the historical memory of the city and its identity, stratified over time. Fragments of Pietrasanta marble and travertine have been used for the flooring of the square, enabling differentiation between the church square and the rest of the urban space. This choice is accompanied by meticulous planning of the green spaces, which include a row of four Norway maples (*acer platanoides*) positioned along the edge of the square to create a natural frame for the whole area.

NICOLAI · IN HONOREM

ISOLATO DEI RIVOCATI
COSENZA, 1997–2001

The complex is part of an integrated programme of interventions for the regeneration of the area of the former fruit and vegetable market in the neighbourhood of I Rivocati, located between the River Busento and the original Viale dei Platani, in a building fabric of nineteenth-century design. The project incorporates the main components envisaged to accomplish a series of functions aiming at the upgrading of the urbanistic, building and environmental fabric. The area where the hospital stands is served by two of the city's important road axes, Corso Umberto and Via Montesanto, the intersection of which forms a trapezoid-shaped block. The intervention becomes the generator for the upgrading of the surrounding building fabric, recovering the sense of a large urban block, almost as though it were a single building. A long bordering element is positioned on the perimeter of Via Pasubio, Via Andreotti and Via Montebaldo, and marks out the boundaries of the block and the part facing onto Corso Umberto. Inside, Via San Martino with the traces of the former fruit and vegetable market defines two spaces of clear public value. The hospital buildings, which are developed over four storeys above ground, are characterised by long sand-blasted red brick walls. The exposed masonry stands on a base of Apricena stone characterised by ample glazed walls protected by the porticoed spaces. Inside, the various intended uses are organised into the linearity of simple building volumes, the transparency of the glass walls, the order of the staircases, the divisions of the white stone shading devices and the regularity and simplicity of the spaces. The competition design originally envisaged the construction of a third phase of intervention, intended for residence, the service sector and commerce to replace private buildings, but the intervention was not implemented.

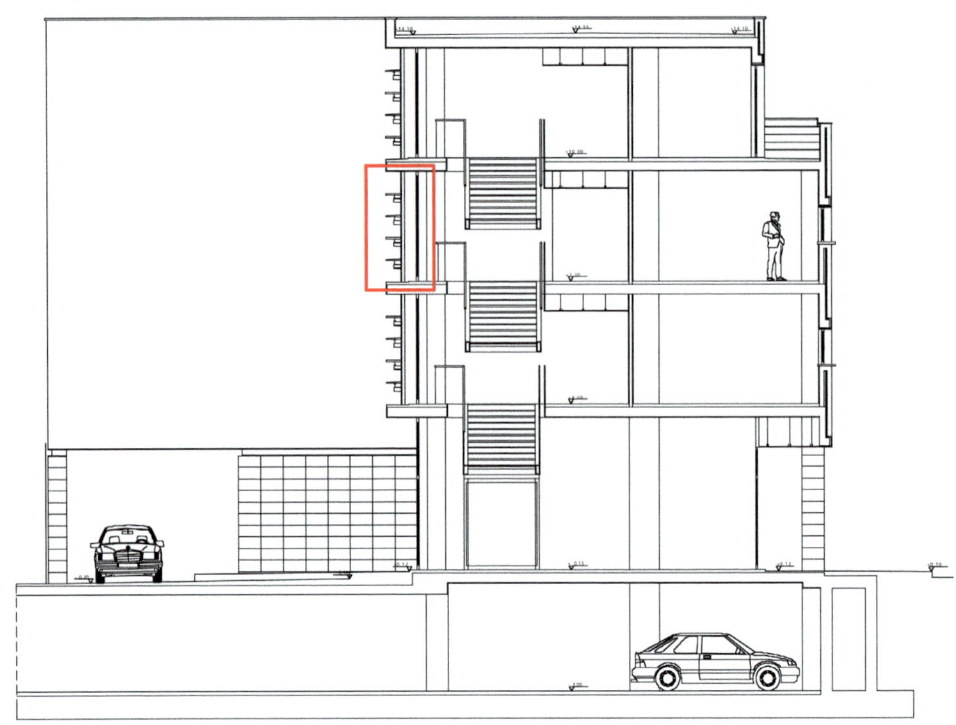

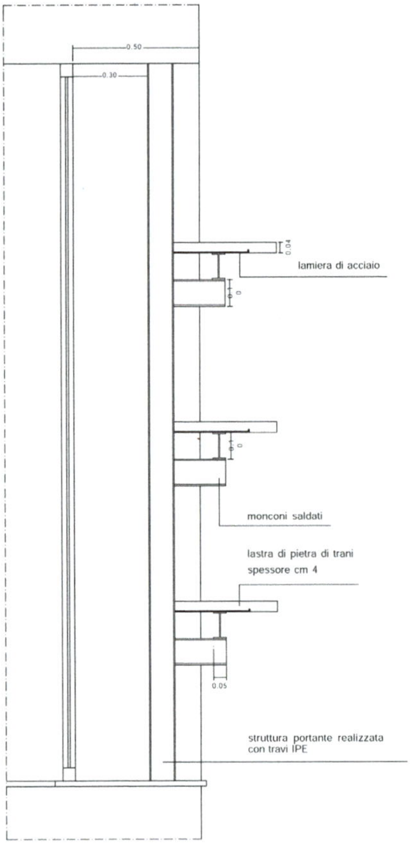

0.50
0.30
0.04
lamiera di acciaio
monconi saldati
lastra di pietra di trani
spessore cm 4
0.05
struttura portante realizzata
con travi IPE

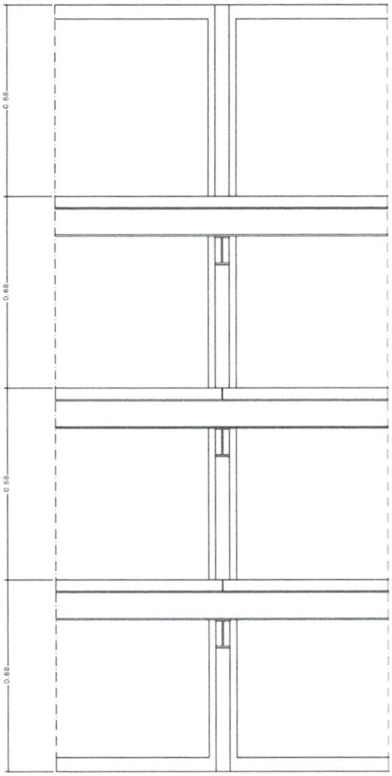

0.68
0.68
0.68
0.68

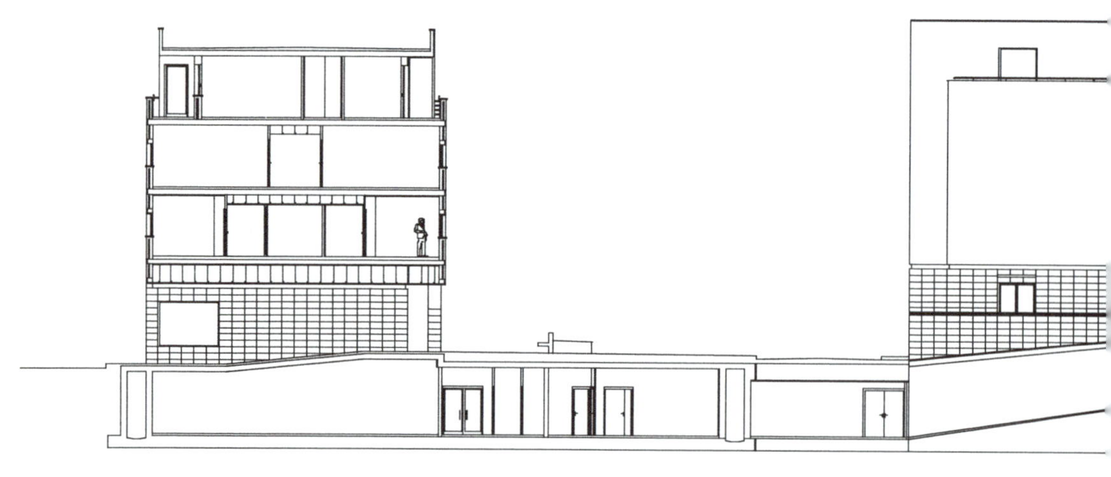

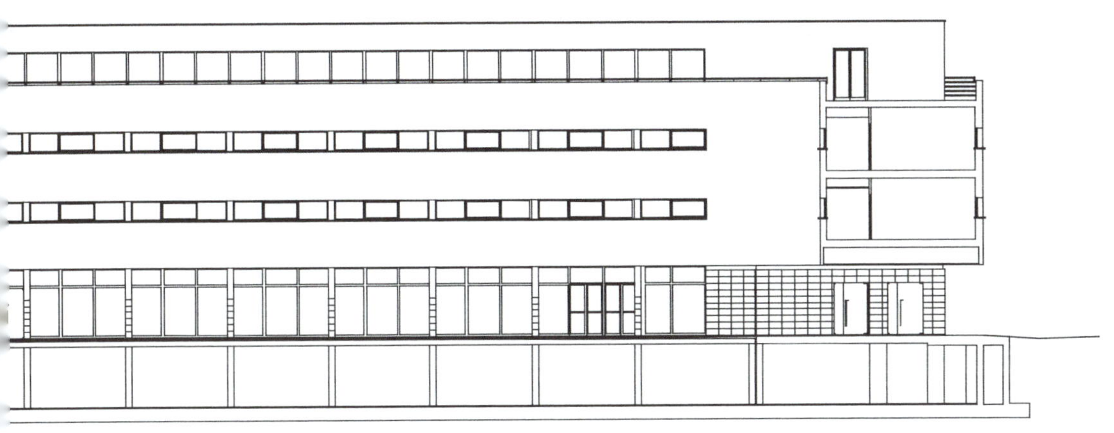

RESTORATION OF THE COVERED MARKET
REGGIO EMILIA
2009–12

The Covered Market is located on land of the ancient Via Emilia, at the intersection between the *cardus* and the *decumanus*, maintaining the traces of the city founded by the Romans. The restoration project takes up the material nature of structures and locations as a system of relationships that presents the old market in all its authenticity, the memory of which takes on the role of principal register of an architectural intervention that is also an intervention on the city. The Covered Market is utilised as a space of connection between existing and new public spaces, defining and revealing the original system of relationships and measurements of the city and its architectures. The organisation of the monument is oriented by the structure of the city, which, reducing itself to the scale of the intervention, has defined the framework of the space of the entire complex, which is capable of also opening up internally through the system of courtyards and gardens. In conserving the specificities and character of the monument, the goal has been set of realising an integrated complex of public interest and social utility that has contributed to triggering and strengthening a process of widespread urban regeneration as an element showcasing and enriching the cultural identity of the city. The new functions and the general distribution system, coinciding with the road network of the historic city, generate a dynamism of spaces, determining a frequency of exchanges between people and things that are typical of the places of the city intended for commerce. A series of 'active actions', with reversible impacts, have given meaning and positioning to the new functions of commerce that live in the monument, assigning to the Covered Market the meanings of a historically symbolic location, a gathering point for the city, inserted into the economic-social fabric, capable of enabling all the pre-existing elements to emerge and at the same time projected into the contemporary world of everyday life.

GALLERIA CENTRALE
coin
coin
New Opening
30 Marzo
2012
coin
New Opening
30 Marzo
2012
coin
TECTON

coin
coin

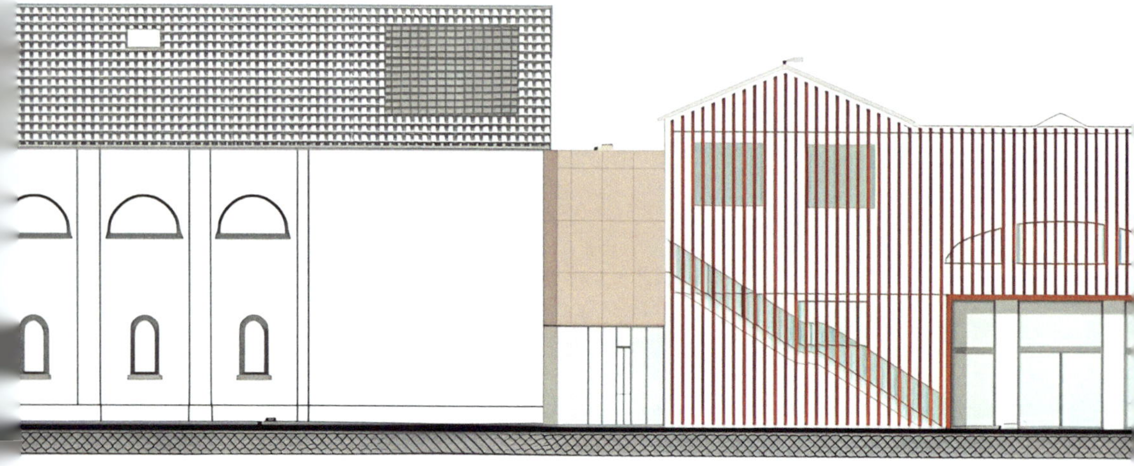

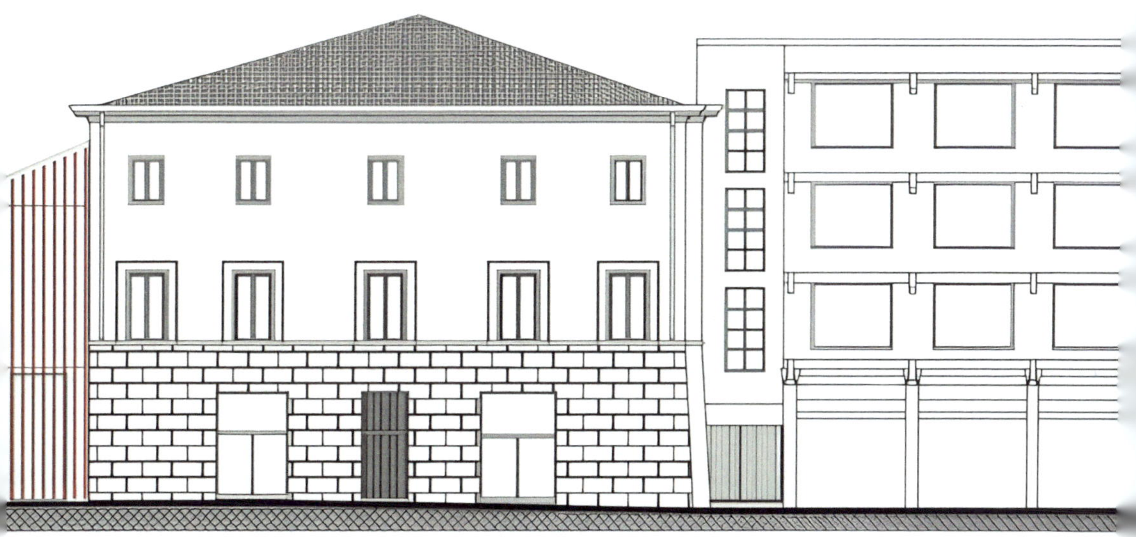

LA CARTIERA SHOPPING AND CRAFTS CENTRE
POMPEII, 2007–12

The project for the new La Cartiera—Integrated Centre for Craftsmanship and Commerce—defines a landscape-building that opens up to its context and registers a new centrality for the town of Pompeii. A number of buildings have been regenerated from the former Aticarta factory that stretched along the right bank of the River Sarno on the stretch between the Traversa di Scafati and the river mouth, in an area delimited by the same river to the south and by the Bottaro Canal to the north. This site presents itself as a marginal location and sets out the conditions for the regeneration of an industrial context that can guarantee appropriate environmental sustainability. The project transforms it into a permeable location that utilises flows of people and goods, transfiguring the enclosure of the former factory, which becomes a space to live, to cross, to inhabit. The profile of greenhouses and large paper spools produced by the old factory is assimilated by the project as the memory of forms deposited over time, which the building interprets, assigning the system of recognisability and unity of the architecture to a general shell.

La Cartiera becomes a place finding spaces for entertainment, shopping, artisan production and dining, intended as public gathering places inserted into a network of existing infrastructures: the motorway, the primary and the local road systems encourage accessibility for the users of the river park and the new activities. The central themes are: a large public space, flexible and with lush vegetation, generated by the thousand-year-old agricultural tradition of these lands, and the major permeability of the entire ground floor. The commercial functions and logistics are moved up to a higher level, guaranteeing the positioning of a significant part of the numerous car parks, also making safe the entire area, which is subject to possible flooding by the two water courses.

LA CARTIERA

MediaWorld

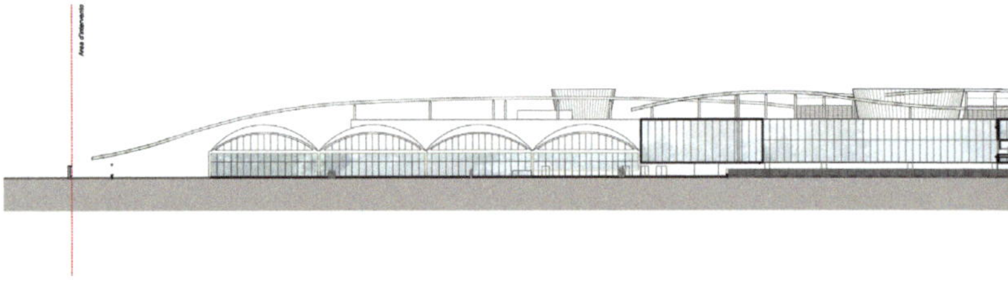

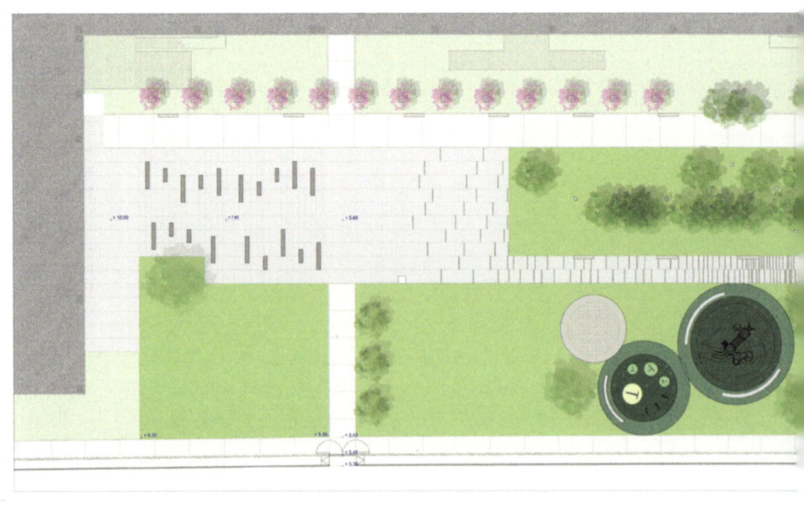

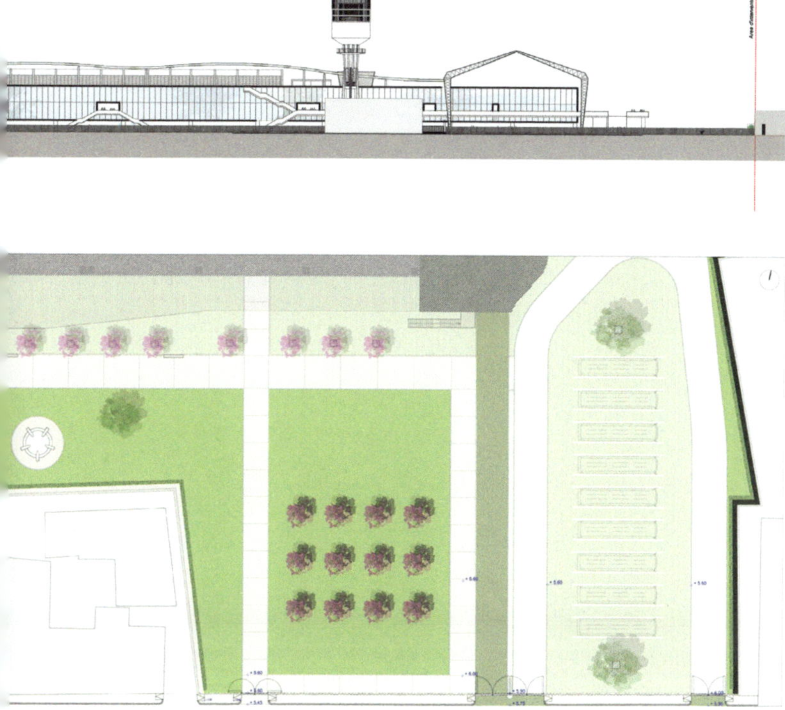

2
MONUMENTAL RESTORATIONS

PAC **In commenting on your first project for Piazza dei Bruzi in Cosenza, you highlighted the importance of your collaboration with a major artist, Mimmo Paladino. I'm interested in further exploring the theme of your relations with contemporary art. Naples is known as one of the European capitals of contemporary art, abounding in artists, collectors, museums and galleries. How has this fertile artistic terrain influenced your choices as architects?**

VC Rather than talk about our meetings with specific artists, I'd like to comment on our relationship with the city, because we recognise this to be the privileged site of a continuous exchange and a historical contamination between art and architecture. 'Contaminations' is in fact the title of an exhibition that we presented in Narni in 2005, and then in Milan, and again at the Galleria Mimmo Scognamiglio in Naples. This exhibition explains architecture as an art that is subject to continuous influences from and interactions with the other visual arts, as well as our pure personal interest in the history of contemporary art. We start with the consideration that one of the secrets of the beauty of the Italian historical city is the fact that the boundary between art and architecture is very blurred, and this makes it difficult to identify where the work of the artist ends and that of the architect begins. We think that the inheritance of contemporary society must take on board this desire for a continuous dialogue, the reason why we endeavour to involve artists, photographers and experts in visual arts in the conception of our projects.

PAC **At the 'Contaminations' exhibition you presented two projects: Piazza dei Bruzi in Cosenza with the large helmet by Mimmo Paladino and the restoration of the Torre delle Nazioni in Naples** [1]**, with the new plinth designed by sculptor Sergio Fermariello. In both cases, the artistic action expresses great symbolic power, associated with the site where it is positioned. In Cosenza, Paladino's helmet evokes the foundation of the city by the ancient pre-roman civilisation of the Bruzi, while in Naples Fermariello's figures replace the original bas-reliefs with a transfiguration with respect to the original fascist rhetoric. In what way does art actually contaminate architecture?**

GM Sergio Fermariello's work doesn't only concern the surface, it gains depth and the work itself becomes the architectural plinth, just as Paladino's helmet gave the project in Cosenza a new spatiality. Fermariello resolves the configuration of the plinth in an artistic but also an architectural vein, replacing the original bas-reliefs from 1940, which Pasquale Monaco and Vincenzo Meconio had created using dark plaster casts, evoking the fascist exploits in the war. The figure of the 'peaceful warrior' proposed by Sergio Fermariello offers a way of interpreting the theme in a contemporary vein: we thought that Sergio was the right person for this discourse on contamination; the artist mustn't be the cherry on top of the cake, rather he's a fundamental figure sitting with us at the table working on the project.

PAC **This project for the Torre delle Nazioni in Naples is particularly interesting, and not only because of this collabora-**

1 TORRE DELLE NAZIONI, NAPLES, MODEL FOR THE PROJECT WITH BASE BY SERGIO FERMARIELLO.

2 HISTORICAL VIEW OF THE MOSTRA D'OLTREMARE WITH THE TORRE DELLE NAZIONI ON THE RIGHT.

3 SKETCH BY MIMMO PALADINO FOR THE TORRE DELLE NAZIONI.

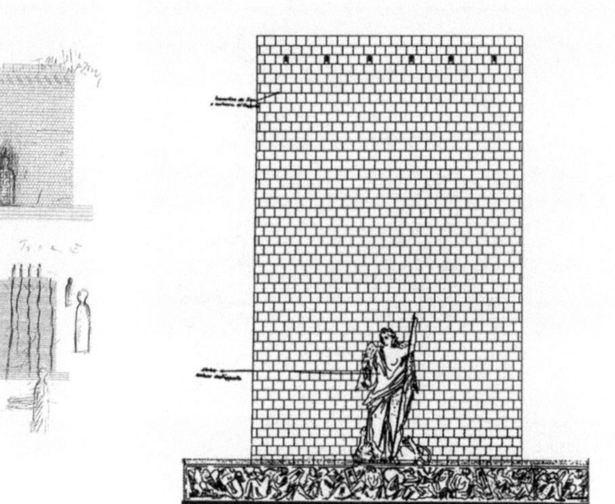

4 HISTORICAL DRAWING OF THE TORRE DELLE NAZIONI, WITH SCULPTURES AND BAS-RELIEFS BY THE ARTISTS MONACO AND MECONIO.

tion with sculptor Sergio Fermariello. It marked your first opportunity to tackle the theme of the restoration of the Modern, in a decidedly monumental context. How did this first assignment on a theme of monumental restoration come about?

VC This project was born in 1994 from the idea, shared with our friend and colleague Luca Lanini, of conducting historical research and organising an exhibition on this extraordinary building **[2]**. Following that job, we received a fiduciary assignment from the then president of the Mostra d'Oltremare, Giulio Albano, to draft a preliminary hypothesis of restoration. The project was presented the following year at an exhibition in the Sala delle Carrozze at Palazzo Reale,[1] with an introduction by Alberto Ferlenga, and became the subject of a publication.[2] Following approval from the Superintendence of Architectural Heritage, we finally drafted the executive project in 2006 with a group of truly excellent professionals and scientific consultants: I'd like to mention in particular, for the structural project, Professors Edoardo Cosenza and Gaetano Manfredi, the current mayor of Naples, but also Andrea Prota, today the director of the DIST–Department of Structures for Engineering and Architecture at the University of Naples Federico II. In 2016 we finally arrived at the tendering for contract and its awarding to the company Brancaccio Costruzioni, but unfortunately the funds had been lost in the meantime, since it involved European financing that was time limited. The idea of involving Sergio Fermariello came after the first restoration project; initially we'd involved Mimmo Paladino, asking him to develop a hypothesis of dialogue between contemporary art and architecture.

PAC **There's only one sketch of this collaboration with Paladino** [3]. **Why was his project not carried forward?**

VC In the fascist period there was a large sculpture of Minerva **[4]** positioned on the plinth, and we had shared the idea with Mimmo of proposing a contemporary interpretation of this in the form of a double vertical white stone sculpture. Subsequently, when we reached the executive phase, we thought it would be more appropriate to involve Sergio Fermariello to rethink the elevation of the plinth, originally the work of the artists Monaco and Meconio, on four sides. It was a work that represented scenes of war and was made of dark plaster panels, masterfully reinterpreted by Sergio from a pacifist perspective with the sign of the 'warrior' that has long characterised his artistic research and his vocabulary.

GM In fact, observing the building carefully, we realised that proposing a sculpture on the plinth once again, as Paladino did, ran the risk of taking on too rhetorical a value, whereas it became more powerful and meaningful to leave the plinth by itself, covered with Fermariello's new corten steel figures **[5]**.

PAC **I agree that the power of the original architecture is reaffirmed in these two large lateral walls, made of stone and totally blind. The presence of a sculpture actually ran the risk of breaking this dimension of absolute abstraction and purity, also of bareness, if we wish to use another term.**

5 DETAIL OF THE WORK
BY SERGIO FERMARIELLO MADE
OF CORTEN STEEL.

6 HISTORICAL NIGHTTIME
VIEW AND MODERN VIEW
(PHOTOGRAPH BY MARIO
FERRARA) OF THE TORRE
DELLE NAZIONI.

VC I must add that Mimmo Paladino was also in agreement on leaving the walls bare. He used a beautiful expression to characterise these walls: he called them 'walls of silence', in opposition to the two other glass walls, for which he used the expression 'walls of chaos'.

PAC **Since you reached the executive project phase, with the hope that construction site could finally begin, I'll ask you a question concerning a problem that's very delicate in monumental restoration projects: how do you guarantee the thermal insulation of the building? How did you resolve this delicate problem, for the blind walls and the doors and windows?**

VC For the blind walls covered in travertine we necessarily had to propose a covering on the inside, increasing the thickness of the infill wall, while for the glass parts we developed a solution with a new design for the doors and windows, using highly insulating thick glass and iron profiles and taking up the measurements of the original design. I may add that the thermal response of the glass façades benefits from the presence of the large reinforced concrete shading devices for the glass wall. It was a building that already presented *de facto* several sustainable characteristics, precursors of the contemporary methods of shading walls to the east and west and keeping the walls blind to the north and south.

PAC **Did you therefore propose new door and window frames because it was impossible to restore the original iron ones? Were they in too poor a condition?**

VC In fact they weren't the original frames; they had already been replaced with very bad iron frames in the 1960s. We conducted some historical research, going back to the drawings of the original façades by architect Venturino Ventura, and using historical photographs **[6]** to understand how the profile of the frame had been made.

PAC **The interior space of the Torre delle Nazioni is organised with an interesting section of offset planes** [7], **which enables a spiral route to be created. On this subject, I read the beautiful interpretation by Luca Lanini, who worked in association with you on the restoration project, and who used the designation 'Guggenheim squared'.[3] The Torre delle Nazioni could in fact become an exhibition space of extraordinary beauty. This theme of the reuse of commemorative buildings from the fascist era for exhibition purposes brings to mind one of your projects, from a few years later, for the Museo del Novecento in the Arengario in Piazza Duomo in Milan. I'm referring to an international competition from 2001, won by Italo Rota, who subsequently implemented the project. Why did you invite the Austrian architect Klaus Kada to take part together?**

GM Our relationship with Klaus Kada came about on the occasion of an exhibition organised by the Architects Register of Naples and curated by Vincenzo in 2000 in Naples:[4] a very interesting and stimulating experience, also because it offered us the opportunity to design the exhibition layout, which Kada had conceived in a wholly innovative way on the theme of the relationship between architecture and multimedia. After the exhibition, we proposed working together for this important competition. The theme concerned the regeneration of the historical building, organised vertically, and its connection with the so-called 'long sleeve' of Palazzo Reale. Kada's projects in Graz had impressed us, particularly the Institute of Physiology of Plants, where a glass-walled bridge **[8]** connects the historic house with the contemporary building. Kada was therefore important in defining the theme of the bridge between the Arengario and Palazzo Reale together.

PAC **Yet Kada wasn't an architect who had actually realised monument restoration projects. Did you bring your own experience into this collaboration, therefore, particularly after the restoration project of the Torre delle Nazioni, whereas Kada had to devote his energies more to the parts with the more linguistic innovation?**

VC We worked on the project in Naples, but always in dialogue with Klaus. I remember a decisive trip to Graz, when we took drawings and physical models with us **[9]**, to define with him all the parts of a project in which the tension between innovation and conservation was consolidated. For us it was also the opportunity to visit his extraordinary architectures and to appraise his capacity to innovate directly, but at the same time to check that the structural project was perfectly consistent with the architectural project. In this regard, I remember that Kada taught architectural and structural planning at the Faculty of Architecture in Aachen.

PAC **We're talking about 2001, and it's a pity that we didn't know each other then, because we could have all met up in Graz! In those years I was a professor and head of the Faculty of Architecture in Graz, and I was also a friend of Klaus Kada, whom I often went to visit in his studio, not far from the university.**

THE RESTORATION OF THE PIRELLI SKYSCRAPER

PAC **The beginning of your career was favoured by your winning important architecture competitions: firstly in Cosenza, with Piazza dei Bruzi and with the Isolato dei Rivocati, secondly in Milan, with the competition for the restoration of the Pirelli Skyscraper, a masterpiece of Italian modern architecture designed by Gio Ponti and Pier Luigi Nervi. How did that project begin?**

VC We participated in two competitions held in 1998 to restore two small yet significant parts of the Pirelli Skyscraper: the auditorium **[10]** in the basement

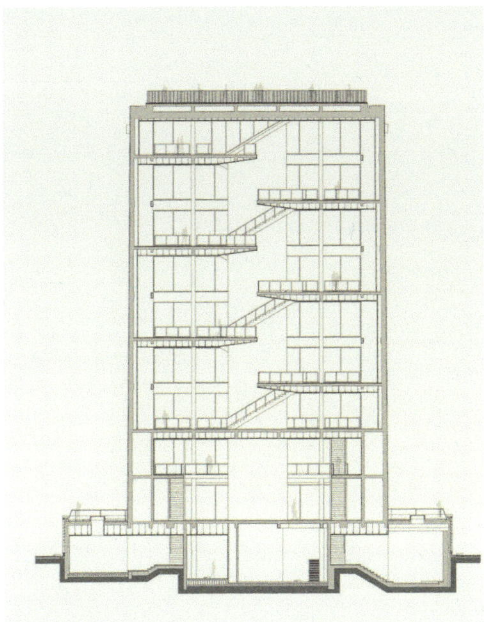

7 CROSS SECTION OF THE TORRE DELLE NAZIONI WITH OFFSET FLOORS.

9 COMPETITION PROJECT FOR THE MUSEO DEL NOVECENTO IN THE ARENGARIO IN PIAZZA DUOMO (WITH KLAUS KADA), MILAN, 2001, DETAIL OF THE MODEL.

8 KLAUS KADA, INSTITUTE OF PLANT PHYSIOLOGY, GRAZ, 1998.

10 THE AUDITORIUM IN THE BASEMENT OF THE PIRELLI SKYSCRAPER, PIRELLI ARCHIVE.

11 THE BELVEDERE ON THE THIRTY-FIRST FLOOR OF THE PIRELLI SKYSCRAPER, PIRELLI ARCHIVE.

12 THE FAÇADE OF THE PIRELLI SKYSCRAPER AFTER THE AIRCRAFT CRASH OF 18 APRIL 2002. ARCHIVE OF THE LOMBARDY REGIONAL AUTHORITY.

and the belvedere on the thirty-first floor **[11]**. These were both restricted competitions based on CVs, so it was necessary to have already realised similar works previously.

PAC **And had you already created an auditorium?**

VC Fortunately we'd already designed the interior layout of the council room of the Campania Regional Authority, in the basement floor of the former Isveimer tower designed by Alberto Izzo and Camillo Gubitosi, one of the interior design assignments we'd fulfilled for Olivetti Engineering. Olivetti conducted planning and turnkey construction work for offices, automation installations and digital management, and with them—again at the headquarters of the Campania Regional Authority—we realised service spaces and the restaurant: an interesting job, published on the pages of *Abitare*, with a beautiful installation by artist Sergio Fermariello.

PAC **So you participated in this double competition, you won with the project for the auditorium and you received the assignment to build it. Was it all easy?**

VC We'd decided to also present some physical models, even though this was not required in the competition brief, which nevertheless did allow this possibility. We learned the importance of models from Alberto Izzo, and subsequently also from Gonçalo Byrne. We had to hire a van to transport these large models from Naples to Milan. And this impressed the jury, which was made up of some outstanding personalities, including the historian Maria Antonietta Crippa and the director of the Superintendence of Architectural Heritage, Carla di Francesco.

GM But I remember that after winning we felt there was a lot of mistrust of us, because we were two young architects coming from Southern Italy.

PAC **And then in 2002 there was the serious incident of the small aircraft that crashed into the façade of the skyscraper. At that time, was your construction site for the auditorium already in operation?**

GM Yes, that day I was in Milan at the worksite. I remember it as though it were yesterday. The images of the incident **[12]** went all around the world; the president of the Lombardy Regional Authority was in India, and people immediately thought of a repetition of 9/11. This incident changed our destiny. Immediately afterwards we had the sensation that everything was over, faced with the seriousness of the event, because, as well as the pilot of the aircraft, two female lawyers from the legal office on the twenty-sixth floor had also died. The construction site was suspended and a major debate was opened on the future of the Pirelli Skyscraper, but then the Lombardy Regional Authority decided that the moment had come to launch an overall restoration of the building. A key role in reaching this decision was played by the technical-scientific commission, which had been formed with many members of the 1998 competition jury, with the addition of other personalities, such as the rector of Milan Politecnico, Giulio Ballio. They were the ones who advised the President Roberto Formigoni to entrust the overall restoration project to the same architects who had won the 1998 competitions: us for the auditorium and Renato Sarno for the belvedere on the thirty-first floor.

PAC **This was hugely fortunate for you; in this case too the politicians overcame their traditional mistrust of young architects.**

GM It always needs to be remembered that we were favoured by a very enlightened clientele, who backed up their decisions based on a group of very authoritative consultants, including Maria Antonietta Crippa, who was the *deus ex machina* of the entire procedure. She was also the one who strongly defended our subsequent decision to restore the original façades **[13, 14]** and not replace them, contributing expertise, archive documents and relations with specialist companies. And in the end she also edited the monograph published by Skira in 2007.

PAC **How did you collaborate with Renato Sarno, who had won the other competition in 1998?**

VC Renato Sarno **[15]** had realised important projects in Milan, so he was already an experienced professional. Working together we were therefore able to combine our enthusiasm, our youth, but also our project culture, with his more managerial, entrepreneurial abilities, and also with his professional experience, which we lacked. It needs to be recognised that he protected us from possible errors, also offering us a great opportunity.

PAC **Did you share all the project work, or did you divide up the various parts of the building?**

GM Once the various activities to be performed were coordinated, we did in fact define the respective tasks, but always trying to find forms of synthesis. For example, we were busier with the interiors, whereas he was more interested in the restoration of the façades, but we always shared all the most important choices. There were also time-sensitive requirements; I remember that the aircraft incident happened in April 2002, and that the auditorium, the façades and the thirty-first floor were completed in April 2004, and the Pirelli Skyscraper was returned fully to its users a year later. This was in record time for Italy.

PAC **The Pirelli Skyscraper was not only returned to its users, but also to the city of Milan. I think, in fact, that the city and its citizens gained a great deal not only from the return of its original architectural image as a landmark of modernity on the urban skyline, but also from the intervention in the public space, particularly along Via Filzi. Previously this was clearly the back of the skyscraper, whereas today Via Filzi has acquired the dignity of a large public space. How did you manage to persuade the authorities on this proposal of yours?**

GM The bottom of the building facing towards Via Filzi was entirely insufficient and not really recognisable, and this was therefore in contradiction with the fact of being the side that had the greater influx and outflow of staff and

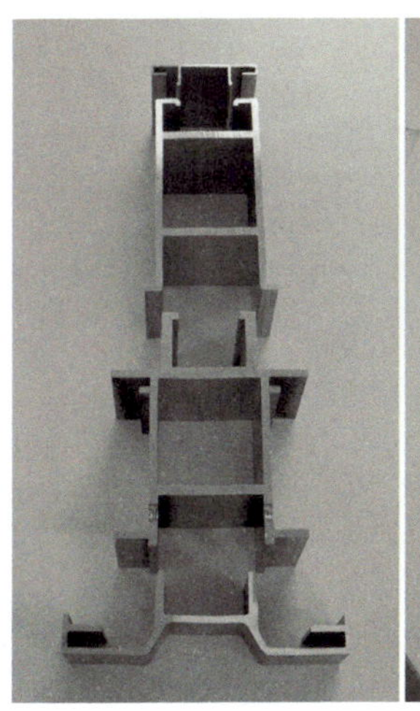

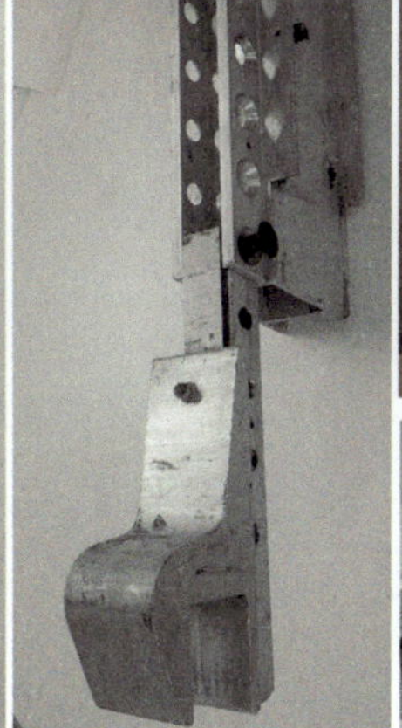

13 ORIGINAL ALUMINIUM ELEMENTS ANCHORING THE FAÇADE TO THE FLOORS, RESTORED AND REINSTATED.

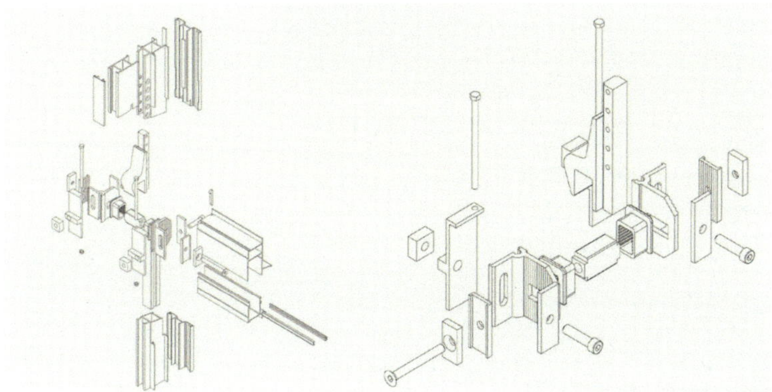

14 CONSTRUCTION DETAILS OF THE FAÇADE, WITH THE REINSTATED ELEMENTS IN THE RESTORATION PROJECT.

15 ABOVE: GIOVANNI MULTARI, RENATO SARNO AND VINCENZO CORVINO AT THE WORKSITE FOR THE RESTORATION OF THE PIRELLI SKYSCRAPER. LEFT: MEETING WITH TECHNICAL–SCIENTIFIC COMMISSION.

the public. I remember a meeting where the president of the Regional Authority was present, a very rare opportunity that we attempted to exploit by introducing the proposal to widen the pavements. Before this meeting, the executives of the Regional Authority didn't want to discuss the merits of the idea, because they said that the matter concerned the Municipal Authority of Milan. During the presentation **[16]**, we had included some images with our proposal, and had pointed out that, compared with an overall budget of sixty million euros, spending another million to implement this proposal affected the overall budget very little, but would have had very important consequences for the appreciation of the building in the urban context. The president immediately recognised that this proposal was interesting and important, asking that it be accepted. We discussed it further with the offices of the Municipal Authority of Milan, with whom we had excellent relations as we were creating the two squares in Milan at that time. After these negotiations between executives of the Regional Authority and municipal offices, we therefore succeeded in realising the definitive project, which widened the pavements not only along Via Filzi, but also along the entire perimeter **[17]**.

PAC **Completed in 1960, the Pirelli Skyscraper became an icon of the Italian economic boom, and of Milan in particular, and it's no coincidence that it appears in the film *La Notte* (1961) by Michelangelo Antonioni, together with other contemporary buildings that enabled the public of international filmgoers to discover how ultramodern Milan had become in those years. The first sequences, with the opening credits of the film** [18], **are extraordinary in that they show us the Milanese urban landscape from high above, with the Central Station and the large voids of the business district, following the vertical movement of a cleaning platform along the glass façade, which partially mirrors the image of the city. A few years after the completion of your restoration, the Pirelli Skyscraper became the location of an action film, *The International* (2009), which director Tom Tykwer imagined returning to its original function as a building representing private capital, such as the headquarters of a merchant bank. What impression did seeing this film have on you?**

GM It was very striking to me to realise that in this case too the film, and the fiction, relied on the pure reality of the architecture, as Antonioni had done with the then recently completed Pirelli Skyscraper. The first scene in Tykwer's film, with the arrival on the square-hill of the two leading actors, is very beautiful, as looking upwards they observe the tower, before entering the atrium with its 'fantastic yellow' floor, go up in the lift and come out on the thirty-first floor. It all happens very quickly, but in this thirty-first floor Tykwer recognises the wholly extraordinary identity of this location, which we have always called the 'Gothic cathedral' of the Pirelli Skyscraper, where Nervi's solid structures are revealed. Tykwer transforms it into a totally open-plan office **[19]**, with few furniture items with elegant designs taken from the collections of the great master designers, such as Mies or Breuer. It therefore seems to me to be a significant method that the director uses to create a scene that is highly consistent with reality, I'd even say with the essence of this extraordinary space, which

16 PLENARY MEETING FOR PRESENTATION OF THE PRELIMINARY RESTORATION PROJECT.

17 VIEW OF THE SQUARE-HILL FROM ABOVE, PIRELLI ARCHIVE.

18 OPENING CREDITS OF THE FILM *LA NOTTE* (1961) BY MICHELANGELO ANTONIONI.

19 THE BELVEDERE ON THE THIRTY-FIRST FLOOR AFTER THE RESTORATION, FRAME FROM THE FILM *THE INTERNATIONAL* (2009).

finds its power in being totally empty, as we wanted to render it with our restoration project. Unfortunately it's no longer possible to see this space on the thirty-first floor as it appears in Tykwer's film, following an intervention—not by our studio, I might add—which significantly modified this beautiful space.

PAC **Why, is it no longer an empty space?**

GM No, a sort of opaque glass bead has been added in the interior, the exact opposite of the geometry of the diamond referred to by Gio Ponti, an intervention that denies the tectonics of Pier Luigi Nervi's marvellous structures, which only return to being exposed concrete structures on this floor.

PAC **In conclusion, how do you evaluate this experience of the restoration of the Pirelli Skyscraper twenty years on?**

GM The restoration of the Pirelli Skyscraper was a decisive experience for the whole of our subsequent career, and today we have the maturity to observe it with a certain critical distance. We've become aware of the fundamental importance of the theme of the restoration of the Modern, but we've become even more aware of the way to design projects for monumental buildings, showing great humility, a huge willingness to understand the context, to understand the location, to understand the specific solutions. For this reason we like to associate the Pirelli Skyscraper with the project for Capodimonte, because the spirit with which we design today is the same as at that time: we don't approach the monument to dictate rules or to impose stylistic features of our own; we're here to learn, to understand and comprehend, observing the building. The Pirelli Skyscraper taught us that.

VC I'd like to add that it's no coincidence that this extraordinary opportunity of the Pirelli Skyscraper was offered to us in Milan, because Milan is a city that is rather special for architecture, for design, but also in general on account of the opportunities it offers. Milan enabled us to encounter a master architect whom we've never met personally, but who has clearly contributed to changing our lives: Gio Ponti, a 'totalising architect', who measured the time of his life through the project, from the sketch to the construction, from the furniture design to the editor's office at *Domus*, from teaching to the construction site. For this reason, I'd place him alongside our first teacher, Alberto Izzo.

PAC **A teacher whose lessons you learned through a building therefore, and not through books?**

VC Yes, that's a particular feature of his teaching, which we grasped in dismantling the façade and observing the original construction drawings, but also in talking to the people who'd worked with him and with his heirs, an extraordinary way to grasp an inheritance directly through the experience of the architecture.

THE RESTORATION OF CAPODIMONTE MUSEUM

PAC **You called upon Mimmo Paladino to collaborate again for Capodimonte. How did you involve him in the design process?**

VC Mimmo is an artist **[20]** with a great capacity to read the space in three dimensions. He usually asks to be able to discuss around physical models, to measure the space, to understand its depth and height. So in his studio he created a large model **[21]** of the reception room on which we and Sylvain Bellenger invited him to intervene. In this way Mimmo investigated the relationship between the lemon montage on the ceiling **[22]**, the hanging sculpture and the other piece positioned in one of the niches of the perimeter wall. He always prefers to enter an architectural dimension before an artistic one in order to imagine his work, as had happened with Piazza dei Bruzi. Artists are rather solitary by definition, whereas we, as architects, also due to our education, have accrued a choral conception of the project work over time. Putting the project in the centre of the table also means valuing the client, who's engaged in the definition of the idea. We like to remember what Filarete said about architecture, that it needs a father—the client—and a mother—the architect.

PAC **In the case of Capodimonte Museum, the Director Sylvain Bellenger can certainly be recognised as having this fundamental role of 'father' of the project. What type of dialogue did you develop about the artists' choices? While you had already worked almost thirty years earlier with Mimmo Paladino, who's become an even more famous and established artist in the meantime, what were the reasons behind the invitation to Christiane Löhr to be involved with an installation on the terrace?**

VC Christiane Löhr **[23]** was proposed by Director Sylvain Bellenger, who had invited her to Capodimonte in 2020 for a solo exhibition as part of a cycle of events entitled 'Sensitive Encounters, dialogue between contemporary artists and the Capodimonte historical collection', curated by him together with Laura Trisorio. Christiane Löhr is an artist who works with very thin, fragile elements, such as wires and branches, and had never come to grips with an architecture project. Sylvain Bellenger saw her as an artist capable of designing elements that initially might even have covered the entire central courtyard, whereas the proposal became more sober during the development of her project, restricting herself to the floor of the large terrace. Her design harkens back to the shadows of the branches of a tree **[24]**, a design that begins inside the loggia to then expand outside onto the terrace, revisiting the relationship between interior and exterior in an extraordinary way.

PAC **What was the occasion when you met Sylvain Bellenger, the director of Capodimonte Museum?**

VC We'd contacted him in 2017 because we wanted to present our monograph *Architecture Experiences* at the Capodimonte Museum. The presentation took place in the Sala Burri on 10 November, with a short introduction by Sylvain Bellenger, whom we'd never met before.

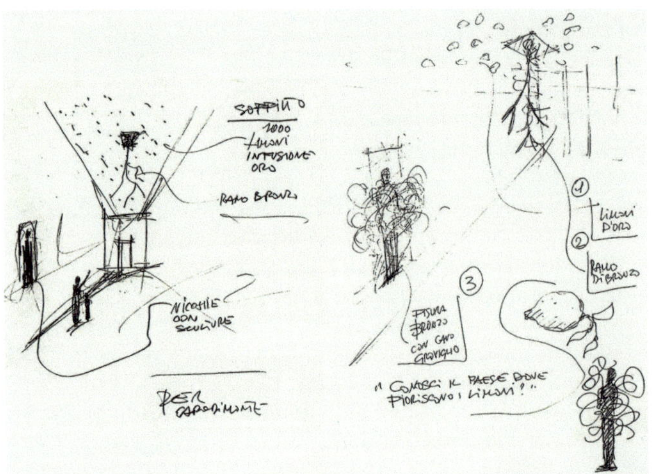

20 SKETCH BY MIMMO PALADINO FOR THE RECEPTION ROOM OF THE CAPODIMONTE MUSEUM.

21 ABOVE: SYLVAIN BELLENGER, FILIPPO CANNATA AND VINCENZO CORVINO STANDING AROUND THE MODEL FOR PALADINO'S INSTALLATION OF THE RECEPTION ROOM. LEFT: VINCENZO CORVINO, MIMMO PALADINO AND EIKE SCHMIDT AT THE WORKSITE OF THE RECEPTION ROOM.

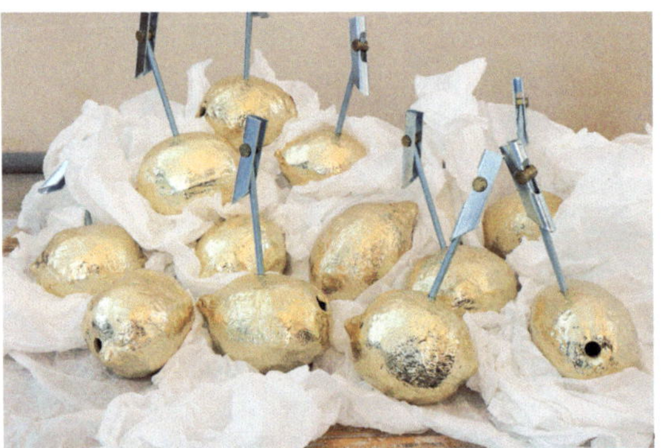

22 THE GOLDEN LEMONS BY MIMMO PALADINO BEFORE THEIR ASSEMBLY ON THE CEILING OF THE RECEPTION ROOM.

PAC **From this first meeting, how did you arrive at being appointed to develop the project?**

VC Everything happened during the 2020 pandemic, when we were all shut up at home, and the museums were all closed, forcing us to create cultural events online. We organised a series of meetings with Pino Scaglione and Raul Pantaleo, structured as forums for work and discussion[5] to which not only we architects were invited, but also artists, politicians, intellectuals and scientists, to discuss certain hypotheses of regeneration of cities, driven by the necessary ecological transition after the serious crisis that had erupted with the pandemic. Sylvain Bellenger had been invited to one of these round tables, on 1 May, together with personalities such as sculptor Mimmo Paladino, landscape architect João Nunes, prosecutor Nicola Gratteri and lighting designer Filippo Cannata. After the meeting, very late in the evening, Sylvain Bellenger called me to thank me for the way I'd described the Royal Wood of Capodimonte in its capacity to become a location of visual, environmental and naturalistic permeability for the city. And immediately afterwards he proposed to entrust our studio directly with the developing of a small project, without specifying what it was. The day afterwards he called me to tell me that he had significant financing available from the Ministry of Culture for relaunching Capodimonte, but that he was unable to spend all of it due to the complexity of the procedures involved. At this point in the discussion I relaunched the proposal, also refusing to be told what the small assignment he was proposing might consist of, to declare instead that we were interested in participating in the major international design competition that was to be launched soon in order to use all the financing. In fact, I didn't want a kind of inappropriateness or conflict of interest to be created if by chance we had already been entrusted with another project for the museum. And so it was that we began to join the conversation about the idea of an integrated project, a multidisciplinary scheme that could also take the various models for managing the intervention into consideration.

PAC **At what point in this discussion did the multinational Engie come into play?**

VC Again in the period of the pandemic, we'd got to know some executives of Engie Italia, and so I got back into contact to ask them if they might be interested in sharing with the museum director a hypothesis of building a public–private partnership to work on the Capodimonte Museum. It must be remembered that Engie is a French multinational, one of the most important in the world operating in the sectors of the production and distribution of natural gas, renewable energies and services, and that Sylvain Bellenger is an intellectual who's very sensitive to the theme of energy transition.

PAC **That's very interesting. Faced with the real difficulties that the museum director had in spending all the money, in view of the complexity of the procedures, you were the ones who tried to place your experience with project financing competitions as architects at his disposal, as had happened, for example, with the Covered Market in Reggio Emilia. I was certain that Engie, as a French company with significant participation by the State, had been contacted directly by Sylvain Bellenger, as a director of French nationality.**

23 SYLVAIN BELLENGER AND VINCENZO CORVINO WITH CHRISTIANE LÖHR IN HER STUDIO IN COLOGNE.

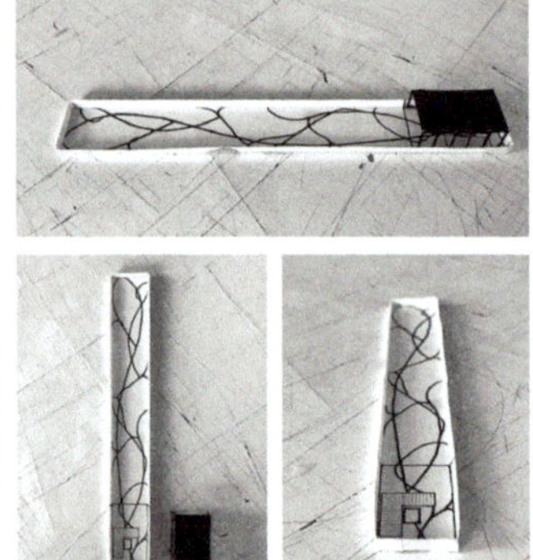

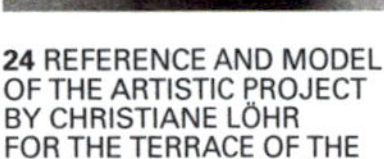

24 REFERENCE AND MODEL OF THE ARTISTIC PROJECT BY CHRISTIANE LÖHR FOR THE TERRACE OF THE CAPODIMONTE MUSEUM.

25 LUIGI SALVATORE GENTILE, VIEW OF THE NEW ROAD IN CAPODIMONTE, 1807.

VC No, it's quite the opposite.

PAC **How did the discussion develop with Engie in order to reach the definitive agreement?**

VC We began with the opening of a discussion between Sylvain Bellenger and Fabrizio Di Battista, director of the South Adriatic area of Engie Italia, to understand how to build up a public–private partnership, and subsequently a two-day workshop was promoted in the Sala Burri, in which various professionals from a number of different disciplines participated, from landscape architecture to engineering, from digital multimedia to the technology of building systems. This workshop was very useful not only in defining the orientations for future design processes, but also in adapting the interventions of a potential project financing initiative to meet their economic and financial needs.

PAC **How much did the public financing available to Sylvain Bellenger amount to?**

VC Altogether, the Ministry of Culture had made around 78 million euros available to the Capodimonte Museum, but only a part of this was spent. Sylvain Bellenger was at the end of his mandate, and up to then only partial projects had been realised; what were missing perhaps were a coordination and an overview for an integrated project. Sylvain Bellenger was prepared to embark upon a wide-ranging and complex project; in the United States he'd had experiences of managing important museum projects, with Renzo Piano when he was curator of the Department of Painting and Sculpture of Europe at The Art Institute of Chicago, and with Rafael Viñoly when he was director of the Department of European and American Arts at the Cleveland Museum of Art. It must be remembered that the Capodimonte Museum was in a state of rather advanced deterioration as regards its doors and windows, the lighting installations were wholly obsolete and inhomogeneous, there was not air conditioning system on the first floor, the areas devoted to services to the public were considerably downscaled, and the terrace with the belvedere on the roof was also unusable.

PAC **I think that this virtuous process at the basis of the restoration project for Capodimonte Museum is exemplary, because all too often we read and we hear tell that in Italy it isn't possible to realise major projects because financing is lacking. There are often resources available, but people can't manage to use them well, because what's lacking is an overall design vision, and what's lacking is a clear managerial capacity on the part of the public institutions. In this specific case, your role as architects was to insist on the need for an overall project and to involve many different players around a common decision-making table.**

VC We actually had to persevere a great deal to stimulate a major energy company, active as a financial global player in many projects, to handle an integrated project in a sphere that was so unusual for them, a major museum in a monumental building. For them it was all new, but since then it seems to me that they're considering establishing a dedicated section to be involved in other museum projects.

PAC **I'm interested now in discussing with you the similarities and differences between this restoration project for the Capodimonte Museum and the restoration project for the Pirelli Skyscraper. Almost twenty years on, have you modified your way of conceiving the restoration project? Are there differences between working on a modern building and working on a building that's mostly 18th-century such as Capodimonte?**

GM There are no fundamental differences in the approach, and I could say today, in all serenity, that the so-called 'restoration of the Modern' is a false problem. The restoration of the Pirelli Skyscraper has taught us that what always counts, at the start of any project, is a very profound act of awareness, to put all the questions that the building poses for us in order, leaving aside the adaptation of the building for new contemporary uses. So we can work on a modern building or on an old building, without distinction. This occurred, for example, in the restoration of the façades of the Pirelli Skyscraper, where we performed an authentic anastylosis: the various pieces were dismantled one at a time, then taken to the workshop to be restored, and subsequently reassembled at the point where they'd been removed, solely adding those fixtures that had been lost following the aircraft crash.

PAC **In fact, you proceeded as has always been done, for many centuries, with the replacement of stone blocks in Gothic cathedrals.**

GM Yes, and we also did so for the small vetrosa based ceramic tiles, which we had to reinstate. In view of the impossibility of finding original tiles, which were produced at the time by Vaccari, which is no longer in existence, we had to have the new tiles produced in India. A similar problem of finding original materials concerned the famous 'fantastic yellow' linoleum floor that Ponti had developed with Pirelli: with it no longer being in production, we had to have the new linoleum, identical to the original, produced in Germany. The real differences in working in a modern or old building concern the functions, because modern buildings come about as very specialised constructions, for example a school as a building type is difficult to transform into something different, whereas old buildings tend to endure forever, passing through the centuries with great ease.

PAC **One of the particular aspects of the Capodimonte Museum is the fact of its being a building with various temporal stratifications in a landscape context of great merit** [25], **with interventions from the 18th century to the late 20th, and so with considerable stylistic discontinuities. How did the discussion develop with the Superintendence of Architectural Heritage as regards the management of these discontinuities, and sometimes inconsistencies, inside the building? I'm thinking in particular of the parts created in the contem-**

porary age, such as the roof and the terrace, or the auditorium on the ground floor, which you proposed to modify. In certain cases, there are Superintendences that defend very ideological positions in stating that all interventions have been historicised, and so must be conserved in their entirety. Or, in contrast, there are positions, equally strongly ideological, such as that defended for many years by Paolo Marconi and by his numerous disciples, the proposal to demolish modern interventions, considered as 'excrescences', and reconstruct the monument in its original forms, defending the need to produce a 'fake historic architecture' when necessary. How did you act, therefore, in Capodimonte in relation to this important issue of historical stratification?

VC When we taught at the Faculty of Architecture in Cesena in the course on restoration of the Modern, between 2005 and 2009, our colleague Giovanni Leoni stated that the architecture project is always a restoration project, if, in order to define it, it's necessary to identify values, starting with a journey of awareness creation, and it's these values that enable the contemporary action to be defined, consistently and in continuity with historical memory. The capacity to innovate is highlighted, even only through an act of subtraction, the removal of excrescences and incongruous parts in order to determine new functionalities.

GM For example, going back to the Pirelli Skyscraper, in order to recognise the importance of the entrance atrium along Via Filzi, we dismantled the parts that had been added by Vico Magistretti so as to obtain a full-height space, considering it more compatible with the original idea of the building. To return to Ponti's project, we had to operate with subtractions and few additions.

VC At Capodimonte we had a very good dialogue with the Superintendence of Architectural Heritage, above all with Director Luigi La Rocca, who agreed with the idea that the intervention could become a pilot project, which would be very useful in Italy, because the energy and digital transition can offer the opportunity to showcase other buildings of great artistic and historical value. One day he told me that until now he had done nothing but reject proposals for photovoltaic panels in historic centres, whereas with our project he'd realised that there are architectural ways of making photovoltaic ambitions and the cultural heritage code compatible. It's necessary to specify that our most innovative interventions concern the 20th-century parts of the building, such as the roof transformed by Ezio De Felice with prefabricated reinforced concrete trusses, the covering of tiles that had already been replaced in 2000, or even the auditorium, created by De Felice by inserting a reinforced concrete floor in the former Royal Chapel, and subsequently replaced recently by Ermanno Guida with Superintendent Nicola Spinosa. The Royal Chapel had therefore already been entirely disrupted by these interventions.

PAC **Your intervention for the large reception room eliminates these 20th-century interventions and reopens the large windows of the former Royal Chapel. On this subject, can we talk of a contemporary form of anastylosis?**

VC It seems to me that that's a really good definition. I may add that we were also thinking, together with our scientific advisor Renata Picone, professor of restoration in the Department of Architecture at the University of Naples Federico II, of restoring some marble fragments of the altar of the Royal Chapel that had been retrieved after the earthquake in 1980. The original curved shape of the altar is recreated in the two new lateral ramps. Our idea is to evoke the former sacred space of the chapel, not to reconstruct it with philological rigour. The most important decision concerns the use of this location at the start of the visit, highlighting the direct continuity between this area, the lifts and the monumental stairway positioned axially, therefore enhancing the axiality with which military architect Giovanni Antonio Medrano had conceived the Palace of Capodimonte in proposing the Cartesian plan of the three courtyards.

PAC **One interesting aspect of the project concerns the technological solutions used to obtain effective energy saving, and the ways of integrating the systems inside a building subject to restrictions, with its abundance of interior decorative apparatuses. On its website, Engie Italia describes the project, specifying that the four thousand five hundred photovoltaic modules are 'fully integrated and invisible'. I'd like to discuss with you this idea that technological solutions should not be on display. Can the invisibility of the intervention be considered a positive value?**

VC I don't like this definition of 'invisibility'; I prefer to use the expression 'compatible' solutions. The inner pitches of the roofs towards the three courtyards are covered in baked brick-coloured photovoltaic modules; this doesn't mean that they're invisible: they can't be seen from the ground, but they will be visible from the belvedere terrace and in the interaction with the landscape in the aerial view. These layers of photovoltaic panels are compatible with the original design of the whole roof and revisit the historical image of blind layers covered with tiles in a contemporary vein. This image had been profoundly changed by Ezio De Felice with the new roof, characterised by large glass skylights providing light to the restoration volumes for positioning the machines of the air conditioning systems.

PAC **Whereas in the exhibition rooms on the first floor you resolved the problem of integrating the air conditioning system into the floor brilliantly, because in this case the intervention is truly 'almost invisible', with a simple grille positioned flush under the large window. How did you arrive at this solution?**

VC In the beginning it seemed almost impossible to air condition the first floor, because the ceilings were frescoed and the original historical floors had to be conserved. We experimented with various hypotheses with Marco Paissan, a designer of air conditioning systems with the engineering company Climosfera, without finding a satisfactory solution. At a certain point, with him we observed the external balconies **[26]** that run along all the façades on the first floor, declared not fit for use by the public, together with the wooden window frames, which in the restoration had maintained a secondary frame sixteen

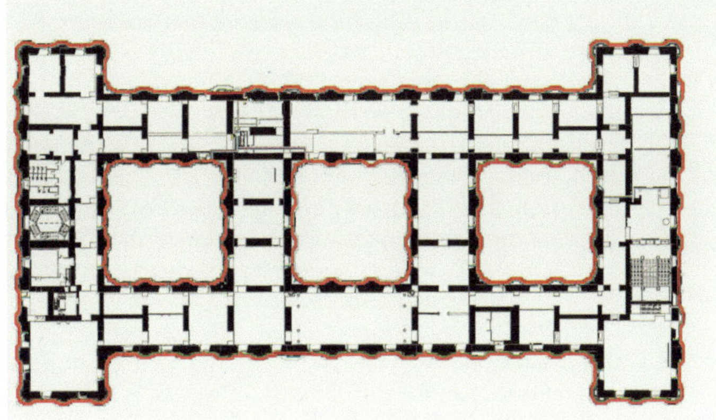

26 PLAN OF THE FIRST FLOOR WITH THE AIR CONDITIONING DUCTS ALONG THE PERIMETER BALCONIES.

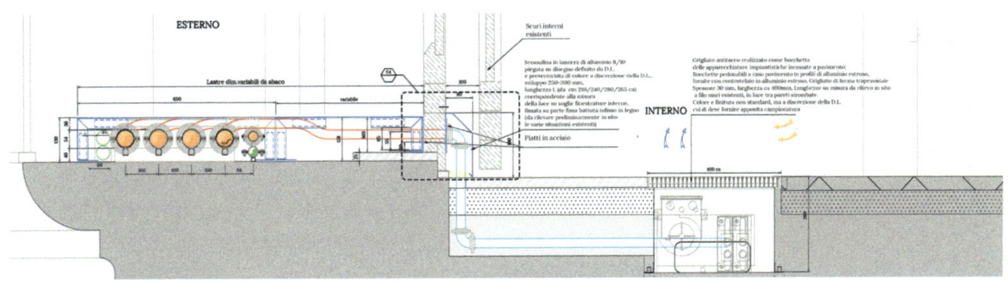

27 CONSTRUCTION SECTION AND CONSTRUCTION SITE PHOTO OF THE AIR CONDITIONING DUCTS HOUSED IN THE PERIMETER BALCONIES.

28 PROTECTION OF WORKS OF ART DURING THE CONSTRUCTION WORK ON THE CAPODIMONTE MUSEUM.

centimetres high for the floor positioning of the window. The possibility therefore existed of creating a technical space outside, on the balcony, which enabled all the air ducts **[27]** to be housed in a truly invisible way. This type of solution is defined on those occasions when a multidisciplinary work forum exists, enabling all the aspects of a technical, plant-engineering and structural nature to be discussed together, to be consistent with the architectural idea. This solution also facilitates maintenance directly from outside, without the need to enter the exhibition rooms; we also verified this during construction, because we were able to keep the museum open while the work on the installations was being carried out **[28]**.

PAC **On the subject of the worksite, how did you manage the need to keep the museum partially open? What type of interaction was there between your project and the management of the worksite by the construction company?**

VC The experience of this large, complex construction site was truly extraordinary, and in this case too there are similarities with the worksite of the Pirelli Skyscraper. It was the first time we'd designed a museum of such dimensions, and so there were not only the Engie technicians and construction site experts at the coordination round table, but also all the figures associated with the clients and users: the director, the museum curators, the restorers of the works, but also those dealing with communication, all extraordinarily skilful people. Everyone always participated in the meetings with the desire to offer answers that were compatible with the need to keep the museum open. I may add that at the start Sylvain Bellenger thought it would be necessary to close the museum for three years or so, and to only reopen it when the work was finished. It was Minister of Culture Gennaro Sangiuliano, when confirming the project, who asked for the museum to continue to be used during the construction project.

PAC **Did Minister Sangiuliano also participate in some of the coordination meetings?**

VC No, never directly. He was kept abreast of the project when the work began, and he was continually updated on its progress. The Ministry indicates the programmatic guidelines, but the person who gives continuity to the action is the autonomous director of the museum: first Sylvain Bellenger, and now Eike Schmidt, who's accomplishing it with the same conviction and determination.

THE RESTORATION OF THE SACRED TEMPIO DELLA SCORZIATA IN NAPLES

PAC **You involved artists once again in the restoration project for the Sacred Tempio della Scorziata in Naples. What were the specific issues that you had to tackle?**

GM We've been working on this project for many years now, in a prestigious context in the heart of Naples **[29]**, in the area of the Greco-Roman Forum. This

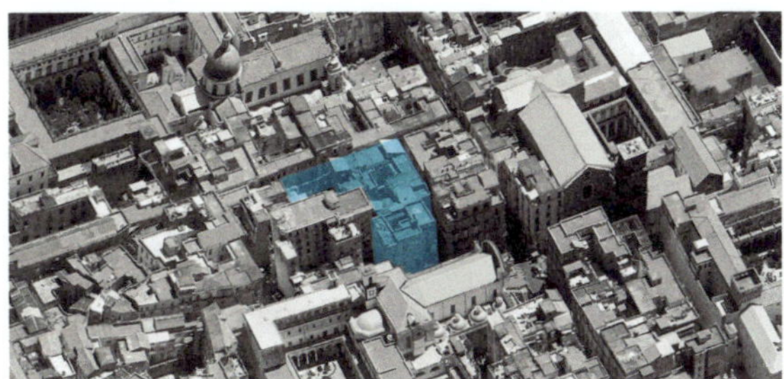

29 THE TEMPIO DELLA SCORZIATA IN THE CONTEXT OF THE HISTORIC CENTRE OF NAPLES.

30 PLAN OF VIA DEI TRIBUNALI WITH ITS MONUMENTAL LANDMARKS, IN THE CENTRE THE BLOCK OF LA SCORZIATA.

31 ALTARPIECE (UNKNOWN, SECOND HALF OF THE 15TH CENTURY) COMING FROM THE TEMPIO DELLA SCORZIATA, NOW IN THE CAPODIMONTE MUSEUM.

32 PHOTOGRAPH OF THE CONSTRUCTION SITE WITH THE WORK BY ZILDA (MEDITATIVE MAGDALENE), REALISED IN 2014 TO REPLACE THE ORIGINAL ALTARPIECE (PHOTOGRAPH BY ANTONIO ACUNZO, WINNER OF THE DESIGN SHOOTING AWARD, NAPLES 2024).

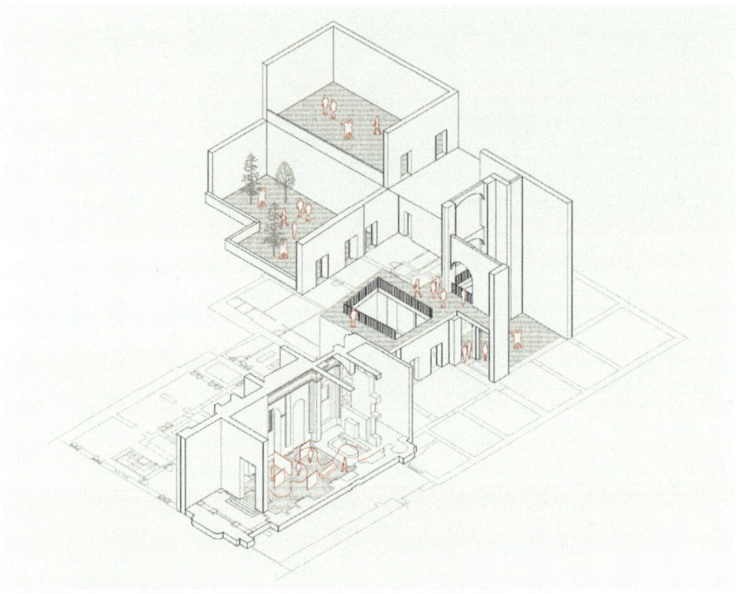

33 PROJECT AXONOMETRY WITH THE VARIOUS USES INSIDE THE RESTORED SCORZIATA COMPLEX.

34 TEMPIO DELLA SCORZIATA: PROJECT DIAGRAMS.

is a group of buildings constructed in 1500 to support women in precarious circumstances. We're currently proceeding with the work to make the structures safe, as they had been in a situation of total abandonment and deterioration for many years. The work fits within the framework of the major project of redevelopment of the historic centre of Naples **[30]**, under its classification as a UNESCO World Heritage site. After years of neglect and a fire in 2012, even the magnificent altarpiece **[31]** had been stolen. Then in 2014 a very fine French street artist, Zilda, entered the church, and decided to hang a very beautiful image of a woman of the people in the empty frame of the altarpiece, the reproduction of a famous painting by Francesco Hayez, *Meditation on the History of Italy*, which depicts a woman sitting on a tall chair holding a crucifix. In Zilda's interpretation, this woman becomes the *Meditative Magdalene* of the Scorziata **[32]**. In this case, it wasn't us who chose the artist, but in our restoration project we'll do all we can to succeed in conserving this extraordinary work as part of the new visitors' itinerary.

PAC **Where does this name, Scorziata, come from?**

GM Scorziata is the surname of a female philanthropist, Giovanna Scorziata, who had imagined this as a place of shelter and inclusion, and in our restoration project it should return to being a community location **[33]**, through its use by associations and the promotion of new residential functions.

PAC **At the moment you're carrying out structural consolidation work to make the building safe, while these new functions are in the process of being defined. How is the debate on future uses of the building developing? Who are the players and the bodies involved in this discussion?**

GM The debate is being conducted in a rather broad context, directly involving the Municipal Administration, primarily Laura Lieto, deputy mayor and councillor with responsibility for urban planning, together with a number of organisations and social workers, also discussing many issues involved in the management models. The building will have to be inclusive, also open to the possibility of hosting meaningful experiences **[34]**, with prestigious partners such as the Apple Developer Academy, in collaboration with the University of Naples Federico II. The historic centre of Naples is undergoing a process of rather significant gentrification, meaning the ground floors of buildings are being used almost entirely for the food retail trade, food and drink consumption and tourism, and many apartments that were once occupied by students have become B&Bs. The Scorziata project should offer concrete alternatives to this process, opening the area up to residential, research and cultural functions.

THE RESTORATION OF THE ARAGONESE CASTLE OF BAIA

PAC **The restoration of the Cavaliere pavilion in the Castle of Baia offered you another extraordinary opportunity to work on**

a building abounding in historical stratifications. During my visit to the construction site in late November 2024, I was able to appreciate how your intervention makes it possible today to experience a genuine 'architectural walk' along patrol pathways, ramparts and terraces, a walk characterised by panoramic views [35] **across the sea and the gulf in Naples. How did the competition enabling you to gain this prestigious appointment take place?**

VC We participated in the competition, called by Invitalia on behalf of the management of the Archaeological Park of Campi Flegrei, with a very wide-ranging planning group including numerous specialist skills, to respond to a very exhaustive framework document. This specified the programmatic and distributional requirements: from the overcoming of architectural barriers to the layout design guidelines for certain rooms, from structural consolidation to the requirements as regarding lighting and air conditioning. We won the competition with a specific design proposal **[36]** and with a group that included, among others, the architect Michele Barone Lumaga, who had restored the Aragonese Castle of Ischia, the architect Fabio De Falco of DFP Engineering, the archaeologist Davide Pellandra and the engineer Carmine Sangiuliano from the studio Sparacio & Partners, an outstanding figure in the field of structural consolidation of monumental buildings.

PAC **I was actually able to ascertain how important the theme of structural consolidation was on my visit to the worksite, for obvious reasons due to the significant seismic activity in the area of Campi Flegrei. In some rooms of the ancient Roman villa, characterised by the presence of the original *opus reticolatum* walls, I saw a rather unusual solution for consolidating the ancient vaults, with a series of small steel ribs** [37] **connected with tension rods. How does this particular structural device work?**

VC These interesting spaces of the original Augustan villa form the foundations of the Cavaliere pavilion, and it's necessary to specify that they had not suffered any particular damage following the various earthquakes. The solution proposed affirms, in a non-camouflaging way, with a statement of constructional sincerity, the principle of a genuinely new structure to respond to earthquakes dynamically.

GM It works as an energy dissipater, absorbing the wave of the earthquake in such a way that the original structure of the Roman vaults has a compatible oscillation. The structural engineers of the Sparacio & Partners are extraordinary experts who are in dialogue with the stones; we're also working with them on projects in Mantua and on the ancient Customs House in Avellino.

PAC **I like this expression: 'In dialogue with the stones.' We could also use it on the subject of the materials that are found in your restoration projects, which are the same ones used in ancient Roman construction: lime, bricks and stone.**

35 RESTORATION OF THE ARAGONESE CASTLE OF BAIA, THE TERRACES AND RAMPS LOOKING OUT ACROSS THE GULF OF POZZUOLI.

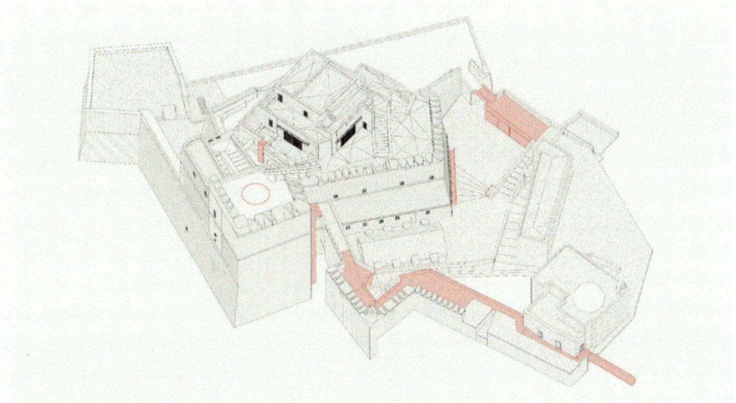

36 GENERAL AXONOMETRY WITH THE NEW PROJECT INTERVENTIONS.

37 ROOMS OF THE ANCIENT ROMAN VILLA, WITH THE STEEL RIBS CONSOLIDATING THE ANCIENT VAULTS AND FLOOR LIGHTING.

38 NEW OPUS SIGNINUM PAVING AND LIME-BASED PLASTERS.

39 NEW BAKED LATH BRICK PAVING ON THE UPPER TERRACES.

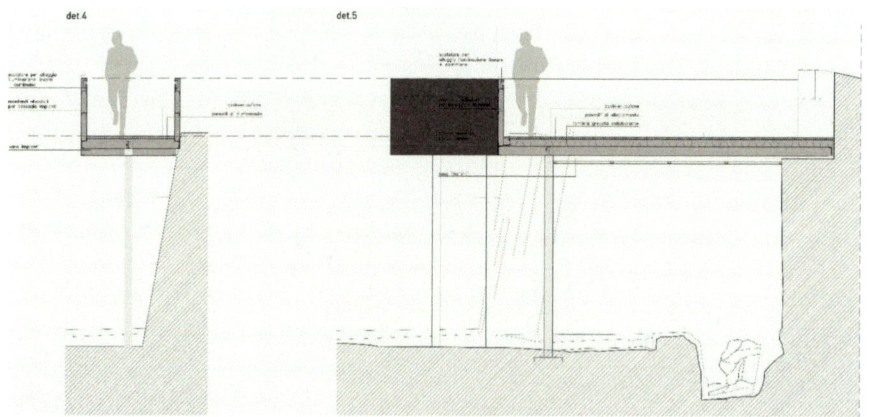

40 SECTIONS AND ELEVATIONS OF THE NEW STEEL WALKWAYS.

VC There was actually the requirement to use lime-based plasters, and not cement, while for the new flooring **[38]** we had very constructive discussions with the archaeologists: with the director of the Archaeological Park of Campi Flegrei, Fabio Pagano, who has always offered us the maximum support, but also with Hosea Scelza, Maria Pia Cibelli, and Francesco Talamo of the Ministry of Culture. It was very interesting to observe the ancient mosaics and the *opus signinum* floors inside the archaeological area with them, to motivate our solutions, proposing the same methods that were used by the Romans to achieve beautiful and durable floors, but in a contemporary vein. This clearly complicated to no small degree the preparation of the metric calculations in order to define 'new prices' without being able to use the normal costs in the lists of charges.

PAC **The new *opus signinum* and baked lath brick floorings in fact create a very beautiful condition of material continuity** [39], **which is in perfect dialogue with the solid colour of the plastered walls. The overall effect reinforces the extraordinary plastic force of the volumes of the castle, which stand out against the azure backdrop of the sea and sky. Opposite the entrance to the Cavaliere pavilion, I noted the presence of some slightly different *opus signinum* flooring, and a doubt came to mind: is it Roman flooring, or a modern one imitating the original Roman flooring? I talked about this to architect Maria Pia Cibelli, who acted as my guide on the visit, and she answered that it was the original flooring. This apparent ambiguity between ancient and modern seems to me to be a really great quality of your intervention.**

VC What you describe as the plastic force of the architecture is perhaps the best compliment to our work. The historical architecture is showcased in its original form, but the new steel structures **[40, 41]** are also considerably integrated, telling the story of the contemporary in this very stratified location. The use of baked lath brick, another characteristic element of Augustan architecture, contributes to this major attention being devoted the colour and plasticity.

PAC **On the other hand, how did you deal with the need to include new technological systems for lighting and air conditioning?**

VC Before developing the project for these systems, we decided to use BIM (Building Information Modelling), and for this the preliminary work by Professor Riccardo Florio was very useful, as he conducted a complete survey, with 3D laser scanners and point cloud, to obtain a very detailed three-dimensional digital model. The challenge was to use this BIM model for the architectural, structural and systems project, achieving innovative and integrated solutions inside the historical structures. In many spaces we used floor-based lighting solutions, designed with the support of Viabizzuno, to bring out the material qualities of the Roman walls with side lighting from the bottom upwards.

41 VIEW OF THE NEW VOLUME THAT HOSTS THE BAR AND A STEEL WALKWAY, WITH THE GULF OF POZZUOLI IN THE BACKGROUND.

42 VIEW OF THE INTERNAL RAMPS CONNECTING ALL THE LEVELS OF THE MUSEUM.

43 DETAILS OF MATERIALS: LAVA ROCK FLOORS, PLASTERED WALLS, EXPOSED BRICK VAULTS, BASEBOARD WITH STEEL PLATE.

PAC **The interior ramps are also very interesting** [42]. **They were created to enable all the levels of the museum to be connected, unifying the routes between the parts already restored and the new parts. Unlike the environments of the Roman villa, you made different choices regarding the materials. Why was that?**

VC In fact the flooring in the ramps was made using lava stone chips, while the walls are covered in white plaster so as to create a strong contrast with the exposed stone vaults. One interesting detail is the skirting board made with a steel plate **[43]**, a solution that is almost a citing of the previous restoration intervention, carried out by Superintendent Enrico Guglielmo at the end of the 1990s. It's a response to a request from the clients, who placed considerable trust in our choices as regards materials, colours and lighting in the new environments, but at the same time they asked us to find a form of continuity with the spaces previously restored in the main building of the museum. It therefore seemed to us to be a good idea to attempt to meet this request with this simple element: flat steel section running along all the walls of the ramps.

PAC **In conclusion, I'd like to highlight the fact that in this restoration of the Aragonese Castle of Baia, as in many other previous restoration interventions, you've always developed excellent relationships of collaboration with the Superintendences of Architectural Heritage. I'll therefore ask you if you have something to place on record in this regard?**

VC In Italy many people complain about the very restrictive guidelines and the actions of the Superintendences of Architectural Heritage, whereas we think that they offer excellent opportunities and make irreplaceable skills available. We're convinced that the Superintendences have remained among the few paladins of the safeguarding and appreciation of the landscapes and monuments of our cities. We've never had any particular difficulties in interacting with the Superintendences, at all latitudes, but also beyond the national frontiers, as has recently happened with the Casa d'Italia in Zurich, because we look at the project as a place of discussion and sharing. We assume our own responsibilities as regards the choices and decisions concerning architecture, but we also retain the humility to listen to those who offer advice and contributions, which almost always prove precious.

1 **Exhibition of the project for the restoration of the Torre delle Nazioni at the *Mostra d'Oltremare*, Palazzo Reale in Naples, and Palazzo degli Uffici della Mostra d'Oltremare in Naples from 6 to 19 February 1995, and subsequently at *Galassia Gutenberg* from 15 to 19 February 1995, and at the *Salone dell'edilizia* from 25 to 28 May1995.**

2 **Vincenzo Corvino, Luca Lanini, *Il restauro della Torre delle Nazioni* (Exhibition catalogue; Naples, 1995); Alberto Ferlenga, 'Progetto di restauro della Torre delle Nazioni a Napoli', *L'Industria delle Costruzioni*, 283 (May 1995), 46-48; Luca Lanini, 'Alcune questioni tra progettazione e restauro', in Roberto Pasqualetti (ed.), *La poetica del restauro. Arte, architettura e paesaggio* (Pisa: ETS, 2017), 53–63.**

3 **Luca Lanini, 'Un Guggenheim quadrato', in Id., *Costruire la bellezza* (Naples, 2004).**

4 **Exhibition *Klaus Kada. Palazzo Multimedia a Graz*, Villa Pignatelli, Naples, from 24 November to 17 December 2000.**

5 **The initiative, entitled 'riaglta. Ripensare, Ripartire, agire. Laboratorio Italia', took place in four parts on 1, 2 and 3 May 2020.**

RESTORATION OF THE PIRELLI SKYSCRAPER
MILAN, 1998–2005

The restoration of the Pirelli Skyscraper in Milan represents an important and significant chapter in the research into the restoration of the Modern. The architecture of Gio Ponti and Pier Luigi Nervi was studied carefully, its spaces observed and surveyed, assigning to the project the theme of the relationship between philological restoration and contemporary intervention. The need for an organic overview of restoration rendered necessary an in-depth investigation of the building using archive and bibliographical sources, orienting the intervention towards conservation goals that best utilise the original design quality and the materials on site, with the aim of guaranteeing the safeguarding of the high artistic and cultural value of the building. Even though it was not yet subject to restrictions in 2002, the Pirelli Skyscraper merited active safeguarding, which was apparent in the decision not to modify the mass, materials and forms of a monument of considerable dimensions that had been realised using industrialised processes. Investigations were conducted on the condition of the aluminium doors and windows, the ceramic tiles and of their support, leading to the decision to restore the original elements and to proceed by solely filling the gaps, introducing technological improvements within an interpretation of the characteristics of the building that would be capable of cohesively shaping new spaces and furnishings, and revisiting the 'fantastic yellow' rubber flooring realised by Ponti. The auditorium, named after Giorgio Gaber, is the place where the theme of the intervention finds an explicit synthesis, with a new independent entrance obtained through a slight depression in the sloping terrain of the hill on Piazza Duca d'Aosta. Access is gained via a new staircase to the reception space, its rhythm marked by slim, black, polished columns, before entering the room characterised by the original plaster-covered system of beams and pillars, interwoven to form a sequence of lozenges typical of the original project design by Ponti and Nervi. Rereading the base of the building, along the entire perimeter, the pavements were widened, particularly along Via Filzi where the entrance atrium was modified in order to obtain a double-height space, considering this more compatible with the original idea of the building, utilising the continuity of the space and the relationship between this extraordinary building and the city.

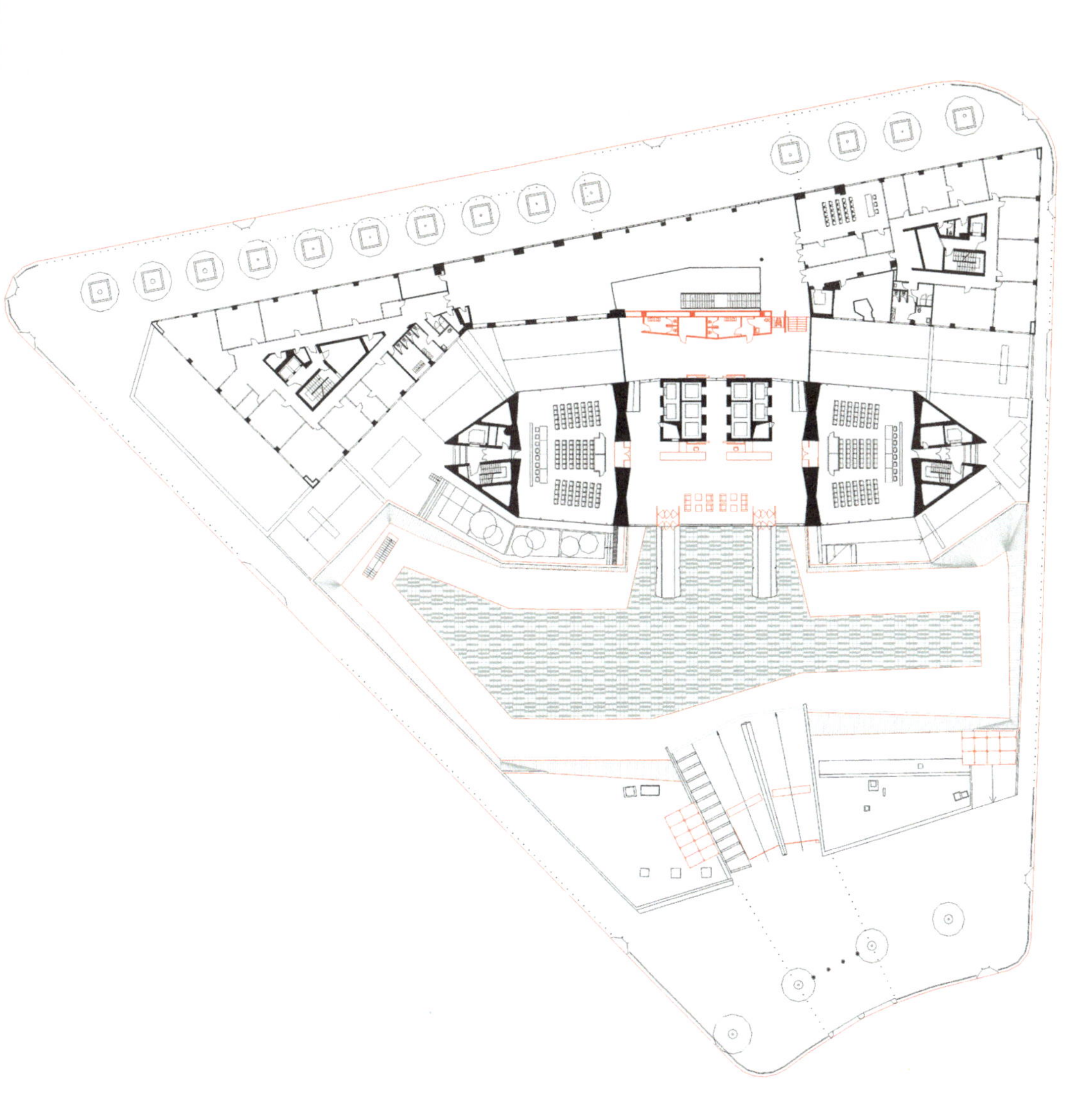

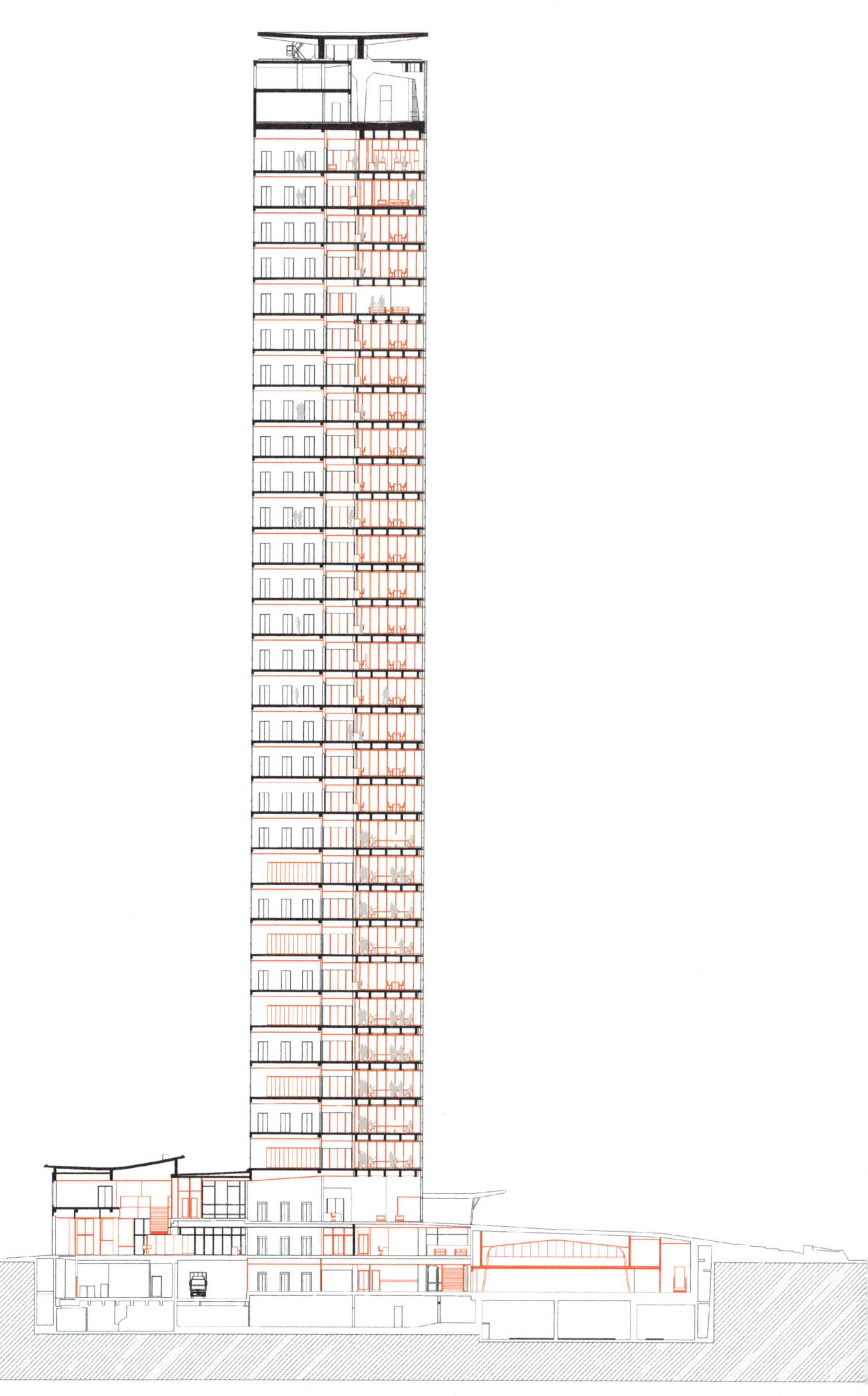

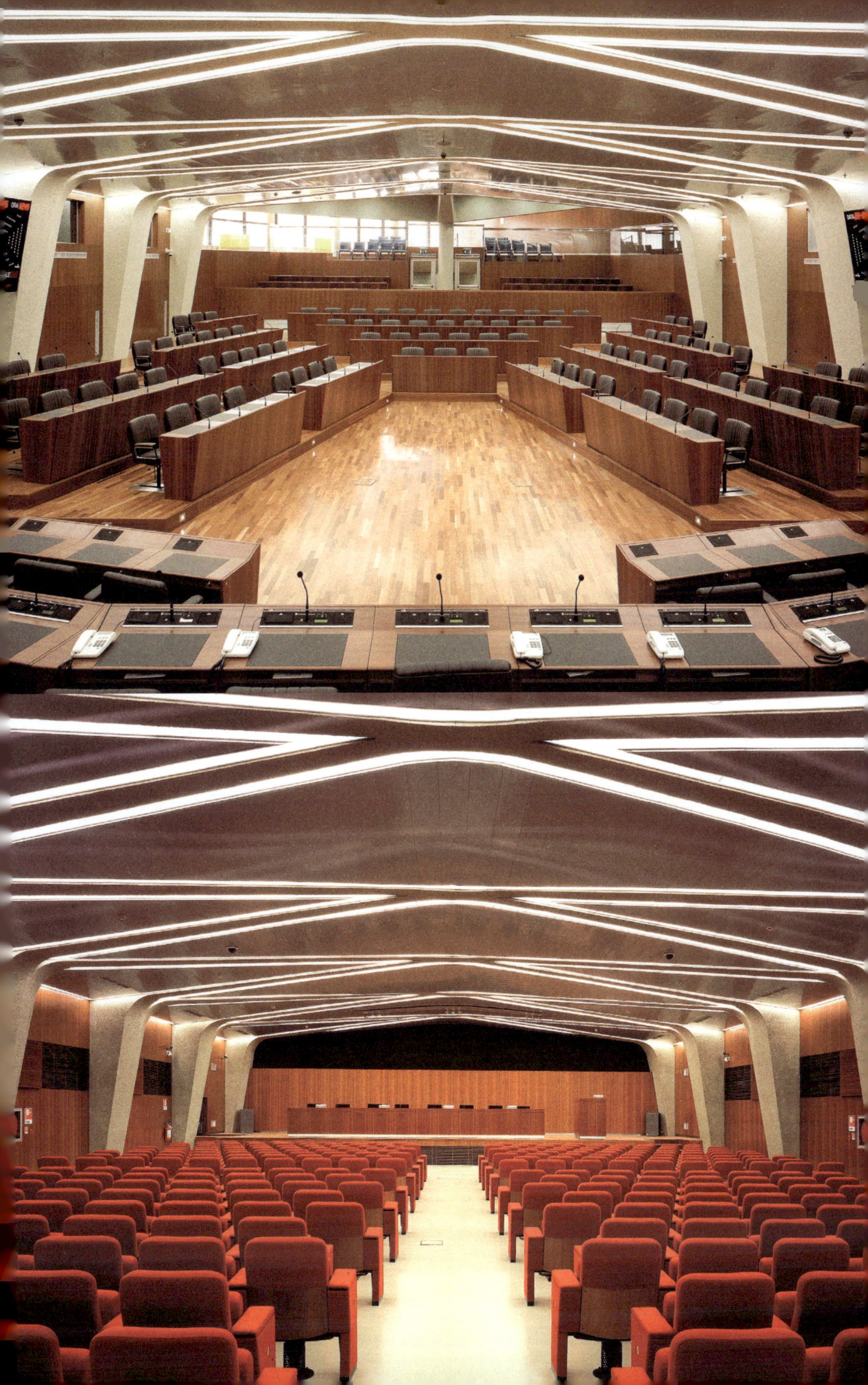

Spazio
Eventi

RESTORATION AND ENERGY UPGRADING OF THE CAPODIMONTE MUSEUM
NAPLES, 2020–25

This is a pilot project on the panorama of Italian cultural assets, the first case of a public–private partnership between Engie Italia and the Ministry of Culture, along with former Museum Director Sylvain Bellenger. Architectural, structural and energy-saving interventions were devised to introduce new ways of utilising the exhibition spaces. Among these, a new reception room for the public, the regeneration of the belvedere terrace and the repurposing of the Causa Room in the basement: three autonomous opportunities to reinterpret the architecture of the building, contributing to the formation of a new experience of the entire complex. On the ground floor, in the northwest corner of the museum, the new reception room takes up the original double-height spatiality of the former Royal Chapel, transformed into an auditorium in the 1950s, and forms the point of departure for the museum route, on the axis with the monumental staircase. Art is integrated into the transformation process as an instrument of dialogue, contributing to defining new atmospheres and spaces. This is evidenced by the installations by Mimmo Paladino in the reception room and those by Christiane Löhr on the roof of the building, intended to enhance the new belvedere terrace. The third intervention concerns the repurposing of the Causa Room, a basement environment constructed in 2006 beneath one of the courtyards of the building, which is transformed into a visitable storage and exhibition space for temporary displays. The architectural choices have been made respecting the value of the existing elements and focusing on advanced technological innovations. One of the main objectives is to improve the energy autonomy of the Capodimonte Museum, reducing consumption by 50% and using mostly renewable energy sources, enabling around 90% of the energy requirement to be met. A significant example is the installation of photovoltaic modules that are chromatically integrated with the baked brick 'coppo' tiles of the courtyard roofs, restoring the formal and chromatic unity of the pitches. Beyond this, plant efficiency interventions contribute to creating a new under-floor air conditioning system in the exhibition rooms on the first floor, and to rethinking the lighting with the innovative concept of 'light for art', guaranteeing improved protection for the works. The continuing work at the site, under the guidance of the current Director Eike Schmidt, has demonstrated the validity of a synergic approach between compositional reflection and technological innovation.

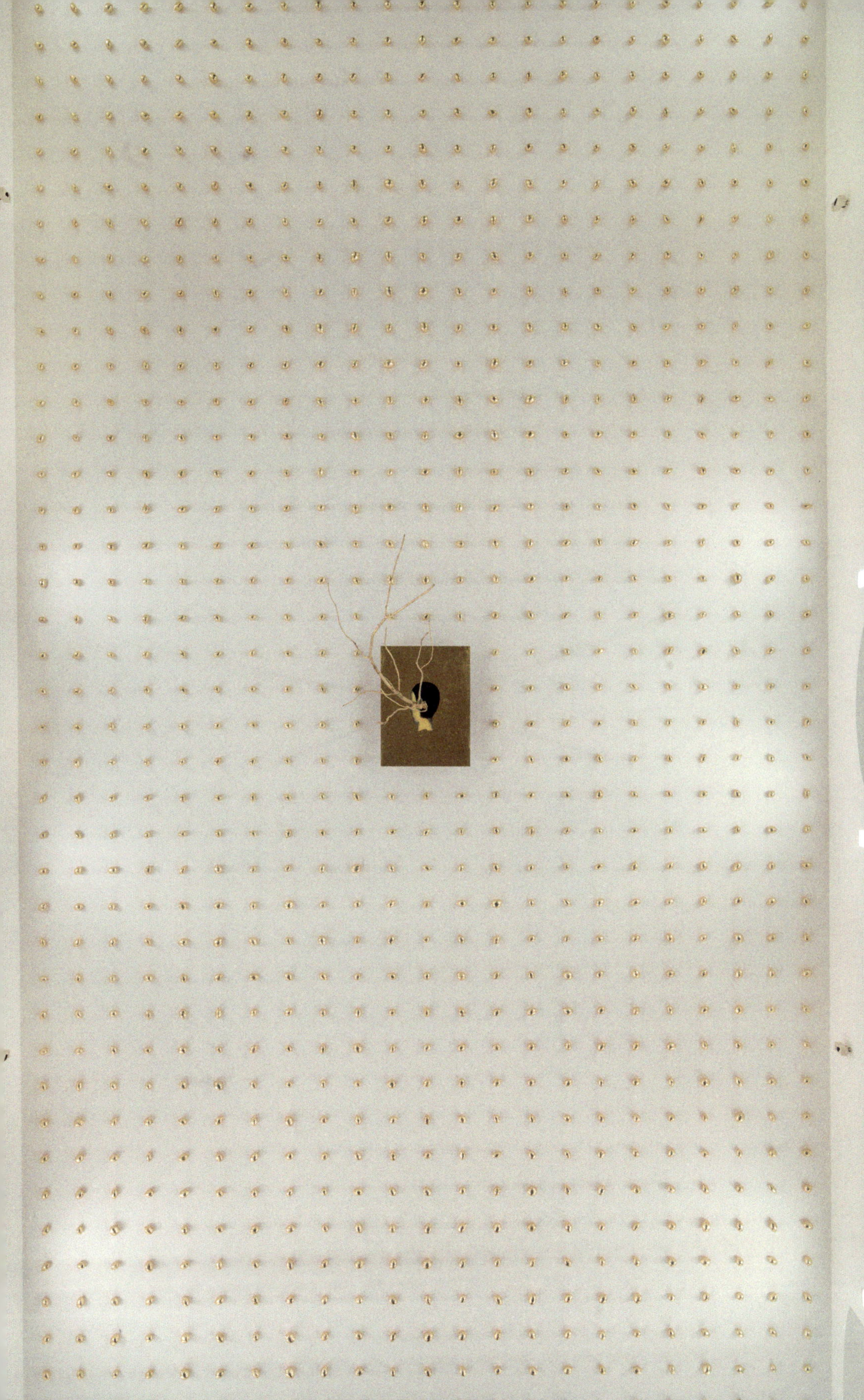

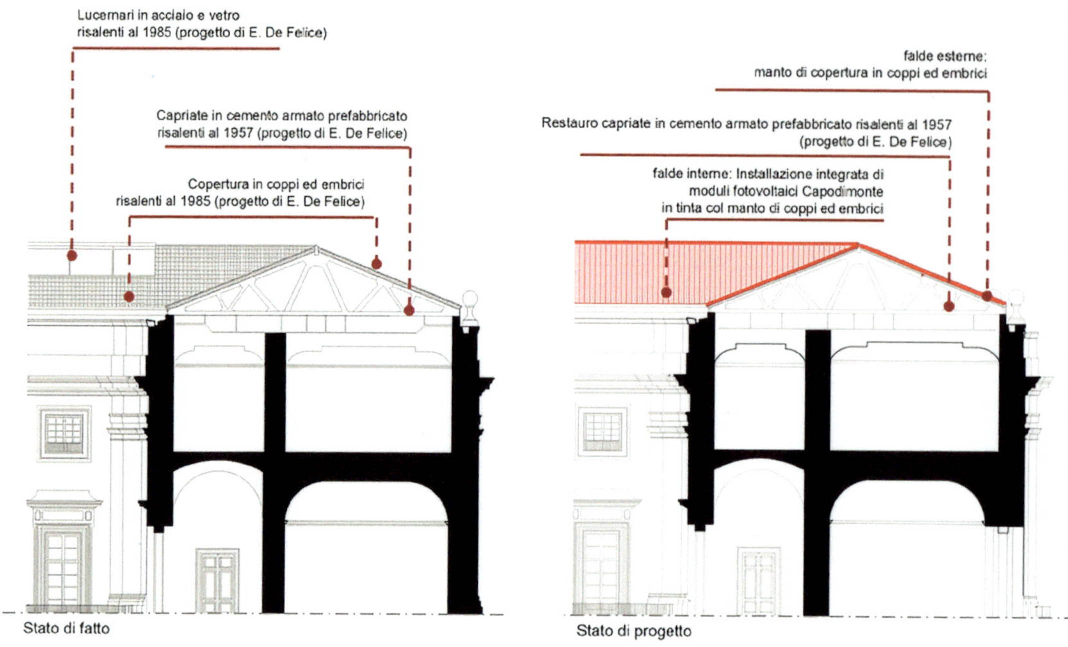

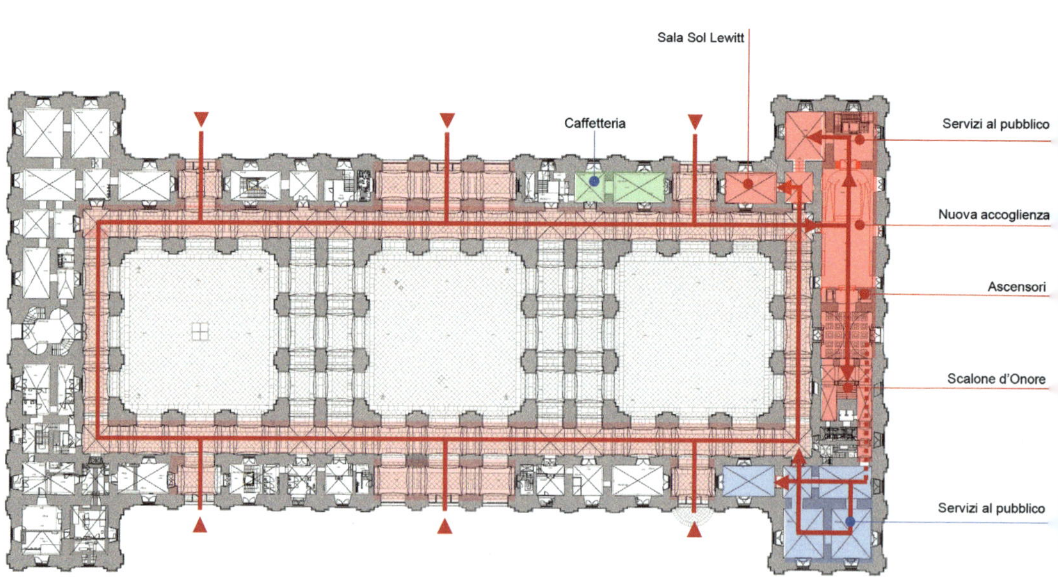

Pianta piano terra: Stato di progetto

3
REPRESENTATION BUILDINGS

PAC **In the same years when you completed the restoration work on the Pirelli Skyscraper in Milan, you also developed a series of projects transforming small buildings without any monumental value. The theme of these interventions was to use architecture as a showcasing instrument, starting from apparently rather unattractive conditions. The first example I'd like to discuss with you is the small office building in Casoria, completed in 2004, in a peripheral industrial context, where you succeeded in transforming the structural skeleton of an unfinished building [1] into the representation office of a small industrial firm. So let's discuss the theme of the representative value of architecture, considering buildings that differ greatly in programmatic and dimensional terms: from buildings for private offices and small interiors to public buildings, such as the headquarters of the Public Procurator's Office of Catanzaro and the Tuscany Regional Authority in Florence, but also prestige buildings representing the Italian State, such as the Casa d'Italia in Zurich and the Embassy in Nairobi. So we won't just talk about institutional representation, because even a private building can present a face of representation in relation to public life. Let's begin, therefore, with this small building in Casoria, a typical example of a 'minor construction' becoming architecture of quality.**

VC This is an experience that's very dear to us. We're in Casoria, at the gates of Naples, where there are some important industries. We were contacted by Andrea Grieco, the owner of GRIEC.A.M, who wanted us to realise his new centre for offices after acquiring this building that had never been completed: a typical 'unfinished' structure, like so many other skeletons that characterise the landscape of the Neapolitan metropolitan area. For us it therefore offered a new opportunity to propose an innovative interpretation of the existing. Not being able to enlarge the building, we decided to radically modify its overall image with a new shell **[2]**, a light skin made of aluminium plates that reconstructs a spatial order, as well as mitigating solar radiation. This clarity of form and geometry creates the representative value of the new architecture.

GM In an almost unknowing way, we were among the first to be interested in the theme of unfinished buildings; they're more rustic than ruins, in the sense that they have no history turning them into ruins with time, rather they are recently constructed elements that have remained in the state of being structural skeletons. Our approach—as has often happened—has been pragmatic, based on in-depth work to gain knowledge, also of the regulatory framework, in order to succeed in dignifying this construction with a measured intervention.

VC It was also an excellent idea by the client to propose that the roof terrace could become an interesting place for employees to relax. To reinforce the image of the building, we extended the new façade in terms of height, creating the motif of a pergola to delimit this space.

1 INCOMPLETE BUILDING IN CASORIA BEFORE THE INTERVENTION.

2 GRIEC.A.M. OFFICES IN CASORIA AFTER THE INTERVENTION.

3 INARCASSA HEADQUARTERS IN ROME, PHOTORENDERING.

4 VIEW OF THE MODEL.

PAC **This successful intervention shows that even a theme that initially seems trivial and rather uninteresting can prove itself useful for experimenting with something new, because ultimately there are no small themes in architecture. I think this was your condition at the start of your career; it's no coincidence that you talked about an open and pragmatic attitude. I find certain analogies between the building in Casoria and the competition project for the Inarcassa premises in Rome, a project from 2002. In this case too you propose radically modifying the architectural image with a new skin consisting of plates.**

GM The opportunity came about from a restricted competition called by Inarcassa (the architects' pension fund), who had bought two residential buildings in a central zone of Rome close to Villa Borghese. The site included some beautiful Lebanon cedar trees, which formed a long-distance dialogue with the trees of Villa Borghese. As in Casoria, this shell generates a new formal unity for the two buildings **[3]**, but at the same time it's lit up to become a lantern on an urban scale **[4]**.

VC I may add that this competition gave rise to the great hope that Inarcassa would highlight its properties through architecture competitions. Even if there was the disappointment of coming second, this project gave us great satisfaction. While in Casoria the plates were aluminium, for this building we proposed using a travertine shading device, a clear reference to an element typical of Italian Modernism.

PAC **This theme of transforming and raising the prestige of buildings that we could qualify as 'ordinary' or examples of 'minor constructions' has been tackled in various other subsequent interventions. I'm thinking in particular of Palazzo Aronne in Catanzaro (2001–7) and the bank in Torre del Greco around ten years later, two examples of a quite different way of acting: instead of adding another skin to a pre-existing building, you acted with a gesture of subtraction, almost of purification of the volume, to value the plastic expression of the building. I'm reminded of the Proto-Rationalist architecture of Adolf Loos, perhaps because the buildings on which you intervened were not entirely devoid of quality as in Casoria; they already possessed a certain dignity of their own.**

GM I think it's right to connect these two interventions, even if they were many years apart. It was indeed returning to the essential, to what we'd recognised as the original nature of these two buildings. Palazzo Aronne is a 20th-century building **[5]**, with some interesting elements, which harkens back to the Rationalist culture between the two wars. We conserved the beautiful internal staircase **[6]**, characterised by the very elegant and original design of the handrail, which we simply extended to adapt it to fit the current regulations. We've always demonstrated this great attention devoted to the materiality of architecture; where possible we always endeavour to recover and adapt elements, from the façades of the Pirelli Skyscraper to the simple handrail of a staircase.

PAC **What kind of condition was the building in Torre del Greco in?**

VC It was a semi-aristocratic agricultural residence that the Banca di Credito Cooperativo had acquired to create a separate branch. The building was not subject to restrictions, even though there is a landscaping restriction in the sphere involving the entire area of the Vesuvian municipalities. We therefore had to ask the opinion of the Superintendence, because the Landscaping Plan did not allow the modification of elevations. We conducted a series of archive searches, which demonstrated that some historical residences possessed a portico as a clarifying element for the architecture. Our building possessed one of these, as an added reinforced concrete element and with a historicist expression with rounded arches **[7]**. Our intervention envisaged realising it in a rational way to obtain an image of essentiality and volumetric purity **[8]**.

PAC **I mentioned Loos because this Proto-Rationalist connotation makes me curious; it takes on a specific value in this context, reconnecting with the great tradition of Mediterranean Rationalist architecture. How do you intervene in the interiors, on the other hand? With which materials?**

VC In this building we also utilised a very beautiful historical staircase, restoring the lava stone of the risers and treads, and we designed pearl grey ceramic flooring that contributed to reconfiguring the spatial quality of each working office.

INTERIORS AS SPACES OF REPRESENTATION

PAC **So far we've discussed projects where the central theme was the metamorphosis of the external image of the building, even if, naturally, you've also acted with transformations of interior spaces. I remember that from the very start of your career you've devoted particular attention to the theme of the architecture of interiors, either alone or also with Olivetti Engineering, and some of these interiors were clearly representation spaces, such as the auditorium of the Lombardy Regional Authority in the Pirelli Skyscraper, and even earlier the Campania Regional Council Room in Tower F13 of the business district in Naples. In the same building, in 2003 you subsequently realised a small restaurant, which I find interesting for two reasons. Firstly, it's a flexible space, which can be used as a restaurant proper, but which also fulfils the role of an atrium and threshold before entering the Council Room. Secondly, you invited Sergio Fermariello, the sculptor you had already involved in the project for the Tower of the Nations, to collaborate in this space. What was the genesis of this project?**

5 PALAZZO ARONNE
IN CATANZARO AFTER
THE RESTORATION.

6 PALAZZO ARONNE,
DETAIL OF THE STAIRCASE.

7 THE BUILDING IN TORRE
DEL GRECO BEFORE
THE INTERVENTION.

8 BANCA DI CREDITO COOPERATIVO
IN TORRE DEL GRECO,
AFTER THE RESTORATION.

VC This job came about immediately after the completion of the Council Room, when the Regional Council of Campania realised that it needed to have its own refreshment space. For us this offered a fine opportunity to act inside basement spaces in the tower designed by our master Alberto Izzo. In that specific case, the space envisaged for the restaurant was previously used as a garage for official cars, and this caused obvious difficulties. It was a space without windows or any kind of ventilation, and it was therefore necessary to immediately call the ASL (local health agency) to verify if the minimum regulatory conditions existed for the exchange of air and emergency exits. The project required numerous systems in the floor and ceiling for ventilation and air conditioning, and this made it necessary to create a raised platform for the restaurant room, with a lateral ramp to overcome the difference in level **[9]**. The invitation to Sergio Fermariello is consistent with the personal commitment of Antonio Bassolino, first as mayor of Naples and at that time president of the Campania Regional Authority, in promoting contemporary art in our city. We were presented with the problem of enhancing the long, narrow space of the ramp, and Sergio Fermariello designed a work of art that could be visible laterally and not frontally, proposing this far-from-ordinary work, which he entitled 'Bum-bum': a chimpanzee that gives the illusion of moving, accompanying visitors going along the ramp **[10]**.

PAC **A few years later, in 2007, you created the offices of Upteam Holding in Naples, another very innovative work where you used an elastic fabric—Barrisol—for the first time to shape walls with a double curvature, transforming traditional corridors into a fluid, dynamic space: in this case it was therefore the space itself that took on the representative value.**

VC This too is a small invention for which great merit must be attributed to a very visionary client, Michele Di Stasio, the owner of a network of travel agencies, who wanted to create the control centre for all his agencies in this location. In the dialogue with the client, the idea emerged of the soft form that would enhance the spaces for circulation **[11]**, opening them up at some points to turn them into small relaxation zones. To achieve the soft forms of the dividing walls between offices and corridors, we decided to use Barrisol, an elastic material that's habitually used to make false ceilings with large-scale lighting, and to experiment with a solution with a double sheet to improve sound insulation. In conducting the first tests, we discovered almost unintentionally that when this double sheet was vertically extended, suspended from curved tracks, it didn't remain straight, but formed saddle surfaces with a double curvature, giving rise to very interesting shapes **[12]**. Later we involved the artist Pierre-Yves Le Duc, who worked on the only two brick walls delimiting the central core of the installations.

PAC **This description of the process that prompted you to experiment directly with the definitive solutions at the worksite is interesting, with a part of almost improvisation, due to the properties of the material that hadn't been fully verified until then. Recently you've also been planning interventions for the transformation of interior spaces for representation offices, I'm thinking in particular of the Lombardy headquarters of the State Prop-**

9 RESTAURANT OF THE COUNCIL OF THE CAMPANIA REGION.

10 SERGIO FERMARIELLO, *BUM BUM* INSTALLATION IN THE RESTAURANT.

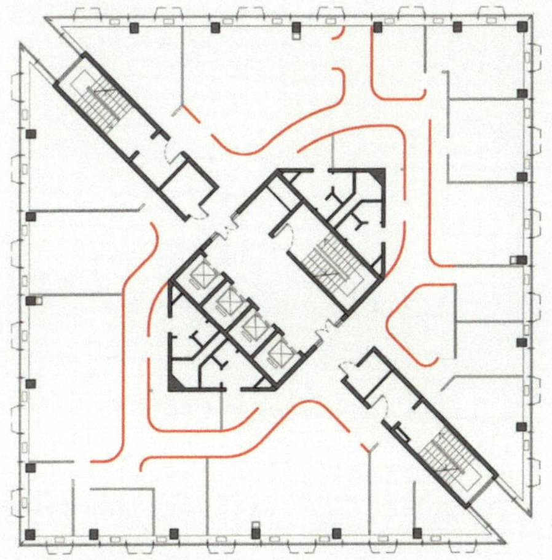

11 PLAN OF THE UPTEAM HOLDING OFFICES IN NAPLES, IN RED THE NEW WALLS DELIMITING THE DISTRIBUTION ROUTES.

12 UPTEAM HOLDING OFFICES, BARRISOL WALLS WITH FLUID FORMS.

13 HEADQUARTERS OF THE STATE PROPERTY AGENCY IN CORSO MONFORTE IN MILAN, PERSPECTIVE OF THE INNER COURTYARD.

14 PERSPECTIVE OF THE BAR ON THE GROUND FLOOR, DIRECTLY ACCESSIBLE FROM VIA DEL CONSERVATORIO.

15 NIGHTTIME VIEW OF THE LIBERTY FAÇADE DESIGNED BY ALFREDO CAMPANINI.

16 PERSPECTIVE OF THE STAIRCASE WITH THE *BIRDS* INSTALLATION BY MARIO AMURA.

erty Agency in Corso Monforte in Milan. One of the interventions you propose is the partial covering of the internal courtyard with a kind of pergola, transforming this courtyard into a space for events [13].

VC The State Property Agency's intention is to redesign this regional headquarters in Milan, where the ground floor will be made available for functions of community interest: in addition to the internal courtyard, there will also be a small meeting room, a coworking space and a bar, which will open directly onto Via Conservatorio **[14]**. In the meanwhile, I'd like to mention that for some years now the State Property Agency has been proving to be an enlightened client. This role originates from a State law that enables the State to optimise the passive costs paid by institutions of various kinds to occupy the various sites, in order to regenerate the public assets. From that moment the State Property Agency has become the guarantor of a series of competition procedures to effectively regenerate its extensive stock of buildings. The peculiarity of the State Property Agency is that it has branches all over Italy; this allows architects to participate in competitions for urban regeneration works in all the regions. Furthermore, it's important to remember the important role played by Alessandra dal Verme as director; she has invested a great deal in the architectural quality of the interventions, defending the principle that these buildings are a State asset, and that they therefore belong to all its citizens. In Milan, the spaces of community interest will therefore be made available to associations of citizens, students and the whole city.

PAC **You're involved in Corso Monforte in an eclectic building designed by Alfredo Campanini, which are the parts where the representative value of architecture is expressed most?**

VC It is indeed a very interesting building, with an elevation characterised by soft concrete forms **[15]**; we've rather jokingly defined it as a work by the Milanese Gaudí. In addition to being an excellent architect, Alfredo Campanini was also a real estate broker, who in the early 20th century bought properties, restructured them and resold them. On the subject of representation, that's a word that the State Property Agency doesn't like to use, because they consider their mission to be an optimisation of public assets; we could therefore talk of a more contemporary, more democratic conception of representation. There are certain spaces of greater merit in which we intervene, for example the main staircase that we propose to continue up to the top floor, which was added in the 1990s and will also host a very interesting work by artist Mario Amura **[16]**. On this occasion too we collaborated very effectively with the Superintendence, who approved what will be the first photovoltaic roof on a public property in the historic centre of Milan. There will also be other innovations in terms of building systems, particularly thanks to a collaboration with Metropolitana Milanese, which will experiment with a heating system obtained from heat exchange with the wastewater from the Milanese sewerage network.

PAC **Your first assignment with the State Property Agency dates back to 2017 and the project for the new Public Prosecutor's Office in the former military hospital in Catanzaro. Have there been recent changes in the procedures for design competitions?**

VC For the Milan project, the State Property Agency introduced a new planning level, which it calls 'concept', in order to better control the process of design and realisation. This was an intelligent decision: a 'concept' must already be developed in a preliminary competition phase, placing various alternative projects in competition in quality terms. The 'concept' establishes the architectural idea, together with the system design and sustainability idea, as well as envisaging an initial estimate of the necessary budget. In our case, after having defined it, the necessary financing was approved by the General Office before commencing the Technical and Economic Feasibility Project (PFTE in Italian), which will establish the contents for further drafting the executive project and announcing the call for tenders. In this way the continuity and cohesiveness between design and realisation can be guaranteed, through the 'concept', PTFE and executive project phases. This is a procedure that we believe the State Property Agency will want to consolidate in the future.

PAC **So far all the projects we've discussed and that you've realised have been Italian projects. With the project for the restructuring and restoration of the Casa d'Italia in Zurich, on the other hand, you've been engaged in an intervention abroad for the first time. How have you managed this need to adapt to another context?**

VC We participated in an international competition called in 2020 by the Italian Ministry of Foreign Affairs, involving the engineering company Rina, as in previous competitions, but also two local partners, Fontana & Fontana, one of the best-known restoration firms in Zurich, and the engineering company ZPF, who for more than twenty years have collaborated with Herzog & De Meuron. You need to remember that the Italian community in Zurich is one of the most important in the world, and that it has long been influential in the urbanistic and political development of the city. The historical building we're working on was built in 1930 as an 'Orphanage and kindergarten for the Italian colony in Zurich', based on a project by architect Otto Gschwind **[17]**, which was subsequently enlarged with the addition of upper storeys. The reinforced concrete trusses that crown the building **[18]** are particularly interesting, and engineer Luis Looser of ZPF reported to us that Jacques Herzog and Pierre De Meuron particularly love this building, to the point of considering it a point of reference in conceiving the Feltrinelli building in Milan.

PAC **Being a building subject to restrictions as a historical monument, you developed a rigorous project of philological restoration, working in agreement with the Office of Conservation of Historical Monuments of the city of Zurich. I've seen that a significant part of this project concerns finding the original colours. What might these colours be?**

VC The restorer Sylvia Fontana has conducted investigations into the materials in the building, to trace the original grey colour, very different from the current salmon colour of the façade. Then we managed to find other tones of grey for the rooms, while traces of an earth red colour have been identified in the main stairwell, which we decided to make good together with the architect Grit Angermann of the Conservation Office. The main restoration will concern the Pi-

17 OTTO GSCHWIND, ELEVATION AND SECTION OF THE 'ORPHANAGE AND KINDERGARTEN OF THE ITALIAN COLONY IN ZURICH', WITH THE EXTENSIONS FROM THE LATE 1930S IN RED.

18 CASA D'ITALIA: VIEW OF THE MAIN FAÇADE WITH THE REINFORCED CONCRETE TRUSSES CROWNING THE BUILDING.

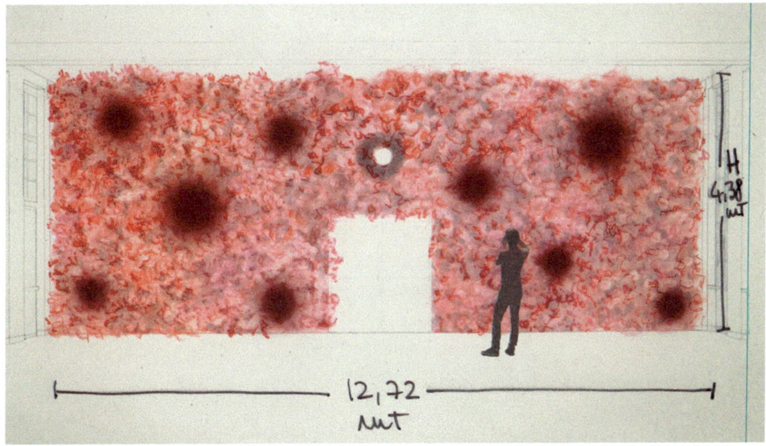

19 FRANCESCA PASQUALI, *ONE, NO ONE AND ONE HUNDRED THOUSAND* INSTALLATION IN THE PIRANDELLO ROOM IN THE CASA D'ITALIA.

randello Room, which for us is an exciting space, also because the great Eduardo De Filippo came to act there: on my first on-site inspection in Zurich, it was very moving for me to suddenly find myself standing in front of a photograph of Eduardo displayed inside this space.

PAC **You also invited the Bolognese artist Francesca Pasquali to that same Pirandello Room for a permanent installation. How did that collaboration come about?**

VC Knowing that the Italian Ministry of Foreign Affairs possesses an amazing contemporary art collection, we suggested that the General Secretary might commission a work of art, and the proposal was accepted by the Ministry and by the Italian consul in Zurich. In my view, Francesca Pasquali is one of the most interesting artists of our time, and we proposed that she might work on the new wall created on the entrance side of the Pirandello Room to host the control room. She therefore proposed a beautiful installation with red spatulas made of recycled plastic **[19]**: red like the Swiss flag, but also like the Italian one, the spatulas emerge from the wall to form a horizontal tube, above the visitors' heads, to accompany them along the route from the space of the atrium to the entrance to the Pirandello Room. The title *One, No One and One Hundred Thousand* is a homage to Pirandello, but also an interpretation of this Casa d'Italia as a unitary place to recognise values of identity, just as there are one hundred thousand souls that have lived in it.

PAC **You also thought about the colour for the nighttime illumination of the façades. How does that work?**

VC We called upon Mario Nanni again to design a lighting system with large numbers of Leds placed on the stringers of balconies, with the possibility of transforming the whole façade into an Italian flag, or a Swiss flag, depending on the occasion. To finish, we also wanted to pay our small homage to Le Corbusier and to his pavilion in Zurich, which we evoke with the purist steel and glass volume of the sentry box, located in front of the main entrance to the building.

BUILDINGS FOR JUSTICE

PAC **So far we've discussed various ways of considering the theme of the representative value of architecture, first in projects in which the metamorphosis of the façade was clear, then in certain interiors, ending with the emblematic example of the Casa d'Italia in Zurich, which came about as a building for caring services for young children and subsequently became a building representing the Italian State. I'd now like to reflect more deeply on the association of the theme of the asset values of historical architecture with that of the repurposing of institutional buildings, in the same way in which we reflected on the major monumental restoration interventions for the Pirelli Skyscraper and Capod-**

imonte Museum. In these buildings the representative value clearly emerges due to the intrinsic monumentality of the architecture. Your project for the new Public Prosecutor's Office in Catanzaro in the former military hospital introduces a variation to this approach: on one hand with a new judicial function you place value on a historical building of great merit, through a conservative restoration intervention that eliminates a whole series of additions and modifications that had compromised the original identity of the Convento degli Osservanti; on the other you respond to the request for enlargement with a new, resolutely contemporary architecture, even if at the same time it is based on a principle of critical interpretation of the figure of the cloister. You therefore create an interesting tension between conservation and innovation, between historical architecture and new architecture [20]**, a tension to which we'll return in the next chapter, devoted to the theme of the 'house inside the house'. Why has this need emerged for a new building as an enlargement of the existing one?**

GM Before answering this question, I'd just like to summon up my memories of being a youngster, when, in the period of medical examinations prior to military service, I found myself in the former military hospital for some checks. I remember perfectly that already then, on account of its historical value, the building represented a cornerstone of the urban development of Catanzaro. Our project actually considers the figure of the cloister as a generating element, and almost by cloning we arrive at the proposal of the enlargement conceived in the form of a 'contemporary cloister' made of steel and glass. The need for an enlargement came about from the decision to demolish certain pre-existing buildings, and therefore be able to reclaim these volumes, as happens in the recovery plans.

PAC **With what functions?**

VC These involve complementary activities with respect to the main offices, which are all located in the historical courtyard. A part of these activities concerns spaces for the police, the CID, while the empty lower floor is for use for parking for official cars.

PAC **In the conception and development of the project, what was the role of Nicola Gratteri, at the time Public Prosecutor of Catanzaro?**

VC Nicola Gratteri **[21]** must take full credit for having the idea of installing the new Public Prosecutor's Office in the former military hospital; he was the one who identified the State Property Agency as the contracting authority, and again it was he who asked the then undersecretary to the Prime Minister Graziano Delrio, in the Renzi government, for financing for the work.

GM On the role of Nicola Gratteri, I must add that in my view he was also the '*in pectore* client', as it was he who directly oversaw the construction site with

20 OVERALL VIEW OF THE NEW PUBLIC PROSECUTOR'S OFFICE IN CATANZARO, WITH THE RESTORED HISTORIC BUILDING AT THE CENTRE, AND THE NEW 'CLOISTER' IN THE BACKGROUND ON THE RIGHT.

21 WITH NICOLA GRATTERI AT THE CONSTRUCTION SITE OF THE NEW PUBLIC PROSECUTOR'S OFFICE IN CATANZARO.

22 THE NEW OVERHANGING VOLUME AND THE FAÇADE WITH VERTICAL SHADING DEVICES.

23 VIEW OF THE GREEN ROOF FROM ABOVE.

the works management, therefore soon becoming a protagonist of this project. This was also very lucky for us, because, being a true leader, he succeeded in running the process and carrying it forward effectively. We had an excellent meeting in Naples, on the occasion of the presentation of the Electa book devoted to the building,[1] in a crowded room of the Fondazione De Felice in Palazzo Donn'Anna. When Gratteri was called upon to speak at the table, he turned towards the screen on which the plans were being projected and began to point out a whole series of organisational, logistic and functional systems that he had mastered perfectly. At that moment everyone understood the extent to which he had immersed himself in the project, how well he understood it and how well he had run it.

PAC **Returning to the theme of the contemporary cloister, we'll see below that you've also revisited the classical figure of the cloister in various other projects, with very diverse programmes and in very different contexts. In the specific case of Catanzaro, I also find a compositional theme that you'd already explored in the first building in Casoria: the building appears like a volume overhanging a base** [22]**, and this image of suspended architecture appears reinforced by the use of shading devices, although in this case in the form of vertical blades and no longer horizontal plates.**

VC I agree that this way of configuring the façade contributes to accentuating the characteristic of lightness of the architecture. The overhangs of the volume are supported by six bearing walls placed at the centre, freeing up the corners, while the vertical shading devices enable daytime illumination to be guaranteed, but also for the gaze to be directed towards the broad horizon of the park and towards the nearby Catanzaro Lido.

GM I'd like to make a final observation on the particular basement of the building, which through the overhang is in dialogue with the difference in height, because in this precise location there is a sloping terrain. A further comment is about the fact that the new building isn't intended to establish itself as an exclusive figure, but rather to become an element within a strongly constructed context, with significant density consisting of very tall private buildings for housing. Hence the need to treat the theme of the roof as a fifth façade, observed from high up from the residential buildings. We wanted to treat this roof as a simple meadow **[23]**, with the value of almost a domestic element belonging to the community of inhabitants.

PAC **This virtuous process that has seen the State Property Agency and the Public Prosecutor Office of Catanzaro involved together was later repeated on the occasion of another competition, which you again won, for the Public Prosecutor's Office of Perugia. The programme was the same, and in this case too you intervened inside a former convent, originally of the Dominican nuns, which was transformed into a women's prison after 1867, with numerous additions and internal modifications. In addition to the conservative restoration and upgrading interventions on the courtyards, which**

become gardens [24]**, you propose an important innovation in the reversing of the public access, which you move from Via Torcoletti to Via del Giardino. Can you explain the reasons for this?**

VC Our project fits within an overall plan of urban regeneration of the former prisons in order to transform them into places of justice **[25]**: in addition to our intervention, Mario Botta is transforming the former men's prison for new use as a court. The theme of the entrance is indeed interesting. Initially we wanted to enhance the current entrance from Via Torcoletti, but from a discussion with Public Prosecutor Raffaele Cantone the assessment emerged that the entrance to a building of high value and public representation such as a Public Prosecutor's Office needed a significant space in front. We therefore studied the possibility of reversing the entrance arrangement, transforming the small piazza on the corner of Via del Giardino and Via del Parione **[26]**, beside the Church of Santo Spirito, where the parking spaces for the official cars had also been located. This new access is positioned on a lower floor with respect to the level of the three courtyards that define the layout plan of the Public Prosecutor's Office, and this enables a more generous, double height entrance hall to be created **[27]**, also forming a filter for control of the public.

PAC **Are there also other significant parts of the building that will be open to the public?**

VC One interesting location will be the former Chapel of the Repentute, which will be transformed into an auditorium, with a separate access from Via Torcoletti. The Public Prosecutor's Office of Perugia felt the need to be recognised by citizens, and this auditorium will therefore not only be used when press conferences are held, but also for events of cultural interest, as already happens in the Public Prosecutor's Office of Catanzaro in the historical cloister of the building.

PAC **In these two cases, a conception is delineated of the places of justice that is perhaps less monumental than in the past, perhaps more on a human scale, more open and democratic, and a key role has undoubtedly been played by two exceptional figures of 'public servants', namely Nicola Gratteri and Raffaele Cantone. On this theme of buildings of justice, you also developed an interesting competition project for the 'Citadel of Justice' of Bari, in which the new architecture is in dialogue with a large linear public park. Was this idea of the park expressly indicated in the call for tenders?**

VC It was indicated, but we were perhaps the only ones proposing a unitary design for the whole area, which we structured into parallel bands **[28]** so as to overcome the obstacle represented by the road traffic, which runs partially in a trench, cutting the plot of the project in two. Our intention was to create an orographic system of reference in relation to the historical city. The landscape continuity is also clear in the stretch of water that separates the city of justice from the park **[29]**, but at the same time becomes a mirror reflecting the new architecture.

24 UPGRADING OF THE COURTYARDS OF THE NEW PUBLIC PROSECUTOR'S OFFICE IN PERUGIA.

25 VIEW OF THE 'CITADEL OF JUSTICE' IN PERUGIA FROM ABOVE, WITH THE NEW PUBLIC PROSECUTOR'S OFFICE AT THE TOP AND THE FORMER MALE PRISON, WHICH WILL BE TRANSFORMED INTO A COURT, AT THE BOTTOM.

26 PERSPECTIVE OF THE NEW PUBLIC ENTRANCE IN THE SQUARE ON THE CORNER BETWEEN VIA DEL GIARDINO AND VIA DEL PARIONE.

27 PERSPECTIVE OF THE NEW DOUBLE-HEIGHT ENTRANCE HALL.

28 GENERAL LAYOUT PLAN OF THE 'CITADEL OF JUSTICE' IN BARI, WITH THE NEW LINEAR PARK AND THE BUILDINGS OF JUSTICE SEPARATED BY AN ARTIFICIAL CANAL.

29 PERSPECTIVE VIEW OF THE NEW VOLUMES PROJECTING OUT ONTO THE PUBLIC PARK.

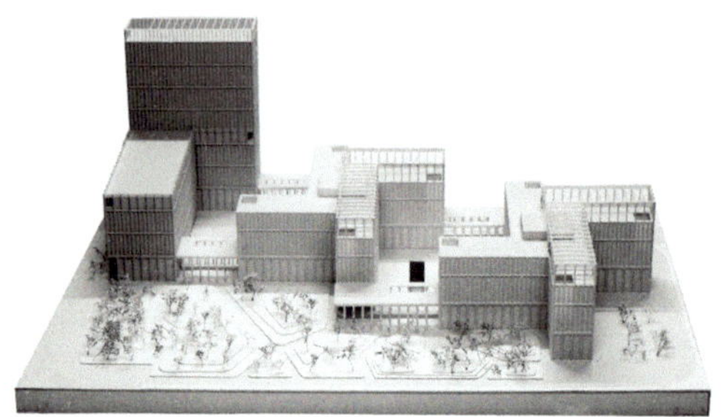

31 HEADQUARTERS OF THE TUSCANY REGIONAL AUTHORITY, VIEW OF THE MODEL OF THE PROJECT: THE NEW VOLUMES CREATE A THIRD COURTYARD LINKING UP WITH THE TWO PRE-EXISTING COURTYARDS.

30 PERSPECTIVE OF THE THIRD TOWER OF THE TUSCANY REGIONAL AUTHORITY.

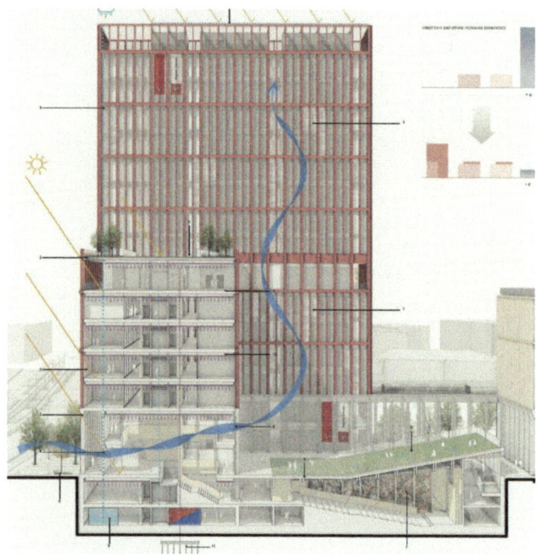

32 PERSPECTIVE SECTION OF THE THIRD COURTYARD, WITH THE UNDERGROUND AUDITORIUM COVERED BY A SLOPING MEADOW.

PAC **This stretch of water forms a kind of naturalistic moat that allows the enclosure wall, which often isolates buildings of justice from the city, generating an image of repression, sometimes even of prison, as happened in many buildings of the Fascist period, to be eliminated entirely. I'm therefore interested in discussing the anti-monumental attitude with which you characterise your architecture, though respecting the clear requirement for security. In the various parts of the programme, you again use the figure of the cloister, even if these 'contemporary cloisters' are no longer closed figures, but become 'U'shaped, opening up towards the park. I also seem to be able to identify a certain continuity with the Public Prosecutor's Office of Catanzaro in your projecting of these 'U'-shaped volumes onto the landscape.**

VC Your observation is quite pertinent; we are indeed attempting to ensure that this building, mostly for offices, can present itself to the city in its most public, I would even say most civic dimension. These front portions overhanging onto the park are intended to coexist with the city, yet without this determining a direct accessibility. In the upper floors, on the other hand, the offices open up onto broad green loggias, also offering those working there a contact with nature though respecting the necessary security. The entire building is covered with a regular square grid system mixing terracotta and photovoltaic modules, on both the façades and the roofs, configured as a large mosaic evoking the floors of the Church of San Nicola. In the basements, which are particularly closed off to avoid direct access, we propose using the local stone.

PAC **Are there particular reasons for the use of the colour red?**

VC We wanted to use terracotta and tuff rock, the colour therefore comes from this desire to use natural materials and these warm colours, with a continuity between façades and internal spaces. We also looked with great interest at the Teatro Petruzzelli, a cornerstone of the historical architecture of Bari, and its beautiful red brick colour; it therefore seemed interesting to us to attempt to use old materials with contemporary methods.

INSTITUTIONAL REPRESENTATION BUILDINGS

PAC **I'd like to return to the conception of the façade as a square grid, observing how this grid characterises architecture with a high degree of geometrical abstraction. Any reference to the number of floors and the real dimensions is almost entirely lost; the architecture is affirmed in the force of its volumetric expression, in dialogue on a large scale with the landscape of the park. I'm interested in this character of abstract purity, which reminds me of the Minimalist sculptures of Sol LeWitt, an Abstractism that goes well beyond your previous references to the great tradition of Italian Modern. This abstraction leads to the building being perceived as**

though it were out-of-scale, a condition not without ambiguity, but it's perhaps this ambiguity that reinforces the architecture's value of institutional representation. I'd now like to discuss the last projects in this chapter starting with this theme of institutional representation. Let's begin with the competition project for the third tower of the Tuscany Regional Authority in Florence, where we find a façade that in its abstraction means the reference to the structuring of the floors is lost. While in the 'Citadel of Justice' in Bari the out-of-scale aspect was affirmed in a closely-woven grid, with three modules per floor, in Florence you introduce a genuine giant order, two storeys high, which produces the effect of lightening the volumetric presence of the tower on the urban skyline [30]. **The competition asked you not only to design a new tower, but also to consider the relationship with the two other pre-existing towers. How did you decide on the position and disposition of masses of the tower?**

GM Our project came about from two observations. On one hand, there was the need to complete the institutional complex in the context of the large San Donato Park in Novoli, with an interesting architectural emergence, the tower of the power plant of the old Fiat factory. On the other hand, being in Florence we began to observe the most significant Renaissance palazzi with great attention, in order to propose an architecture that was without doubt contemporary, but at the same time in a relationship with this extraordinary urban context. In particular we studied Palazzo Davanzati, Palazzo Guadagni and Palazzo Rucellai, naturally not to propose a literal translation of them, but rather to glean operational indications in linguistic terms, proposing an architecture based on the tripartite structuring of base, body and crown, together with the use of large loggias. We also considered the typological system, starting with the observation that the first two buildings formed two courtyards in a chain: more than a third tower, we in fact wanted to build the third courtyard **[31]**, rising on one side of which is a large blade, narrow and tall, positioned on the urban axis. Due to various aspects, it is a very simple, rational architecture, with a concrete supporting façade, mass-coloured with iron oxide pigments and the load-bearing bracing points positioned so as to eliminate all the intermediary pillars.

PAC **Beyond this reference to a kind of Renaissance Classicism, the tower establishes a good dialogue with the two pre-existing buildings, the façades of which you've modified, proposing to adopt the same design of a giant order. I can also observe your proposal to cut the tower in half with a free floor, a kind of large loggia at the level of the crown of the pre-existing buildings. Does this loggia take on a public value?**

GM We actually located the council room and the spaces for meetings with journalists at this level; it therefore becomes to all intents and purposes a public floor above ground with large terraces. We wanted to increase the amount of community and public locations, which the competition brief only envisaged on the ground floor. The courtyards are also conceived as spaces that are available to the community of the neighbourhood, as you can see with the treatment of the auditorium below ground, covered by a sloping meadow **[32]**. Along the road, we enclosed the courtyards with connecting propylaea, which take up the same giant concrete order, in this case grey, that we use to wrap the pre-existing buildings.

PAC **That same year, 2022, you participated in another interesting international competition for the upgrading of Building E at the United Nations headquarters in Geneva, in the context of a 'Strategic Property Plan'[2] involving the whole complex. There's much that could be said about the ambiguity of this plan, which envisaged the partial demolition of this beautiful Modernist building** [33] **designed by Eugène Beaudouin, the author of the stupendous Maison du Peuple in Clichy (with Marcel Lods, 1935–39), together with Basil Spence, the architect of the famous Modernist Coventry Cathedral (1962). How did this competition take place?**

VC It was a competitive dialogue, a kind of tendering for contracts in which large international construction firms were invited to take part. We participated with the Pizzarotti company of Parma. The procedure was interesting, because during the competition procedure certain meetings were envisaged with the clients, according to a process of dialogue and interaction with the participants.

PAC **I'm familiar with this procedure that's used in Switzerland for complex projects, in particular for urban regeneration; they call it 'parallel study assignments', a procedure recognised by the professional registers,[3] which provides that the competition jury, in which the clients' representatives also sit, should meet a number of times with each competitor in order to suggest modifications or prescriptions between one phase and the next of the design process.**

VC This dialogue with clients is fundamental. Our idea, which was a very strong one and was shared by Pizzarotti, was that we could act with a restoration of the building, in contrast with what was envisaged in the preliminary project drawn up by the US studio SOM, which proposed demolition without taking the evident qualities of the existing architecture into consideration. I must add that we were the only ones who proposed a restoration; we'd invited Giovanni Carbonara, the great professor of restoration at 'La Sapienza' University of Rome, to join us in the planning group, and he was enthusiastic that we could act almost outside of the competition. We also had the support of a professor at the EPFL, Franz Graf, an expert in the restoration of the Modern, who has produced a detailed study to this building.[4] When we met the UN officials, we had the impression in the more heated dialogues that some understood the importance of the building, while others, particularly the Americans, were almost shocked by our proposals, which were not provided for by the competition rules.

33 EUGÈNE BEAUDOUIN AND BASIL SPENCE, BUILDING 'E' AT THE GENEVA HEADQUARTERS OF THE UNITED NATIONS, 1968–73, ARCHIVE PHOTO.

34 PERSPECTIVE OF THE WEST FAÇADE WITH RIBBON WINDOWS FITTED WITH MOVABLE PHOTOVOLTAIC ELEMENTS.

35 PERSPECTIVE SECTION OF THE BUILDING: THE 'VERTICAL FARM' AND THE BELVEDERE.

36 NIGHTTIME VIEW FROM THE OTHER SHORE OF THE LAKE, WITH BUILDING 'E' ILLUMINATED WITH THE BLUE AND WHITE COLOURS OF THE UN.

PAC **What arguments did you try to convince the clients of the need for a restoration with?**

VC We wanted to offer the certainty that through the restoration approach we could realise the work with definite timescales, avoiding the need for removal of the rubble caused by the demolitions and the subsequent environmental clean-up in a landscape context of great value. We then proposed the modification of the ribbon windows with a device with mobile photovoltaic elements **[34]** that open and close automatically depending on the intensity of the sunlight. We also proposed transforming some storeys of offices, which they wanted to demolish, into a 'vertical farm' **[35]** that could become a research centre and a showcase for the UN's agricultural and environmental policies.

PAC **I saw that you also proposed transforming the top floor into a belvedere, perhaps remembering your intervention in the Pirelli Skyscraper in Milan, which at night became a huge lantern.**

VC We thought it was important to affirm the presence of the building in the urban landscape, also in views from the other shore of the lake **[36]**, through lighting with the two colours of the UN—white and sky blue—so that it could represent the rebirth of this extraordinary building. It still appears truly paradoxical to us today that the UN should want to demolish a building of such quality.

PAC **The last project we'll consider here is the Italian Embassy in Nairobi. As we saw earlier about the project for the Casa d'Italia in Zurich, you again tackle the theme of the representation of Italy abroad, no longer inside a pre-existing building, but with a newly constructed architecture. The first topic that I'd like to discuss concerns the relationship with a geographical context of great quality. If I interpret your intentions correctly, you wanted as far as possible to respect the original topography of the site, characterised by steep slopes, with a series of terraces and earth embankments on which a series of rather small buildings stood** [37]. **This choice makes it possible to limit excavations and filling with earth, but also to characterise the architecture with an anti-monumental dimension, which we could describe as picturesque and almost domestic.**

VC We actually interpreted the construction of the new embassy as an opportunity for safeguarding this extraordinary environment of the Karura Forest **[38]**, which we consider to be the true monument. Our proposal was appreciated by the competition commission for the way in which the buildings are arranged on different levels, respecting the contours. Nevertheless, I must specify that the orientation document for the design process indicated this new conception of embassies no longer as individual buildings, but as a cluster of buildings differentiated according to their functions.

PAC **The architecture of the buildings proposes façades characterised by a rapid rhythm of pillars, giving depth and shade to**

the full-height apertures; these are concrete façades that remind me of those of the tower of the Tuscany Regional Authority in Florence on account of their similar connotation of abstract Classicism, even though in this case they're organised in an anti-monumental vein, because the principle of a giant order is entirely lacking. How important is it for you to think of an architectural language that can evoke a representative value of Italian architecture abroad?

VC We did indeed want to render an image of Italian architecture, but also to make it coexist with the element of the large raised roof that shades the buildings, typical of tropical architecture. We also used the marvellous red earth of Nairobi **[39]**, which we included in the concrete as aggregate, with the addition of white cement parts to evoke the statuary marble that we often find in Italian embassies. The buildings are all composed starting with a square module that's repeated in various forms, but always with a central void for the natural rising of warm air.

PAC **In some aspects, the figure of the cloister also returns, with a distribution of rooms around the central void, but I also interpret this choice of the square module as a revisiting of a very Classical compositional theme, used by Palladio and even taken up in contemporary architecture: the theme of the square that is decomposed into nine squares, a theme that forms the basis of compositional exercises in many schools of architecture all over the world, particularly in the United States; I remember in particular John Hejduk at the Cooper Union School of Art in New York. With different dimensions and different intended uses, all five buildings propose variations on this compositional theme.**

VC We really didn't want the decomposition of the programme into a number of buildings to betray the visual unity of the complex as a whole. In the subsequent executive development of the project we learned that when you work in Africa you need to make a virtue of necessity, and so we'll have to limit the importing of materials and equipment as far as possible, also due to the customs costs. We therefore conducted a careful analysis with our local partner on the availability of materials and decided to realise cast-on-site floors, both inside and outside, with red earth aggregate, but also to use very essential plasters for the walls and ceilings, with the same earth colouring to give chromatic unity **[40]**, giving the impression of a space dug into the hill. The work should begin in late 2025.

1 Marco Mulazzani (ed.), *Costruire nella città / Building in the City. La Procura della Repubblica di Catanzaro / The Catanzaro Public Prosecutor's Office* (Milan: Electa, 2023).

2 Office des Nations Unies à Genève, Plan stratégique patrimonial, 2015, cf. https://www.ungeneva.org/fr/about/palais-des-nations/shp.

3 Cf. Regolamento dei mandati di studio paralleli d'architettura e d'ingegneria, Norma SIA 143, 2009.

4 Cf. Franz Graf, Giulia Marino, *Le siège de l'ONU à Genève, L'agrandissement du Palais des Nations, Étude patrimoniale* (Lausanne: Laboratoire des Techniques et de la Sauvegarde de l'Architecture Moderne, Ecole Polytechnique Fédérale, 2016).

37 PERSPECTIVE OF THE NEW ITALIAN EMBASSY IN NAIROBI, WITH THE VARIOUS BUILDINGS RESTING ON ARTIFICIAL TERRACING.

38 BOB MATHENGE AND VINCENZO CORVINO DURING THE FIRST VISIT TO THE NAIROBI SITE.

39 LOCAL MATERIALS USED FOR CONSTRUCTION: RED EARTH AND WHITE STONE, USED AS AGGREGATES FOR THE CONCRETE FAÇADES.

40 PERSPECTIVE OF THE CENTRAL ATRIUM OF THE NEW EMBASSY, WITH THE TYPICAL NAIROBI RED EARTH COLOURING.

OFFICE BUILDING
CASORIA, 2002–4

The context into which the project fits is an area of industrial expansion characterised by the absence of pre-existing constructions at the margins of the consolidated city fabric. Facing on one side towards an intersection of the median axis and on the other side towards the first constructions of the urban centre, the intervention is prompted by the aim of transforming an existing construction left in a rustic state due to neglect over time. The building is structured into a basement floor for parking and storage and three floors above ground for use as offices.

The intention to return the building to a rediscovered unitary disposition of masses is fulfilled through the use of a system of shading devices enveloping the building around the two most representative elevations: the south elevation, with the large glass windows of the offices and operational spaces, and the east elevation, the head of the main entrance. The curtain of shading devices, consisting of extruded aluminium plate elements with curvilinear sections, is characterised by the presence of horizontal cuts in the areas of the fenestrations on both sides, and by a lightening of the crown achieved by spacing out the plate elements. The shading device is turned horizontally on the top level, creating a pergola at the edge of the terrace. The plate system, which makes the surface of the building appear to oscillate through an interplay of light and shade, inverts the light ratio during the nighttime hours thanks to the presence of lighting units arranged in the areas of the glass apertures, making the building alive and illuminated from inside.

The internal operational spaces, organised over three floors, are arranged in such a way as to receive the light filtered by the shading devices along the perimeter walls, leaving the area of connection and service at the centre of the building. Natural light penetrates directly into the building through the south elevation and indirectly through a genuine 'chimney of light' consisting of the entirely glass-covered lift space, which, running through the entire building as far as the basement floor, spreads the light captured above from the glass opening present on the tower of the stairwell. In this way, depending on the time of day and the season, in each environment there are different qualities of light determining a perception of the spaces that is always different.

gnec.a.m.

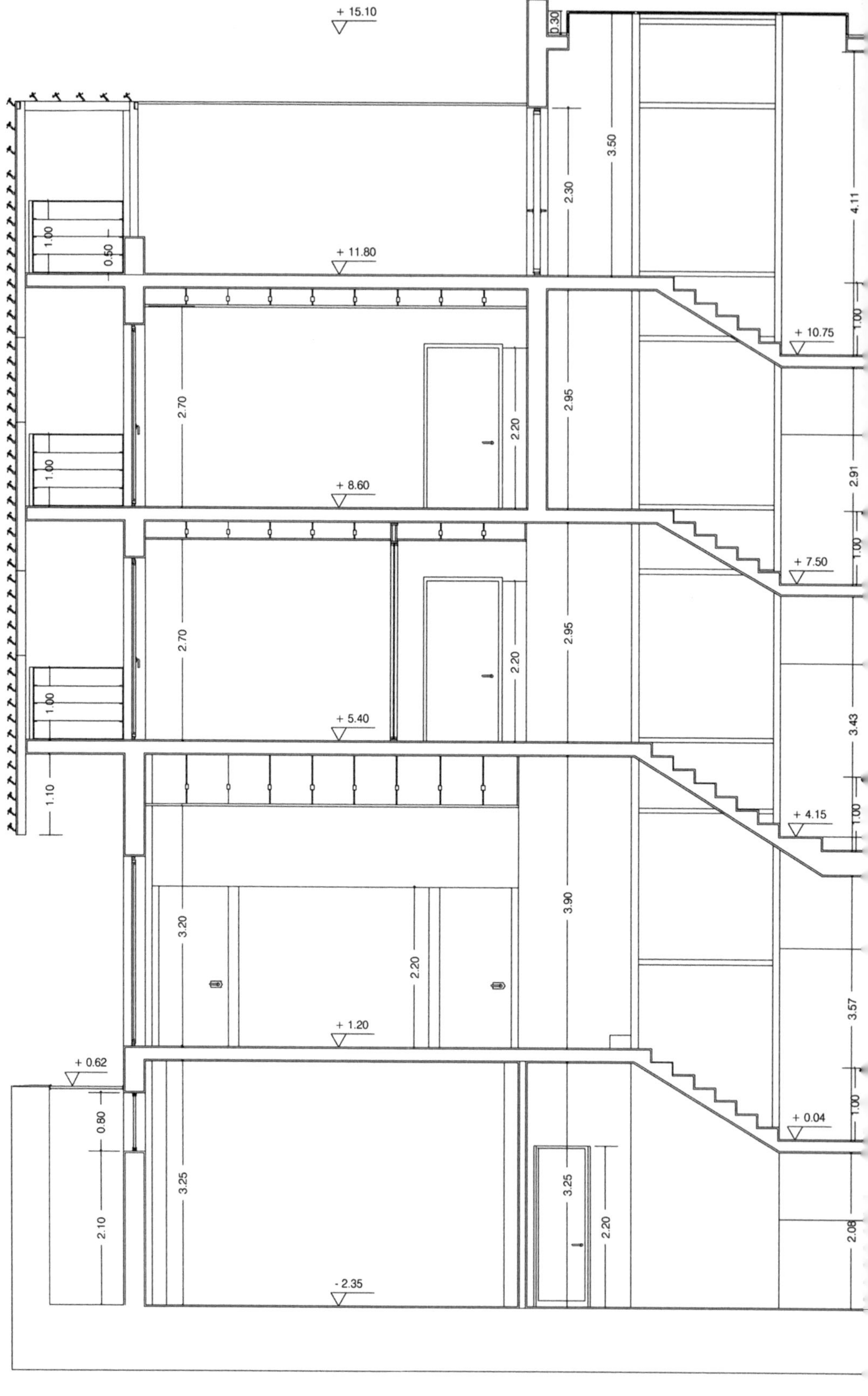
+ 15.10
0.30
3.50
2.30
4.11
1.00
0.50
+ 11.80
1.00
+ 10.75
2.70
2.20
2.95
1.00
2.91
+ 8.60
1.00
+ 7.50
2.70
2.20
2.95
1.00
3.43
+ 5.40
1.10
1.00
+ 4.15
3.20
2.20
3.90
3.57
+ 1.20
+ 0.62
0.80
1.00
+ 0.04
3.25
3.25
2.20
2.10
2.08
- 2.35

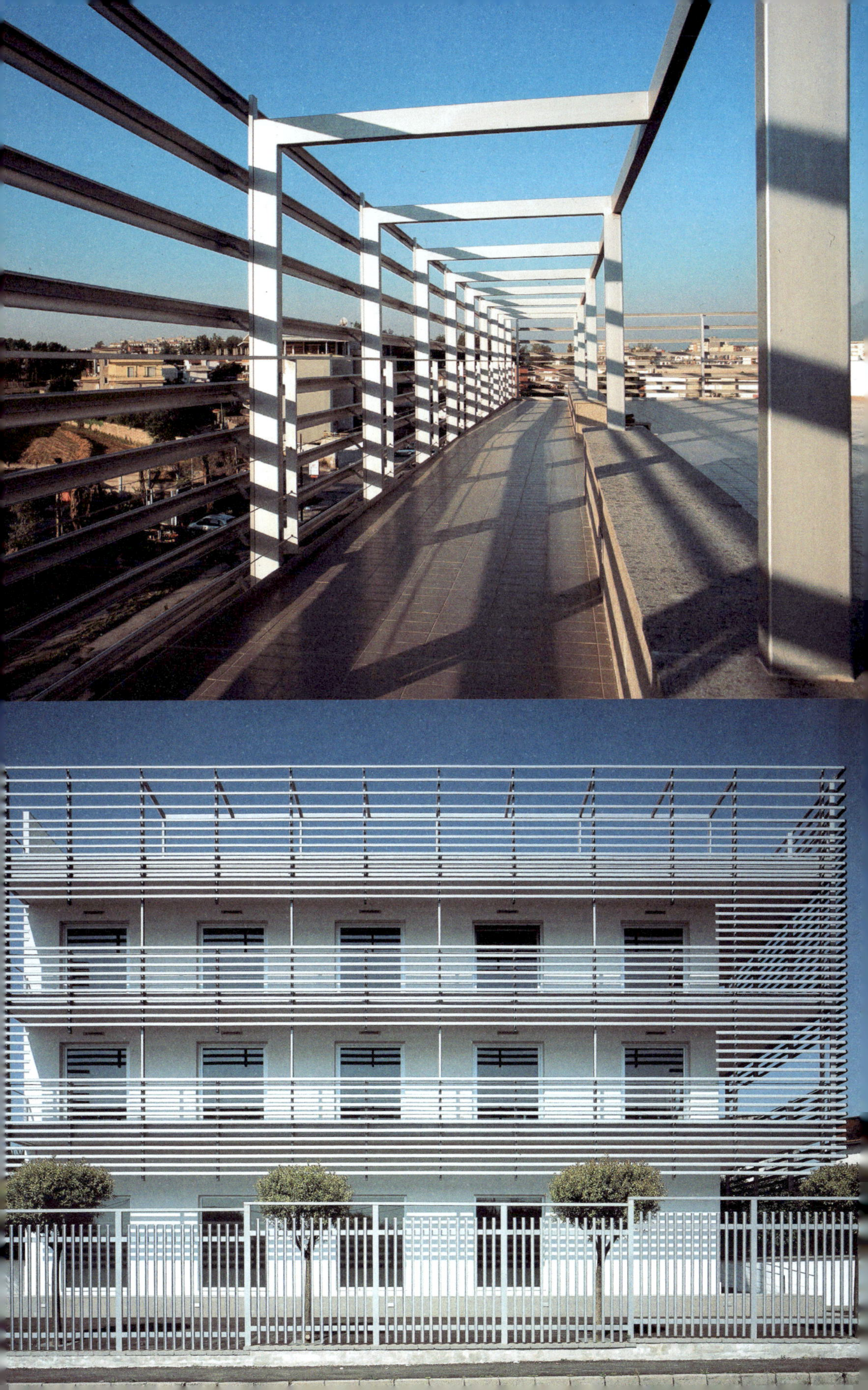

NEW PUBLIC PROSECUTOR'S OFFICE IN THE FORMER MILITARY HOSPITAL
CATANZARO, 2017–22

The complex of the former military hospital in Catanzaro, built in the 15th century as the Convento degli Osservanti, has undergone various transformations over time. In the 19th century, part of the convent and the church were used for military purposes. In 2011 the monumental complex was declared a site of historical-artistic interest, while in 2016 the Municipality of Catanzaro allocated part of the complex to the Ministry of Justice for conversion into the headquarters of the Public Prosecutor's Office.

On one hand, the overall project concerned the architectural restoration, the conservative redevelopment and functional redesigning of the historical courtyard, which is freed of building additions, restoring legibility to the original configuration of the convent. The interventions on the elevations are limited to the restoration of materials and the replacement of fixtures in order to improve its energy efficiency, while the internal circulation routes have been reorganised, creating new vertical connections to remove architectural barriers and provide added security staircases in the existing bays. On the structural level, the project included static consolidations and seismic improvements, while for the technological systems the restoration focused on criteria of efficiency and sustainability with the maximum use of renewable sources.

On the other hand, several volumes of limited architectural value were demolished and a new extension was created, called a contemporary courtyard, which is respectful of the architectural characters of the historical monastery. The new building is structured with a plan with a central courtyard, partially projecting into the landscape, which reinterprets the convent typology with a contemporary entirely glass façade protected by aluminium shading elements. All the external areas have been upgraded, returning to their historical uses as ornamental garden and orchard, with the planting of new trees that are consistent with those of the past. The new building also contributes to fitting harmoniously into the landscape, thanks to the flat roof appearing like a meadow, offering the inhabitants of the nearby houses views that are in continuity with the other terracing. The intervention has thereby returned historical and functional value to the complex, adapting it to meet contemporary needs without denaturalising its identity.

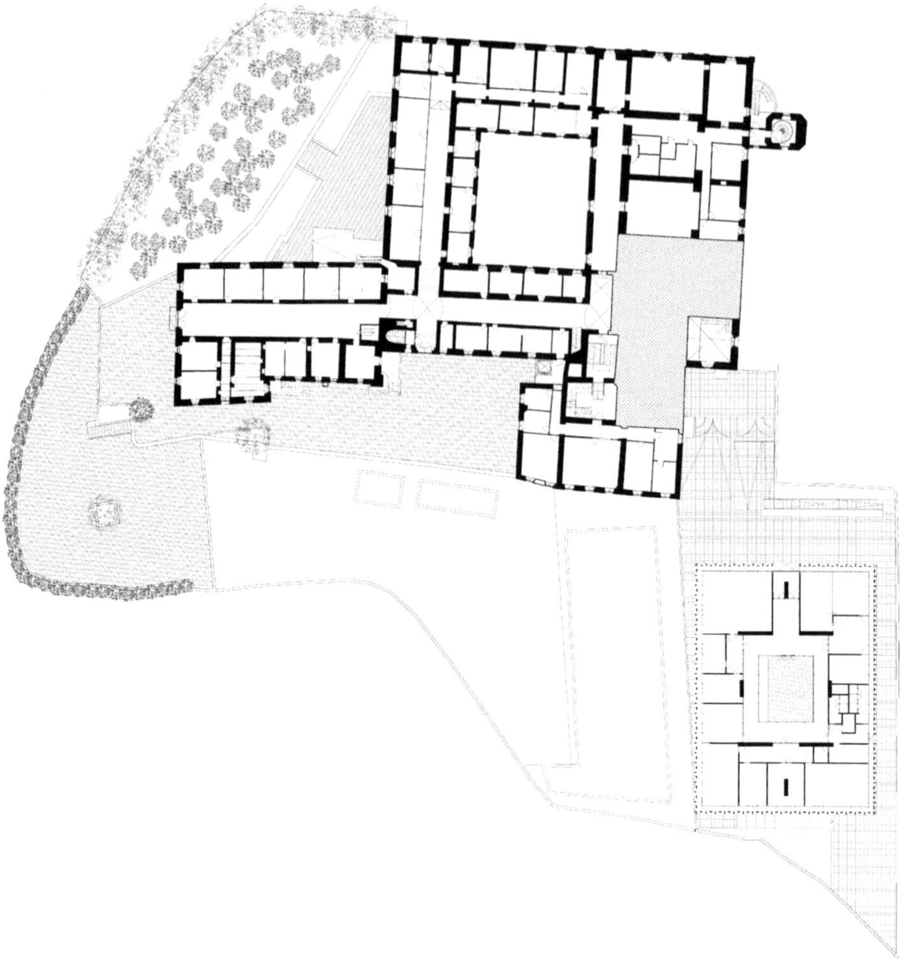

PROCURA DELLA REPUBBLICA
DI CATANZARO

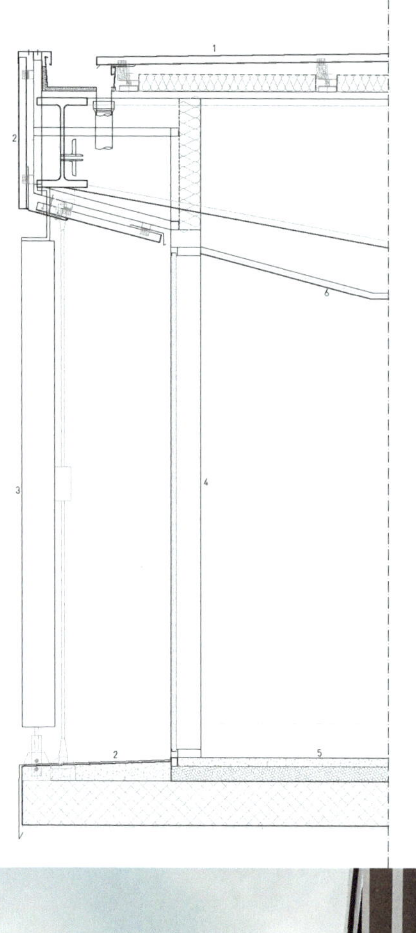
1
2
6
3
4
2
5

RESTORATION OF THE CASA D'ITALIA ZURICH, 2021–26

Commissioned by the Italian community in Zurich, the building was constructed in 1932 from a project by Otto Gschwind and was initially used as a language school and cultural centre. In 1935 it became property of the Italian State and was transformed by the Consulate General into the Casa d'Italia. The building is protected at municipal and federal level on account of its historical and artistic value.

The restoration project follows the principles of recognisability, reversibility and distinguishability, as agreed with the Superintendence of Zurich. The external spaces have been reorganised with separate accesses for the school and the consulate, and upgraded with uniform flooring, the restoration of the enclosures and utilisation of green spaces, with conservation of the chestnut trees and new plants. For the façades, the restoration includes the making good of the plaster and the wooden fixtures, with the addition of new windows respecting the original dimensions, returning the northeast frontage to its condition prior to 1939. The restoration also involved the making good of the zinc-titanium roof and the realisation of a new handrail on the balcony.

The repurposing of the building attributes the south part to the school and the north part up to the second floor to the consulate, while the attic rooms are occupied by the Italian Institute of Culture. The distribution of the environments has been maintained, with modifications to optimise spaces and circulation routes by means of the insertion of two lifts and the reorganisation of the attic rooms with a central corridor. The school canteen has been maintained on the basement floor, while the gymnasium has been converted into an archive for the consulate and the changing rooms into a storeroom. The ground floor hosts the kindergarten with dedicated spaces, while the north part with the Pirandello Room remains practically unchanged. On the first floor the school environments are optimised, while the front office is enlarged in the section devoted to the consulate. On the second floor, the planned uses are confirmed, with the school to the south and the offices of the consulate to the north. On the attic floor, the reception office of the school is sited to the south and the offices of the Italian Institute of Culture to the north. The interior finishes envisage rubber granulate flooring for most of the environments, concrete for the technical rooms and wood strip parquet and wood panelling in the Pirandello Room. The new access control sentry box is realised with bulletproof glass and equipped with a steel cantilever roof with blackout curtains.

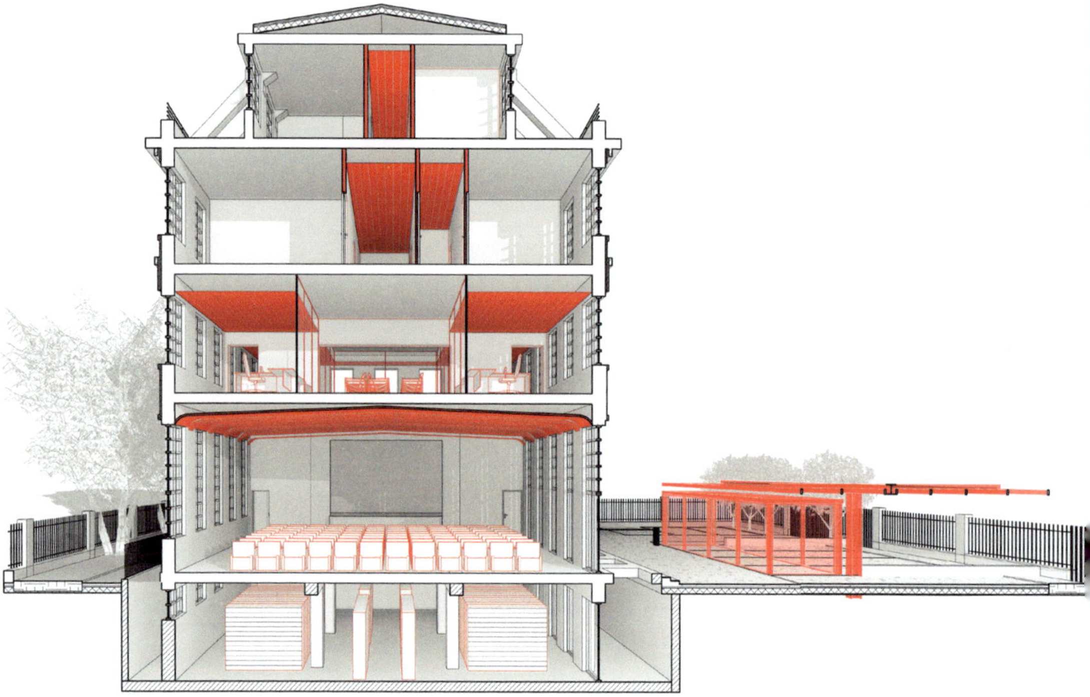

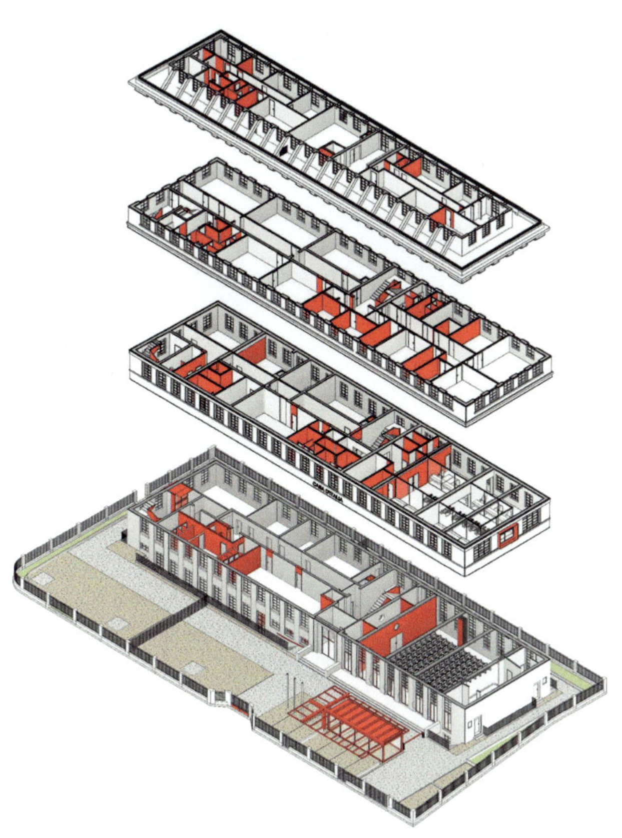

THIRD TOWER OF THE TUSCANY REGIONAL AUTHORITY
FLORENCE, 2022

The competition project for the third tower of the Tuscany Regional Authority has been located inside the business district of Novoli with the aim of modernising and reinforcing the institutional image of the Regional Authority, creating an architecture that reflects authoritativeness and the accessibility of institutions. The new building is integrated into the existing structures and defines a relationship of continuity and cohesiveness with the surrounding area, proposing a solution that redefines the urban curtain between Via di Novoli and Viale della Toscana by means of a system of propylaea, courtyards and gardens. The project adopts an approach that challenges the monolithic nature of institutional architectures, offering a solution that develops vertically but that is structured horizontally at the same time, creating a series of courtyards and propylaea that favour the connection between the various sections of the complex and facilitate public access. Thanks to the ecological network and pedestrian and cycle paths, the project provides for good integration with the San Donato urban park and other community facilities. The building thus forms not only an important administrative pole, but also an element of urban cohesion, destined to become a point of reference for the city and the Tuscany Regional Authority.

The project for the building is marked by simplicity and modularity, making reference to the principles of order and formal rigour that are typical of the historical city, but also to the traditional tripartition into base, central body and crown. The new building is conceived as an open space that is usable by the community, with public and multi-purpose areas for events, conferences and cultural meetings. The ground floor hosts public spaces such as the public relations office, dining areas, an exhibition room and the auditorium, while the upper floors are earmarked for the administrative offices, with a number of more prestige spaces on the sixth floor, such as the council room, the press room, the reception room and an exhibition space linked to a spacious terrace on the seventh floor. These spaces are organised in a flexible and modular way to meet the future requirements of the regional administration.

ITALIAN EMBASSY IN KENYA
NAIROBI, 2021–28

The new complex of the Italian Embassy in Nairobi is located in the Muthaiga district, a historic residential area adjacent to the Karura Forest. The site, Italian property since 1965, covers an overall area of 32,500 square metres, and the intervention involves three lots of this, making a total of 10,250 square metres. The terrain has a difference in level of around 25 metres and is characterised by rich biodiversity, with numerous autochthonous species typical of the nearby forest.
The project has the preservation of the existing vegetation and harmonious integration with the environment as its main objectives, using sustainable construction techniques and local materials. Access to the complex is guaranteed by a vehicle entrance and two separate pedestrian entrances, for the public and for staff. Independent circulation routes are envisaged for public functions, so as to minimise the interaction with the areas reserved for staff.

The architectural design takes account of the orography of the terrain and biodiversity, reducing the need for earth moving. The orientation of the buildings has been optimised based on solar studies, and the compact form of the buildings reduces dispersions of energy. The roofing is designed to guarantee protection from direct sunlight, to collect rainwater and allow natural ventilation. The project is inspired by a sober, elegant architectural language, which reflects the Italian tradition, particularly Rationalism, but is also integrated into the local tradition and the naturalistic context through the use of the typical red coloration of the local earth. This approach contributes to making the building a symbol of Italian culture abroad, at the same time respecting the surrounding environment. The main building of the embassy is designed on two floors marked by the colours red and white, with the ground floor earmarked for the areas of greatest public use (helpdesks, auditorium, halls) and the first floor for the areas with less need for access by the public. The orographic conditions of the sloping site allow panoramic views, both from the surrounding areas and inside the complex, integrating perfectly into the natural landscape. Photovoltaic panels are not envisaged on the main buildings to reduce the visual impact and to respect the environmental restrictions, while a photovoltaic system will be installed on the canopies of the car parks in order to meet the energy requirements of the complex.

4

THE 'HOUSE INSIDE THE HOUSE'

PAC **I'd like to begin today's conversation with a drawing by Le Corbusier, developed on the occasion of his project for the reconstruction of the town of Saint-Dié, when had been totally razed to the ground by the Nazi Army in November 1944. Although his urban planning project proposed a radically new plan that didn't consider pre-existing elements, Le Corbusier devoted particular attention to the ruins of the old Cathedral of Romanesque origin, rejecting any hypothesis of philological reconstruction. What he proposed was very distinct from the conservative positions expressed by the 'architect-restorers' of the academic culture, because he considered it necessary to maintain the physical presence of the ruin, as a testimony and future memory of the drama of war. In a sketch of extraordinary beauty** [1], **he represented his simple idea: instead of completing the destroyed parts, he kept the shape of the ruin intact and built a new structure with slim concrete pillars bearing a flat roof.[1] The interval between the uppermost part of the ruined walls and the new roof is closed off by full-height glass walls, through which the landscape of the Vosges mountainous chain can be admired. I propose that we use this sketch by Le Corbusier as a reference to introduce a reflection on the way in which you intervene as contemporary architects inside ancient buildings that have been ruined by the neglect of time. I'd therefore like to begin with your restoration project for the Temple–Cathedral in the Rione Terra in Pozzuoli, developed for an international competition in 2004: a project that I consider to particularly exemplify the desire to create—precisely as Le Corbusier did—a significant tension between the pre-existing elements, which must be protected and showcased, and the new architecture, which must take on its own autonomy of construction and expression. The new liturgical room that you proposed to realise had an entirely independent structure to support the new roof, detached with respect to the colonnade of the Roman Temple. Do you agree with this association with Le Corbusier's sketch?**

GM This observation of yours arising from Le Corbusier's sketch seems to me to be very pertinent, because our project for the Temple–Cathedral of Pozzuoli was indeed our first experience of the theme of the insertion of a contemporary structure inside an old building. The theme was complex and fascinating: the late-Baroque church-cathedral had been built on the remains of the Augustan Temple; its nave was destroyed by a tragic fire in 1964, then subsequently the 1980 earthquake led to the total abandonment of the monument and to further deterioration **[2]**. How do we reconstruct an ancient structure that had suffered so many historical vicissitudes in a contemporary way? The project needed to confirm some elements associated with the original state of the building, but at the same time it was this space left open that needed to be repaired. We wanted to act outside of any act of mediation, proposing a very rational new structure, which from the interior reaches the top to form the new nave, contained in a pure parallelepiped.

PAC **What decisions did you take regarding the reconstruction of the apsidal part of the cathedral?**

GM In this case too we relied on the use of pure geometries and forms, in clear contrast with the historical structure. Instead of reconstructing the collapsed roof with a spherical or semi-spherical dome, we wanted to affirm the presence of a pure prism **[3]**, a raised box-like element that we had jokingly called a 'cubola'. For us this 'cubola' meant a contemporary way of enabling the origins of this monument to emerge, with all its historical stratifications. This was clearly our idea, one that represents well what became a feature of our design in the years that followed: to always endeavour to create a work that in distinguishing itself was not invasive, that didn't go beyond the value and beauty of a complex history. Then the proposal by Marco Dezzi Bardeschi won, and was subsequently realised.

VC I should also point out that this new cubic prism crowning the upper part of the presbytery—our so-called 'cubola'—doesn't exceed the height of the steeple of the other domes, following the desire, which in some ways characterises all our work, to always be very discreet, but at the same time powerful and clear in the use of such essential forms.

PAC **I find the decision to configure the new nave as an independent volume emerging above the eave line of the Roman colonnade particularly interesting, for two reasons. Firstly, it reinterprets the theme of the cell of the temple as a genuine 'house inside a house', leaving the perimeter route free. Secondly, the greater height of this new 'cell' compared to the colonnade and the Roman wall enables a junction of light to be created between old and new: the sun penetrates during the day, while at night the new structure is illuminated like a large lantern when perceived from afar. How did you configure this new structure?**

GM The structure consists of large frames, which respect the intercolumniation of the temple but at the same time characterise the spatiality of the church with a new rhythm. I might add that this new space was enhanced by a beautiful work by Nino Longobardi: a large cross **[4]**, five metres high, bearing the engraved figure of Christ on both sides, with the idea that this element was two-sided. This cross was suspended from the large arch separating the nave from the area of the presbytery, and the fact that the thin figure of Christ is duplicated was a way of looking at the history of the Temple–Cathedral in all its depth and complexity.

VC I'd like to add a consideration concerning the relationship between architecture and archaeology. I'm pleased to recall that in this work we'd involved Professor Bernard Andreae, an archaeologist of extraordinary expertise, very well known for his excavations in Sperlonga, Pompeii, Baia, Pergamon and Villa Adriana. We'd discussed this idea with him of enclosing a millennial history within the essential form of a display case, and considering the contemporary intervention as an opportunity to design a work of continuity with history. The access to the church was conceived as an archaeological itiner-

1 LE CORBUSIER, SKETCH FOR THE RECONSTRUCTION OF THE CATHEDRAL IN SAINT-DIÉ, JUNE 1948. FROM: PIERRE SADDY (ED.), *LE CORBUSIER LE PASSÉ À RÉACTION POÉTIQUE* (PARIS: CAISSE NATIONALE DES MONUMENTS HISTORIQUES ET DES SITES, 1987), 101.

2 VIEW OF THE TEMPLE–CATHEDRAL OF POZZUOLI IN THE LATE 1990S, WITH THE DISCOVERY OF THE ROMAN TEMPLE FOLLOWING THE FIRE IN 1964. PHOTO BY LUCIANO ROMANO.

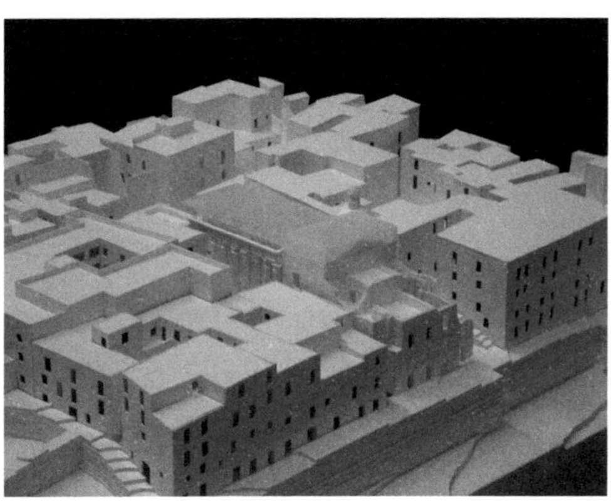

3 MODEL OF THE COMPETITION PROJECT, 2003.

4 SKETCH BY NINO LONGOBARDI FOR THE CRUCIFIX IN THE NEW LITHURGICAL ROOM.

ary: from street level visitors went up to the level of the church along a staircase-walkway, from which the fragments of the archaeological dig could be glimpsed. I recognise a major analogy in Le Corbusier's sketch, in looking at the palimpsest of fragments not only as finds, but as elements from which to start in order to design the new architectural composition.

PAC **It can clearly be read in the longitudinal section that you defined the level of the floor of the new nave at the same height of the base of the Roman colonnade, a level that is raised with respect to the floor of the presbytery. How did you resolve the problem of the connection between these different levels?**

GM We wanted to extend the flooring of the new nave as far as the presbytery, in order to unify the liturgical space, but at the same time this new floor, made of metal grid, enables all the other levels of this rich historical stratification to be glimpsed. There is a rich underground system of archaeological areas throughout the Rione Terra in Pozzuoli, all visitable and connected together, the culmination of which is clearly the Cathedral, because it was the temple of Augustus. In addition to constructing the religious space, the project was also obliged to connect all these levels together.

VC We wanted to enhance not only the use of the new nave, in fact, but also the perception of the underground Roman level. This also corresponds to our much broader way of understanding the concept of archaeology: not referring to finds associated with a given dating, but also irrespective of this, of understanding it as a reference to the historical context upon which first of all to express a value judgment, to find out which elements are intelligible, and in what way contemporary architecture can be the guarantor of an opportunity for continuity.

THE OLD CUSTOMS HOUSE OF AVELLINO

PAC **We began this conversation by commenting on the sketch by Le Corbusier on the reconstruction of the Cathedral of Saint-Dié, and his critical attitude underlined in the proposal of a new independent and contemporary structure inside the ruins. This theme of the 'house inside the house', to which you referred in your project for the Temple–Cathedral of Pozzuoli, also clearly characterises your intervention for the reconstruction of the old Customs House in Avellino, currently at the construction site stage. Personally, I appreciate this project on account of its qualities of great maturity and harmonious tension between preservation and innovation. How did the opportunity for this project come about?**

GM Even if there are many years between them, it's true that some insights emerging on the occasion of the project for Pozzuoli became very important and were further developed in the project for Avellino. The project came about thanks to community financing, through the PICS (Integrated Programmes for Sustainable Cities) Fund of the Campania Regional Authority, which tied the reconstruction of the old Customs House to the creation of a centre for young people. The old Customs Building is a very important monument for the city of Avellino **[5]**; it dates back to the year one thousand and was embellished in the 17th century with the monumental façade designed by Cosimo Fanzago, before undergoing a process of tragic decline: transformed into a cinema in the 1920s, it was destroyed by a fire in 1992, leaving only the façades standing, and since then it has been totally abandoned. We began to have discussions with the municipal administration, exploring three different scenarios. The first hypothesis, perhaps the most radical, was to only reconstruct the façades without doing anything inside, to obtain a large room in the open air.

PAC **A kind of 'piazza inside a piazza?'**

GM Yes, a kind of internal piazza in continuation of Piazza Amendola. The second hypothesis was to reconstruct the building in its original form, with a large pitch roof, while the third, which was the one that was subsequently developed, was to propose a contemporary spatiality, as had happened with the Temple–Cathedral in Pozzuoli, working with a more rational, autonomous profile.

PAC **How was the new steel structure inside the perimeter defined by the façades conceived? Were there particular difficulties in the foundations?**

GM With the support of our engineer colleague Carmine Sangiuliano, we established that it was very important to return the historical walls to their original dimensions, but at the same time that it was necessary to release them from bearing any further structural loads. The idea of the 'house inside the house' **[6]** also finds a technical justification, therefore, because unfortunately Avellino is also an area known for earthquakes. The new foundations were constructed with one hundred and four micropiles sunk down until they reached the tufa stone bank, but these micropiles have the characteristic of working not only under compression, but also in traction in the case of seismic events, absorbing horizontal stresses. The new steel structure works a bit like a stake supporting a tree, it's attached precisely to the original structure of the walls, which remain self-supporting, to then rise up to the roof, which, unlike the other elements, is a wooden structure.

PAC **How did the Superintendence react when presented with this very innovative proposal?**

GM The proposal was very well received, and we immediately discussed the issue of the excavations for the micropiles, and the eventuality of archaeological finds. We then proceeded to conduct a very unusual investigation, a geoelectric investigation, used in our case to rule out any pre-existing elements in the subsoil. It was feared, in fact, that, with it being a central zone of the historic city, possible finds might invalidate the micropile solution. On the subject of the monumental safeguarding restrictions, one of the most interesting aspects of this project concerns the responsibility for reconstructing such a significant monument for the city. On this theme of the reconstruction of a ruin, we recognise the lessons of great master architects such as Linazasoro, Grassi and Távora. There are three works in particular that we consider to be paradigms of a contemporary attitude towards the monument: the Sagunto Theatre by Giorgio Grassi, the 'Casa dos Vinte e Quatro' Tower by Fernando Távora, alongside the Cathedral of Porto, and above all the interventions by José Ignacio Linazasoro, such as the Escuelas Pias Cultural Centre in Madrid. In fact, we feel closer to the sensibility of Linazasoro when he reconstructs the church with a strategy of fragmentation that makes clear the reading of the tension created between original historical elements and contemporary elements. Though being a small building, the Customs House in Avellino takes on a very high value for the collective memory: for us it's the quality and not the quantity that counts, with our responsibility to deliver to the city the inheritance of an architecture for an entire community.

PAC **Another interesting aspect of the project concerns the fact that the structure of the new roof, due to the fact of not resting on the façade, remains in a set-back position, and a sort of perimeter courtyard is created around the top floor. This space, compressed between the upper part of the historical façade and the new volume, offers a fascinating image, which evokes in me the interpretation of the Classical figure of the peripteros temple, with cell and perimeter colonnade. This interval between the existing and the new also allows natural light to penetrate diagonally into the full-height central space, creating a very evocative atmospheric light. I might add that this tension between existing and new is also perceivable in viewing the building from below. From the piazza it is evident that the historical façades have undergone a conservative restoration, but at the same time, observing the corner of the building, it can be seen that the historical cornice at the top is interrupted almost brutally: the lateral façade is clearly cut and lowered to make the new volume emerge, crowned by its own cornice, in a set-back position. The design strategy of the 'house inside the house' therefore also becomes perceivable from the outside.**

GM I agree with your observation, but I'd also like to add that this choice to insert an autonomous volume also offered us the opportunity to reach the new roof level, which is utilised as a public terrace **[7]**. We also proposed flooring recalling the long history of this extraordinary building, a dedication to Cosimo Fanzago, taking up his traditional design for the flooring in the sacristy of the church of the Certosa di San Martino in Naples **[8]**.

VC In addition, as architects, we seek increasingly often to devote special attention to this theme of the fifth façade, in the sense of not considering only the experience of the roof as a threshold space between inside and outside, but also to create a continuity with the history of the city through a visual or perceptive reference.

5 19TH-CENTURY VIEW OF THE OLD CUSTOMS HOUSE IN AVELLINO IN PIAZZA AMENDOLA.

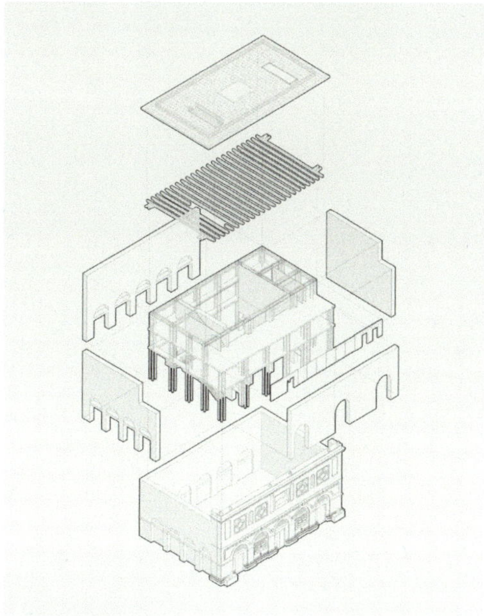

6 PROJECT DIAGRAM, WITH INSERTION OF THE NEW STRUCTURE, TOTALLY INDEPENDENT FROM THE HISTORIC WALLS

7 THE NEW ROOF USED AS A BELVEDERE TERRACE DEDICATED TO COSIMO FANZAGO.

8 FLOORING OF THE SACRESTY IN THE CHURCH OF THE CERTOSA DI SAN MARTINO IN NAPLES, FROM A DESIGN BY COSIMO FANZAGO.

9 THE RESTORED BUILDING OF THE FORMER CENTOLA TOBACCO FACTORY IN PONTECAGNANO FAIANO.

10 COMPETITION PERSPECTIVE, WITH THE GLASS VOLUMES HANGING IN THE VOID OF THE FORMER TOBACCO FACTORY.

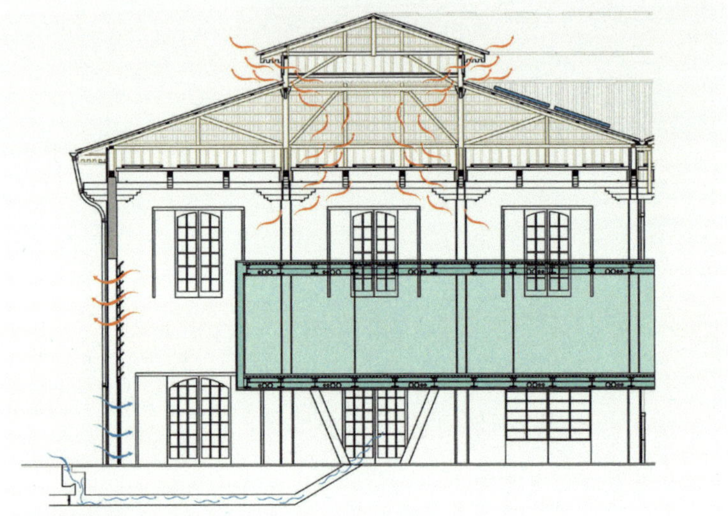

11 COMPETITION SECTION, WITH THE NEW GLASS VOLUMES SUPPORTED BY AN INDEPENDENT STRUCTURE.

12 COMPETITION MODEL OF THE WHOLE AREA OF THE FORMER TOBACCO FACTORY.

PAC **You talked earlier about a structure of steel columns, but I see that in the perspectives the roof seems made of wood. How did you conceive this hybrid structure?**

GM In effect the roof is made using a structure of laminated wood beams, which are also used for the two coupled tall columns present in the large central hall: in the perception of the central space, full height, we wanted the wooden roof to be seen resting on these two columns, to obtain a tectonic continuity between the beams of the roof and the two columns themselves.

PAC **In other perspective views, the steel columns can't be seen, and the walls also seem to be covered in wood. Will it be like this in the final realisation?**

GM In order to comply with the regulations on fire safety, the structures have been protected with a continuous covering, which will be finished with a layer of resin. This regulatory prescription offered the opportunity, however, to obtain a continuous plasticity for the architectural space. Even if it is a cladding, in this way we'll obtain a significant thickness for the walls, in dialogue with the ancient masonry.

PAC **This project for the old Customs House in Avellino in some ways reminds me of a project of yours from more that twenty years ago: the project for the European Centre for Emerging Creativities in Pontecagnano Faiano. This small town in Campania, which neighbours the city of Salerno, had announced an international competition in 2003, with a programme that was aimed at valuing 'emerging' businesses and talents, and for this reason I see certain analogies with the Avellino programme, aimed at young people. You won the competition with a very complete and extensive proposal, but one that was only partially realised. What were the conditions of this competition?**

GM In 2003 we found ourselves in this very successful season of national and international competitions, which we've already mentioned, and which offered us all our initial design opportunities at the beginning of our career. In this case too the Municipality had guaranteed itself a jury of the utmost quality, with Alan Balfour, head of the Faculty of Architecture of the Rensselaer Polytechnic Institute in the United States, and with the famous art critic and historian Achille Bonito Oliva. The administrators wanted to link the tourism development of the town, thanks also to the future presence of 'Costa di Amalfi' Airport, inaugurated in 2024, with the very interesting theme of the redevelopment of the Centola Tobacco Factory, previously acquired by the Municipality. The competition offered us the opportunity to work on a broader urban scale, but it was clearly very difficult for a small municipality to guarantee the financing of the work, the reason why we only realised a part of the project, with the redevelopment of the main building **[9]**. Luckily, this building was later used by the Municipality itself, by the community and by various cultural bodies. For example, when Vittorio Sgarbi curated the Italy Pavilion at the Venice Biennale in 2011, he later decided that the exhibition would travel all around the national territory, and, to our amazement, when the site in Campania was chosen, the exhibition was staged in this building in Pontecagnano. For us it was an interesting moment of confirmation that this industrial building could be adapted to fit various temporary uses.

PAC **In some perspective views of the competition project, some glass-walled volumes can be seen** [10] **inside this industrial building, suspended in the large full-height void, conceived to host the new cultural and production functions. To all intents and purposes, I interpret this intervention of yours with the same principle of the 'house inside the house', as in Pozzuoli and Avellino. Was it a wholly autonomous structure, or were these 'glass boxes' in reality attached to the tall pillars bearing the roof?**

GM We'd actually imagined this structure as totally independent, even if, unfortunately, the project had no follow-up and we therefore never went beyond this preliminary vision, represented in the perspectives and the sections **[11]**. The project idea was in effect to add new volumes inside the pre-existing, well preserved volume of the old tobacco factory; a very different situation, therefore, from Avellino, where it was a matter of reconstructing a building in ruins.

VC I may add that we participated in the competition while we were involved in the project for the restoration of the Pirelli Skyscraper, for which we were interested in the theme of artificial topography, which was evident in Gio Ponti's extraordinary invention of the 'hill square'. We therefore wanted to go beyond solely redeveloping the tobacco factory, to attempt to intervene on a broader urban scale, including the building in a system of connections and crossings, both above ground and at below-ground level, which was rendered explicit in the compositional gesture of raising folds in the terrain **[12]**: a genuine artificial topography, useful for hosting the underground car parks, but also for defining the new enclosure of the whole system, which creates relationships with the surfaces of the urban context.

THE STADIUM INSIDE THE STADIUM

PAC **We find this theme of the 'house inside the house' again in a recent project for the restructuring of the municipal stadium in Florence, following an international competition called in 2021. I consider it a very significant project, for various reasons. Firstly, you find Pier Luigi Nervi once again twenty years after your experience with the Pirelli Skyscraper in Milan, and you take on the difficult challenge of designing a new stadium, to meet the requirements and regulations of contemporary football, respecting the extraordinary masterpiece of Rationalist architecture** [13] **created by Nervi between 1929 and 1932. Secondly, for this competition you form an association with Kengo Kuma,**

one of the great masters of contemporary Japanese architecture, who had recently completed the new Olympic Stadium in Tokyo, to replace the stadium for the 1964 Olympics that was demolished in 2015. How did that association with Kengo Kuma come about?

GM The competition notice placed precise restrictions on being able to participate, associated with previous experiences, both in the field of restoration and in that of major sports installations, but also in relation to the requisites inherent in the economic aspects, and under these conditions the need was quite clear to propose ourselves with a very strong international group. We formed a team with architects and engineers from Florence, and it was precisely thanks to a colleague from Florence, Daniele Lauria, that we were able to invite Kengo Kuma to join our group. Beyond the specifically project-related component, with us as group leader, if we were to win the competition the engineering component also had to be very well prepared in order to guarantee the total reliability of the project management. We therefore involved the engineering company Rina, with whom we had also worked on Capodimonte Museum.

PAC **Nervi's stadium had already been extensively modified for the 1990 football World Cup, with the elimination of the athletics track and the lowering of the football pitch to obtain a greater capacity, but also unfortunately with a series of building additions that had partially compromised the original structure. Precisely what did the competition notice ask for?**

GM The stadium no longer met UEFA's needs, and so a transformation was necessary in order to hold games at international level. The notice expressly asked to be able to achieve a covered seating capacity of 42,000, and it was therefore necessarily to densify the space available.

PAC **The great interest of your project is clearly evidenced in the radical proposal to build a new stadium inside the pre-existing stadium [14], with the spectacular gesture of the new curved terraces rising up, like huge unfurled wings, above the ridge line of Nervi's architecture, reaching double the height. The new architecture is affirmed powerfully, contributing to the perception of a monumental presence for the distant observer, but at the same time the force and clarity of this gesture enables Nervi's architecture to be preserved almost in full, with its terraces, its helical staircases and its spectacular cantilevered roof. How did you interpret the Superintendence's safeguarding restriction?**

GM Even if it was possible to eliminate these recent building additions, we clearly had to conserve the characteristic elements of Pier Luigi Nervi's original structure. We began the project by exploring various scenarios, including perhaps the riskier one that proposed building a kind of clone, another stadium for contemporary football activities, beside Nervi's stadium returned

13 PIER LUIGI NERVI, MUNICIPAL STADIUM IN FLORENCE, 1929–32. ARCHIVE PHOTO.

14 COMPETITION PERSPECTIVE WITH THE NEW STADIUM INSERTED INSIDE THE PRE-EXISTING STADIUM.

15 VIEW OF THE AMBULATORY SPACE BETWEEN THE NEW TERRACES, LEFT, AND THE HISTORIC TERRACES BY PIER LUIGI NERVI, RIGHT.

to its original state, to be used for other public activities. Then we arrived at the solution of this insertion of the new stands inside the void delimited by the historical structure, utilising Nervi's large porticos as continuous frames, which we wanted to open up completely towards the public park.

PAC **The perspective views illustrate very well this beautiful idea of transforming Nervi's structure into a large urban portico. How did you interpret this possibility of strengthening the link between the stadium and the city?**

GM In our project idea this urban portico changed from a boundary to a threshold, a permeable threshold to be used as place for activities throughout the week. It was a way of giving a meaning to the project in relation to the neighbourhood of Campo di Marte, but also to all the citizens of Florence. While inside the stadium a new arena was formed, one autonomous and devoted to football, outside a new space was gained between Nervi's old terraces and the new ones for concert, entertainment and outdoor cinema activities. The stadium therefore acquires its own permanent life, beyond the ephemeral moment of the football match, becoming a very generous urban machine.

PAC **It can be clearly seen in the perspective views that the old terraces no longer overlook the football pitch, but rather look onto this fascinating space** [15]**, which, on account of its large dimensions and the rather mysterious light, evokes the ambulatory of a cathedral or the monumentality of a Roman cryptoporticus. Returning to the theme of the 'house inside the house', I'd like to understand better how the structure of the new part works, remaining entirely independent and projecting out over Nervi's architecture, which remains entirely complete. How did you succeed in avoiding any new support pillars outside?**

GM In fact the structure is very innovative in creating a sort of continuous cage, a network of cables that realises the entire roof of the whole ring, but at the same time stabilises the system of huge reinforced concrete ribs bearing the new terraces.

VC With respect to the winning project, which develops horizontally, we wanted, rather, to bring out the huge scale of the new structure, consistent with the principle of monumentalising the presence of Nervi's stadium in the urban landscape, making the mark of the new architecture visible and recognisable, also at a great distance, with respect to the historical context of reference.

PAC **On this subject, I've seen that you've developed very long territorial sections for the competition, over the whole plain of Florence, which show the relations between the heights of the new stadium and the natural and built emergences of the landscape, from the hills to Brunelleschi's dome. This way of representing architecture in its relations with the city and the landscape is typical of your way of considering the project on all scales, from the territorial to that**

of the structures and the construction. I'd like, therefore, to associate this discussion on the project for the stadium in Florence with a previous project, which you proposed in 2012 for the stadium in Naples. It was a project financing proposal, developed with Arup Italia, envisaging two interventions in parallel: the construction of a new football stadium in a peripheral area in Ponticelli and the restructuring of the old plan of the San Paolo Stadium in Fuorigrotta. In what way was this previous experience useful for the project in Florence?

GM For this previous project in Naples we'd divided up the responsibilities, between Arup for the new stadium and ourselves for the restructuring of the San Paolo Stadium. There's a clear continuity in our project attitude as regards these major modern architectures, from the Pirelli Skyscraper to Nervi's stadium in Florence. Our idea for the San Paolo Stadium in Naples was to restore the building to return it to the splendour of the original construction **[16]**, eliminating all the additional constructions built on the occasion of the 1990 World Cup, which had weighed down and concealed the elegant reinforced concrete structure designed by Carlo Cocchia **[17]** in 1959. In particular, the removal of the roof gave form and vitality back to the original bowl, a genuine arena. It's no coincidence that we made reference to Roman amphitheatres, such as those of Arles and Verona, to underline the need to create a very strong relationship between the stadium and the neighbourhood of Fuorigrotta, thanks to the creation of a large public piazza **[18]**, completely pedestrian, open on the axis of the Mostra d'Oltremare.

VC I think it's a priority today, at a time when we're talking about building new stadiums, to defend this theme of the restoration of existing stadiums, also significantly renovating them, as in the case of Florence, because this offers a great opportunity to value the principles that inspired these facilities, often designed by great architects.

PAC **I fully agree with this statement; in Milan too people should fight against the idea of abandoning the San Siro Stadium, which should in fact be restored and upgraded.**

THE CHURCH IN DRESANO

PAC **So far we've seen that you've tackled the theme of the 'house inside the house' in projects that differ considerably from each other, also with very different programmes, but always having in common the strong tension that is created between the historical building and the new architecture placed inside it. To conclude, I'd like to discuss the project for the church in Dresano with you, which presents certain affinities with the other projects, even if in this case it's an entirely new building. I'm interested in considering the spatial device of the church, as a whole, as a 'house in-**

16 RESTORATION PROJECT FOR THE SAN PAOLO STADIUM IN NAPLES IN ITS ORIGINAL FORM.

17 CARLO COCCHIA, SAN PAOLO STADIUM IN NAPLES ON THE DAY OF INAUGURATION, 6 DECEMBER 1959.

18 PERSPECTIVE OF THE NEW PEDESTRIAN SQUARE AROUND THE RESTORED SAN PAOLO STADIUM.

side a house', that forms a relationship between two fundamental figures in the tradition of Christian religious architecture: the round temple and the cloister [19]**, two figures that, even in their geometry, reference an idea of purity and formal autonomy, including one inside the other. Why did you propose the figure of a church with a central plan, rather than the more common figure of the basilical plan? What role did the liturgist play in accompanying this proposal?**

VC We participated in the restricted competition, called by the Italian Episcopal Conference in 2008, with a liturgist—Don Antonello Giannotti—and an artist—Nino Longobardi, as was required by the competition brief. Don Giannotti is a parish priest in Caserta who has a great awareness of the role of the community inside ecclesiastical architecture; he's much loved by his congregation and as a liturgist he offered a meaningful contribution when we began to discuss the form of the liturgical room. As you quite rightly said, the circular church is an integral part of an enclosure. I nevertheless have a clear difficulty in distinguishing between new building and restoration. To build a new architecture in this location in the countryside, on the edge of the province of Lodi, also means restoring the landscape. There are some very beautiful photographs of the church in the fog by Cappelli and Criscuolo, which highlight the fact that the building is also in dialogue with the climate and the temperature of this location.

GM There are various reasons behind our choice of the circular form. A first reason is associated with the liturgical prescriptions of Vatican Council II, which see the assembly as participating in the religious act, ideally with the priest at the centre and the congregation all around. Another reason concerns the fact that the church would have been dedicated to Our Lady of Graces. Talking with Nino Longobardi, we'd observed that this Virgin Mary is characterised figuratively by the image of a mother's embrace of her child, and this figure of the embrace pushed us towards the circularity of the plan. Furthermore, visiting the original historical church, San Giorgio Martire in the small historic centre of Dresano, we found that this was a church with a central plan with an ambulatory, a genuine *circulum* surmounted by a dome. To finish, considering that when faced with these great themes it's necessary to measure oneself against the great architects of history, Alberti states that the *circulum* is the most reliable figure for building the temple. Convinced that this circular form could be the famous 'reliable form', as we jokingly called it amongst ourselves, we then had to propose an innovative interpretation of the theme, so as not to run the risk of falling into the banality of the analogy. We therefore interpreted the circular form with the idea of a double drum, with the outer one higher so as to filter the light from above and make it bounce towards the centre of the room through the ambulatory. In the end, with a certain awareness but also with doubts and uncertainties, what we imagined in the competition phase found confirmation in the completed work, because the main material of the church is light, that element that enables the space to be transcended. In short, light is always the true theme. I always tell my students that a project ends when there's nothing more to be removed, because as long as you're adding, you're not finishing the project, you're complicating it. When, on the other hand, you've slimmed it down, you've reduced it to the essential, as happened in Dresano, the project is heading towards completion. This circular room that stands on the land of Dresano, together with the large church square, came about from the interweaving of forms that eloquently met all the demands of the competition brief, and subsequently the demands of the community.

PAC **Can you confirm, therefore, that the project did not undergo modifications between the competition and the construction?**

GM In reality there are significant changes in the façade. In the competition project, the façade took up a motif typical of rural architecture, the baked brick latticework that characterises the walls of barns **[20]**, perforated to guarantee the circulation of air. We used the same bricks, crossed to form a kind of large tent. Then in the realisation we realised that it was very complicated to use such small elements as these, and so we enlarged the motif to form lozenges from the rural architecture to obtain unitary structural elements, in the form of giant 'X'-shapes three metres twenty high **[21]**, closing off the perimeter of the whole building. Every element is prefabricated in the workshop, using a concrete coloured red with iron oxide pigments, and assembled on site with threaded bolts, so as to create this motif of a perforated façade in dialogue with the Lodi countryside.

PAC **This account is very interesting, because it explains very well how important it is to transcend the most immediate reference to the traditional rural architecture, to obtain a less literal and freer interpretation. In this way, you create a new relationship between the interior and the countryside, establishing a necessary critical distance from the reference to the traditional crossed bricks of Lombard farmhouses. This reworking of figurative references also fuelled your relationship with sculptor Nino Longobardi, with whom you'd already worked on the occasion of the competition for the Temple–Cathedral of Pozzuoli in 2003, for which he'd proposed a beautiful figure of Christ. How did the dialogue take place with the artist in the realisation of the church in Dresano?**

GM It was a great experience, also at the level of human relations, in the moments shared, such as travelling together or going to the foundry to witness the birth of the two sculptures **[22]**. Also the transporting of these huge works **[23]** to Dresano, and their positioning when the building was not yet complete; these were extraordinary moments. I also remember the meetings in which he expressed himself, as a non-believing contemporary artist, in the search for a secular, non-atheist intervention, because his black Christ without a cross, and his Cross engraved negatively in the façade, represent very decisive acts from the point of view of spirituality. With his gestures and with the materials he uses, such as lead paint, he relies on figures from an ancient art that he transfers into the contemporary. We too, as architects, attempt to bring ancient figures such as that of the cloister into the contemporary. Our personal relationship with Nino was therefore very important, marked by ex-

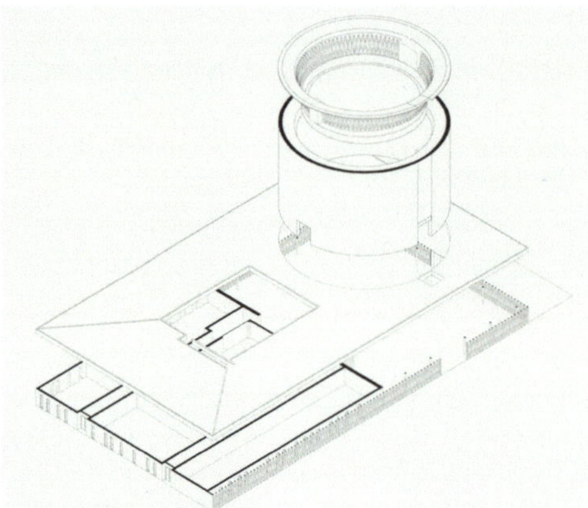

19 PROJECT DIAGRAM WITH THE PRINCIPLE OF INCLUSION OF THE ROUND TEMPLE INSIDE THE RECTANGULAR ENCLOSURE.

20 THE TYPICAL TRIANGULAR BAKED BRICK LATTICEWORK, A MOTIF OF VERNACULAR ARCHITECTURE IN THE FARMS OF THE PO VALLEY.

21 THE 'X'-SHAPED PREFABRICATED CONCRETE ELEMENTS THAT CLOSE OFF THE PERIMETER OF THE BUILDING.

22 GIOVANNI MULTARI WITH NINO LONGOBARDI IN THE WORKSHOP OF THE FONDERIA NOLANA.

23 THE TWO HUGE SCULPTURES BY NINO LONGOBARDI IN THE FOUNDRY, READY FOR TRANSPORTING.

treme simplicity. During the ceremony of consecration of the church, I saw Nino, he a convinced atheist, making the sign of the cross, not because he'd become a believer, but because unexpectedly his decency and humanity had made him feel part of the religious rite.

PAC **Can you explain better how your early ideas for the church were developed with the artist?**

VC When we were together at the drawing table, while we were discussing the liturgical aspects with the priest, Longobardi never spoke; then at a certain point he began to draw, developing Virgin and Child figures that seemed like those of Michelangelo. Beautiful drawings emerged, created by a skilled hand, and he began to say: 'Careful, we're working with a complex subject.' He didn't immediately try to go on to the contemporary; he begun with the richness of the figures. I'd like to add that our desire to work with contemporary artists also represents a way of not disregard a law on public works that's in force in Italy, which has existed since 1949 but has often been forgotten: the so-called 'two percent law',[2] which envisages artistic interventions according to a very cohesive view of a State that might, on the occasion of the realisation of public buildings, be enriched with works of contemporary art. In our case, we don't consider these works to be a superficial decoration; we endeavour to engage artists in the project ideas, as has always happened in the historical Italian city.

1 Commenting on his sketch, Le Corbusier wrote: 'Mass could be celebrated inside this extraordinary, synthetic, symphonic decoration: this pulsating human construction, all torn up, is positioned there like an epic in the midst of everyday idiocies. The modern technique enables all this to be saved; it enables it to be used; it enables the memory of the very recent tragic past to be registered there. All that would be necessary would be a concrete deck, held up high on thin pillars outside the cathedral, which would serve as a roof. Saint-Gobain glass would allow views of these perspectives that I have indicated at various points: of nature, of sky, of architecture.' Cited in: Pierre Saddy (ed.), *Le Corbusier le passé à réaction poétique* (Paris: Caisse Nationale des Monuments Historiques et des Sites, 1987),101.

2 Law no. 717/1949 containing regulations for art in public buildings. Since the law has often been disregarded over time, the Interministerial Commission MIBACT-MIT, first in 2006 and subsequently in 2017, issued guidelines providing a precise interpretation of the Law, adapting its prescriptions to meet the current technical and project-related requirements of public works. Cf. https://duepercento.cultura.gov.it/la-law/.

RESTORATION OF THE TEMPLE–CATHEDRAL IN THE RIONE TERRA
POZZUOLI, 2004

The restoration of the religious monument takes on particular relief in the historical predominance of the Temple–Cathedral building in the general context of the Terra Murata (Rione Terra), as a central symbolic, representative element of the entire ancient high ground standing sheer above the sea from the Republican Age to the 11th century, when it was elevated to being a cathedral dedicated to the martyr of Pozzuoli, Saint Procolus, until the Baroque rebuilding (1632–47) at the wishes of Bishop Martin de León y Cárdenas. The Temple–Cathedral is composed of wholly distinguishable and recognisable architectures, which reveal to visitors the Christian temple on the remains of the pagan temple.
The new architecture consists of extra-clear glass walls and thin white cement structures standing on the new structural plane and support the new shape of the cathedral.

The cathedral can already be visited by the faithful via the cathedral square and the historical side entrance. Its volume is contained within the outline of the temple, but it is elongated as far as the Baroque structures and is permeated by the tension of the spaces of the temple, illuminated by the natural light filtering from above. The new construction, consisting of the nave and the liturgical room, lies inside the two orders of columns, standing on the Republican temple and raised to support the new roof. The void therefore becomes a building that is dilated in a new floor, which is first a vestibule, then a nave, then a presbytery. Around it is its history, which, with the ancient finds, participates in the definition of the contemporary construction dedicated to Saint Procolus, allowing the light to filter towards the liturgical space.

The nave elongates the plane towards the ancient choir and frames the remains of the apse, marking the location of the table of the Eucharist and the cathedra in a space measured by the large hanging bronze cross, the work of sculptor Nino Longobardi. The liturgical room is connected to the baptistery, realised in the spaces of the former sacristy, to the Eucharistic chapel, formerly the chapel of the Holy Sacrament, and to the existing and reconstructed spaces that conclude the cathedral on Via Duomo.
The levels of the city are taken up onto the ancient high ground and the discovery of its heritage of archaeology and history: it is in the Temple–Cathedral that the two cities coincide, the archaeological one and the inhabited one, constantly visible and perceivable through the Corten steel grid floors, which are also connected by mechanical systems for people with disabilities.

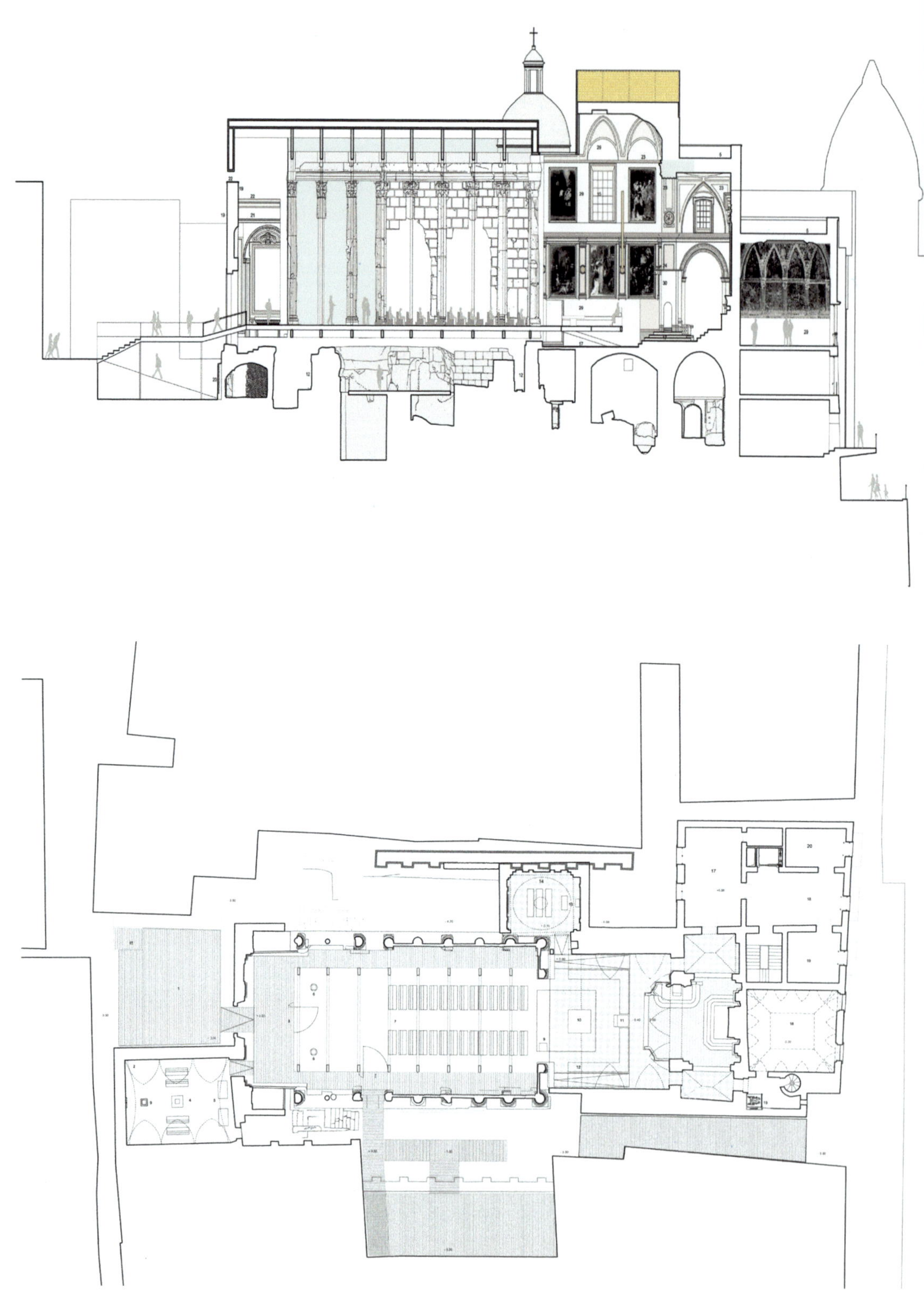

RESTORATION AND UPGRADING OF THE OLD CUSTOMS HOUSE
AVELLINO, 2022–26

The Customs Building, constructed in the 17th century, is one of the symbols of the city of Avellino. The restoration and upgrading project envisages its transformation into a services centre for young people, intended to support entrepreneurship, culture and the development of skills, in the context of a broader plan for urban regeneration, to improve the environmental, social and demographic conditions of the city.

From the architectural–compositional point of view, the intervention is characterised as the insertion of a new structure inside the perimeter defined by the historical façades, which survived the 1992 fire that destroyed the roof and the internal spaces. The building is structured on three levels. On the ground floor we find the so-called 'theatre of the Customs House', a full-height multi-purpose hall that can lend itself to various uses, a storeroom to serve the room, a space for production and meetings, the staircase and facilities. On the first floor there are shared spaces for co-working overlooking the room below, together with service spaces. On the second floor access is gained to the open promenade, from which the pre-existing walls and the sculptural apparatus by Cosimo Fanzago can be observed. From this outdoor space, a last staircase enables the roof-terrace overlooking Piazza Amendola can be reached, a belvedere space from which to view the monumental projections of the city of Avellino. The flooring of this belvedere terrace takes up the well known two-colour scheme that is typical of the architecture of Cosimo Fanzago. From the structural point of view, the intervention envisages the construction of a new internal metal frame, also used to prop up the historic façades, which supports the intermediary steel floors and the laminated wooden roof.

The intervention falls within the guidelines of the *Avellino, inclusive city* programme, which aims to improve the offer of services to the community, reinforcing the social and economic role of the historic centre and the surrounding areas. This regeneration is part of a broader vision that sees Avellino as a sustainable, innovative, competitive and inclusive city, destined to become a point of reference for young entrepreneurs and the showcasing of cultural heritage.

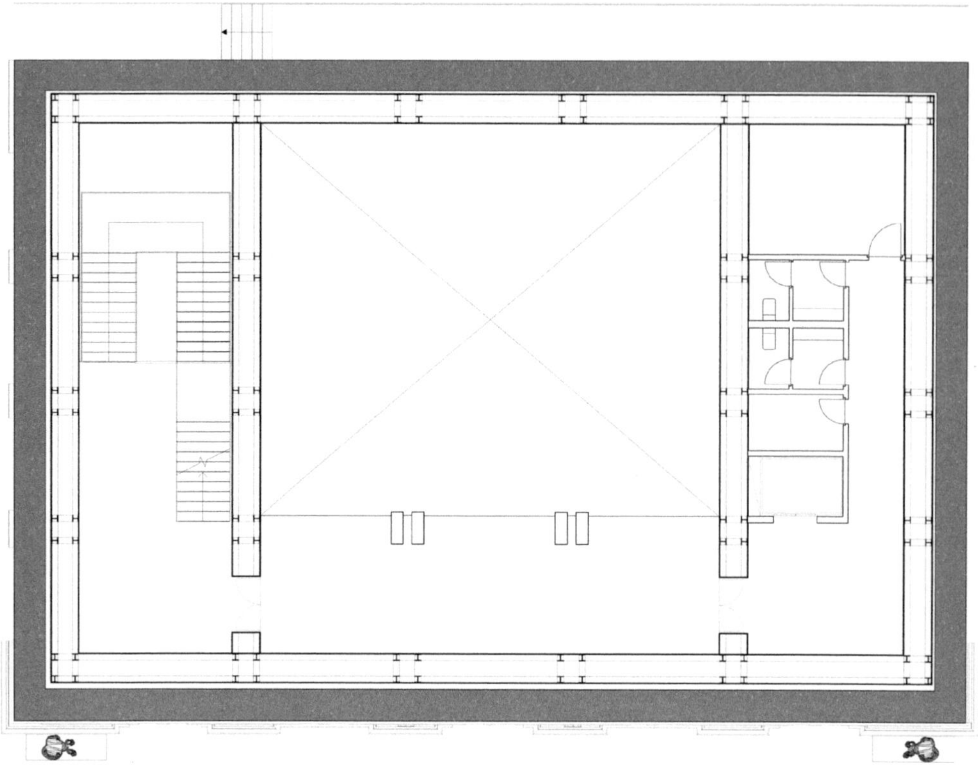

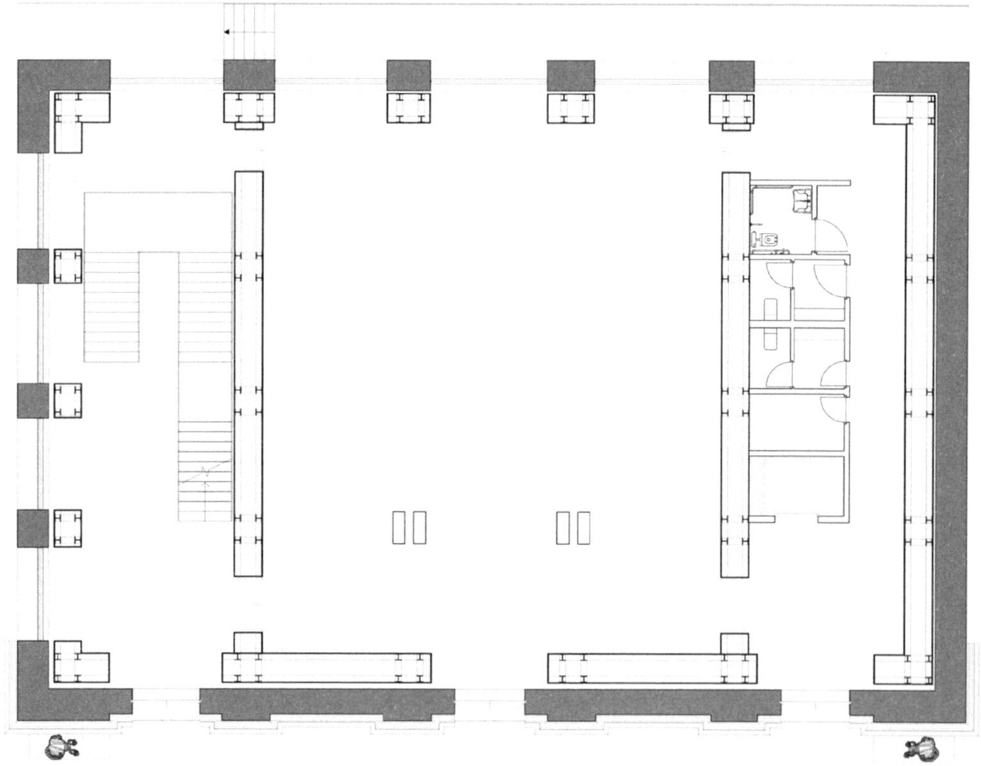

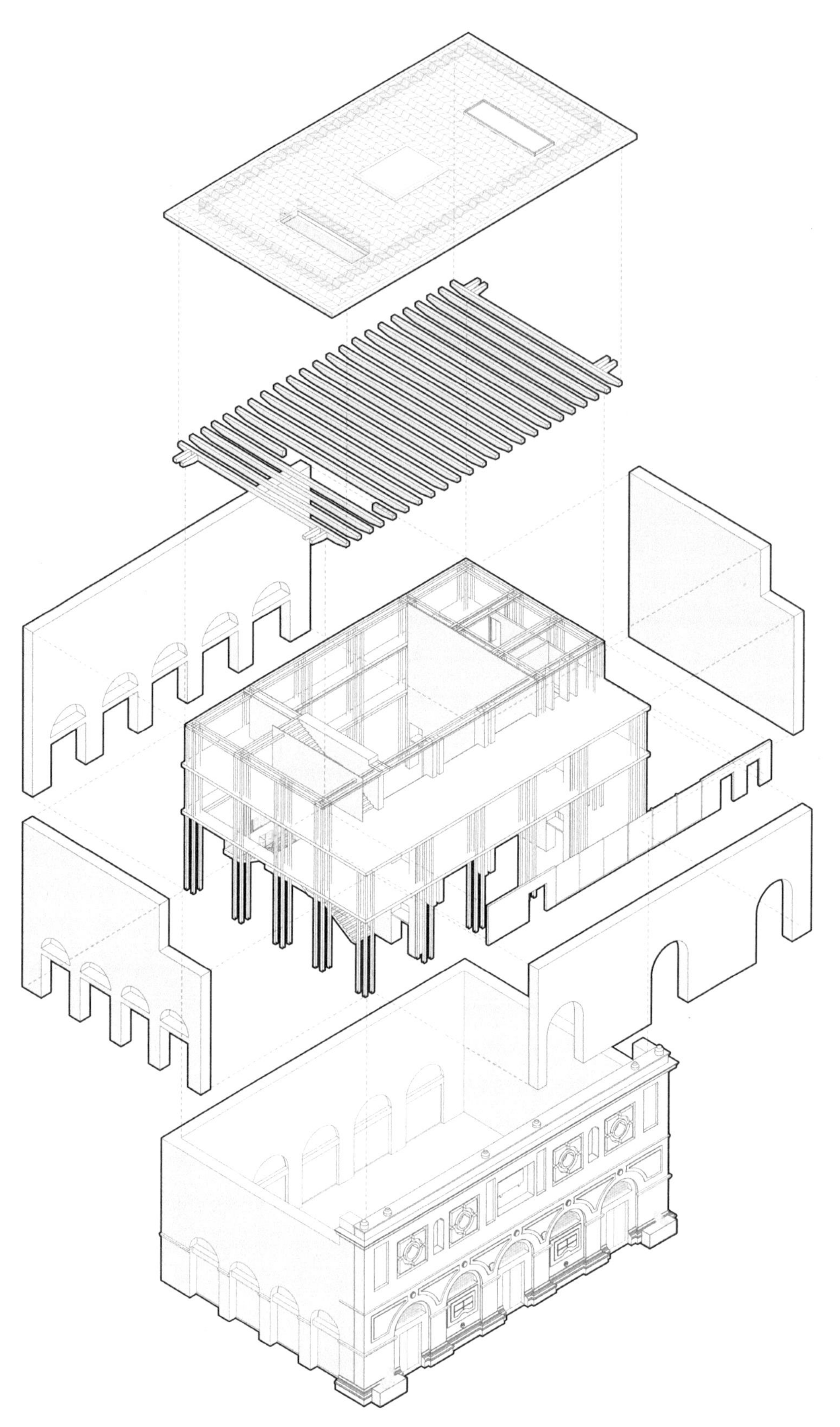

RESTRUCTURING OF THE MUNICIPAL STADIUM
FLORENCE, 2021–22

In the awareness of the importance of the architectural values of Pier Luigi Nervi's work, the proposal regarding the Municipal Stadium in Florence is moved by the firm intention to satisfy the stringent functional requirements of the competition brief, and at the same time to preserve and value the historical evidence of Nervi's work. The new profile of the stadium converges onto the Torre di Maratona and the projecting platform, highlighting these two salient elements of the *cavea*. The horizontal plane in the area at the top of the existing terraces separates the lower and upper rings of the grandstands, guaranteeing visual permeability between the interior and the surrounding landscape context. For the roof, a tightened membrane solution has been adopted, with minimum impact towards the outside; it is positioned on the new upper edge of the terraces and anchored in a spread-out pattern, thus avoiding recourse to invasive structural elements. Subvertical external edge cables ensure the equilibrium and non-distortability of the system, figuratively characterising the sober elevation of the added volumes. The external spatial continuity of the original structural ring, together with the highly original helical stairways, is entirely conserved and showcased, both by the meticulous restoration of the exposed concrete and through a new lighting engineering design intended to bring out the spatiality of the rhythmic series of frames. A methodological approach of critical–conservative restoration has been followed in the formulation of the design proposal, which has the conservation, protection and utilisation of an architectural asset with heritage value as its object. With a view to the transmission of the historical and figurative values of the monument, communicated through the conservation of the materials of the work, the proposal falls within the perspective of the permissibility of a contemporary insertion inside a stratified historical palimpsest. The lively and respectful relationship between the new and the existing is governed by a design choice proposing intervention with an appropriate connecting architecture. The conservation of the values referred to and the integration of contemporary elements provide a rigorous solution, consistent with the theme of the competition, a solution that is summed up in a project capable of meeting the demand for a stadium to suit its time.

STADIO

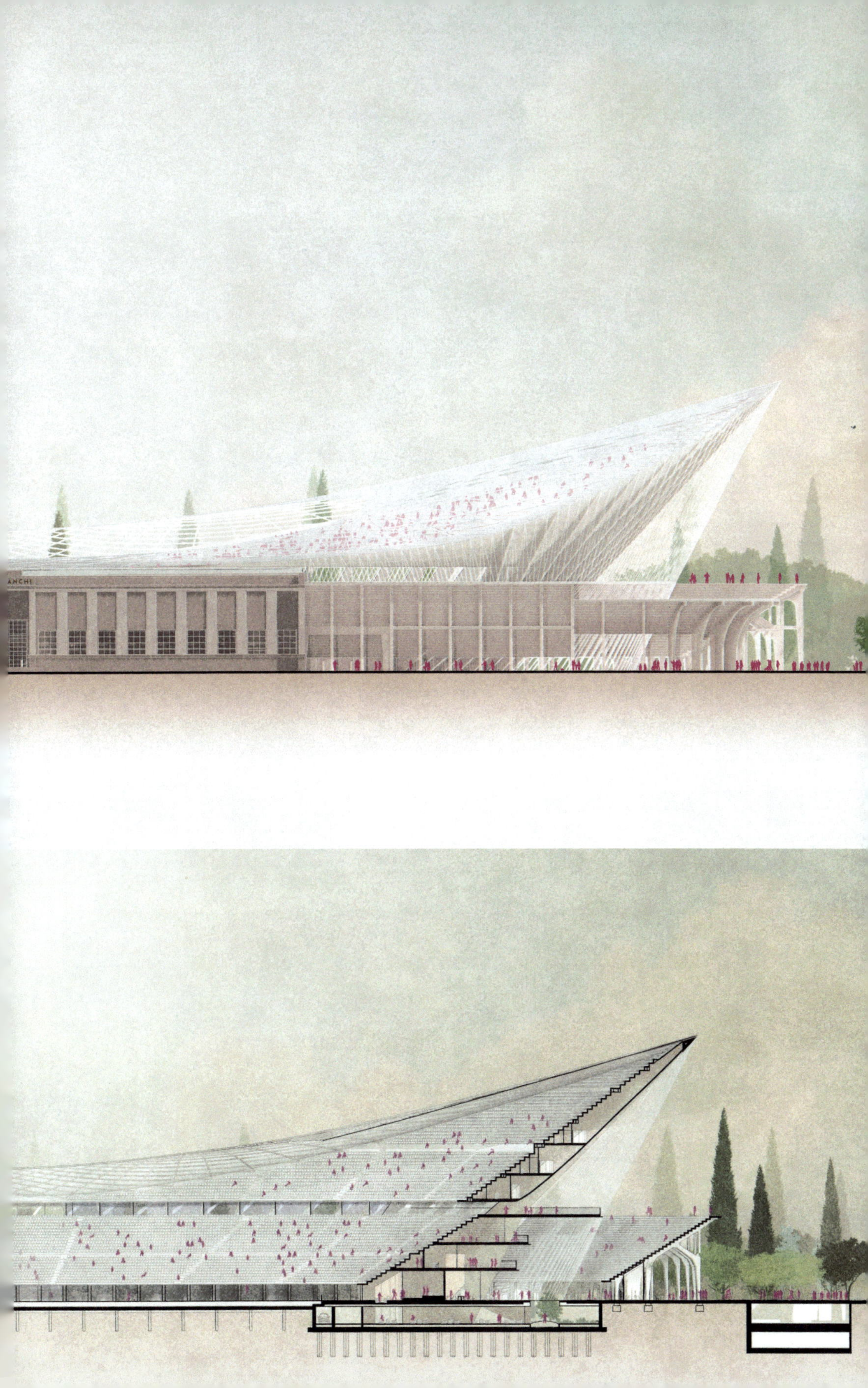

PARISH COMPLEX MADONNA DELLE GRAZIE
DRESANO, 2009–17

The architectural structuring of the parish church complex arises from the composition of two elementary geometries: the circle, the pure form par excellence, standing on which are the ecclesiastical building, the location of the celebrated Eucharist, and the rectangle of the base volume, characterised by a central cloister around which the rooms of pastoral ministry, the site of the lived Eucharist, are arranged.

The volume of the church, characterised by a double height, is located at the centre of the entire composition, giving rise to the long church square with reconstructed stone flooring. The base volume is the size of the entire plot in an east–west direction, developing on a single level, and is characterised by an interweaving of reinforced concrete elements with iron oxide pigmentation, to give the procession of elements the characteristic brick tile colour, which, like the agricultural constructions on the lowlands south of Milan, filters the necessary illumination to the internal spaces.

The two volumes are combined in the area of the church square, giving rise to a perimeter pronaos, welcoming the congregation and filtering the relationship between the public space and the sacred place of the celebration. The liturgical room is based on a plan consisting of two concentric circles. The inner circle hosts the room defined by the convergent arrangement of the benches towards the presbytery, while the external circular volume designs an ambulatory that envelops the entire assembly, with strong natural zenithal lighting that illuminates the central room indirectly. This space hosts the liturgical sites: presbytery, casing of the Eucharist, baptismal font and penitentiary. The position of the presbytery, at the end of the perspective sequence church square–door–liturgical room–apse, adds another fundamental symbolic element to the centrality of the circular plan: the axiality of the space, which culminates in the large statue of the Crucifix by Nino Longobardi.
On the façade of the church, on an axis with the church square, there is a large burnished bronze plate on which the artist has engraved a huge cross.

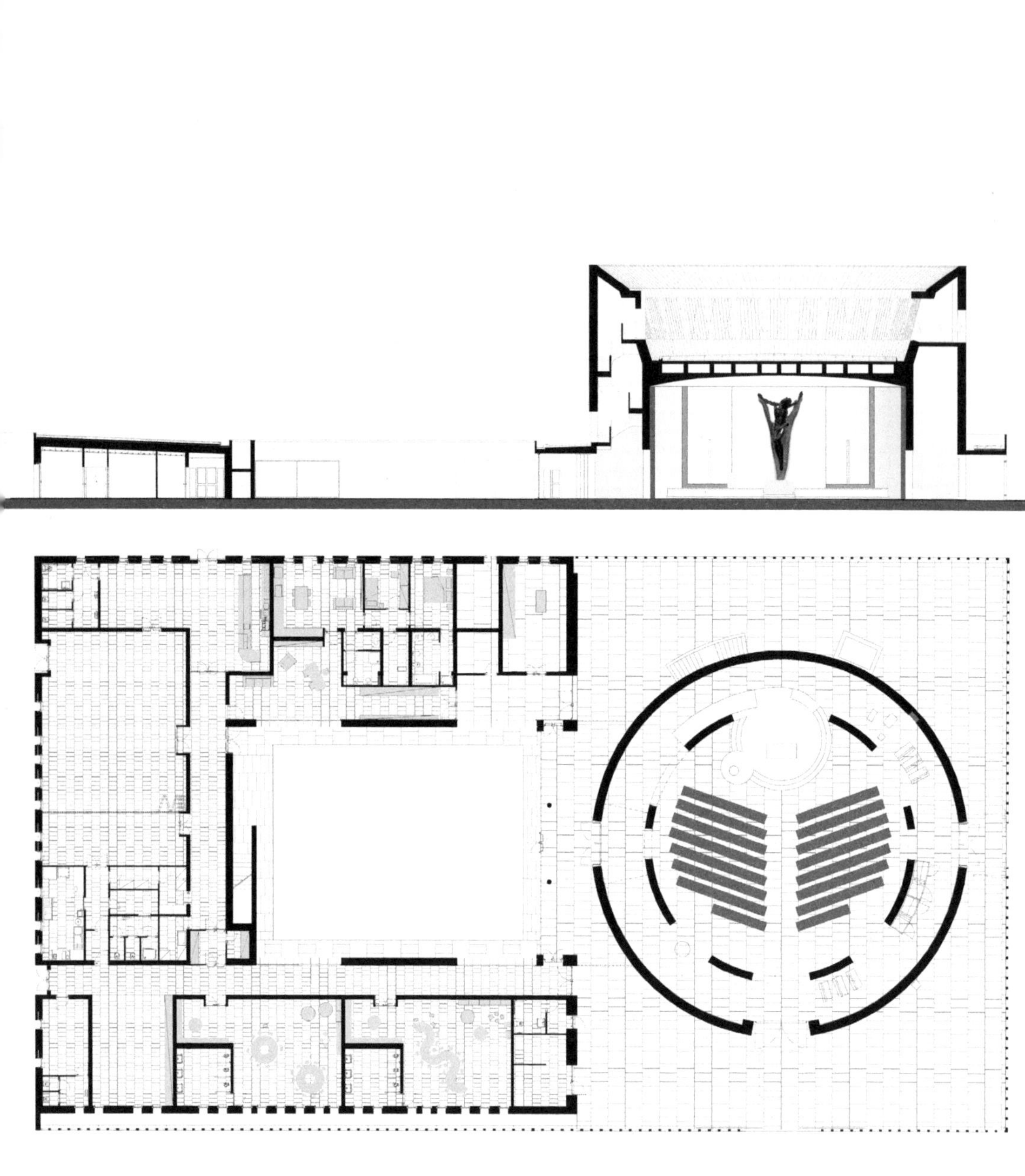

5

THE FUNCTIONS OF INHABITING: RESIDENCES AND SCHOOLS

PAC **In our previous conversations, you've often explained that there are no fundamental differences between new interventions and restoration and restructuring interventions, because in all of your projects you always seek to value first and foremost the relationship of the architecture with the city, irrespective of the functional programme of the building. In this conversation I'd like to look more deeply into your way of intervening in residential projects and those for schools, most of which are new buildings. I'd like to start with the Isolato dei Rivocati in Cosenza, completed in 2001, remembering that the overall plan envisaged the realisation of a residential building along the street** [1]**, closing off the block and replacing a series of old buildings. Even though this residential part was never completed, it appears clear that in this case the residence served an overall urban design, based on the idea of the crossing of the block by pedestrians and complementarity between the various public and private functions. A few years later, between 2002 and 2006, you realised your first residential intervention in Piazza Molino, again in Cosenza, with a similar design strategy that again envisaged the overall reconfiguration of an urban block. Even though in this case the client was private, I find it interesting to discuss the similarities between the two projects: a mixed functional programme, with residences, shops and offices, a system of public and semi-public through-routes, on this occasion organised on two different levels. How did this project come about?**

GM In those years the city of Cosenza was undergoing a historical phase of profound urban transformation, and there were also private operators alongside the actions of the public administration. We were contacted directly by a private company, Molino Bruno SpA, who had moved their production plant to the peripheral industrial areas and wanted to restructure their site in the city centre, being able to take advantage of the possibility offered by the town planning scheme to convert the industrial volumes into residential volumes.

PAC **Was the urban planning instrument therefore the drafting of a redevelopment plan?**

GM Yes, a redevelopment plan associated with an architectural project with building licence, maintaining the original volume. This private client had also consulted various other architecture studios, and their idea was to create a kind of comb with a number of buildings in this long, narrow plot. We were immediately critical of this idea, because we realised that the comb solution would deny views and light to a sizeable part of the dwellings. As an alternative, we therefore proposed concentrating the buildings on the edges of the plot, around a raised central piazza **[2]**, opening up the apartments towards the sun and towards the Sila Mountains. This alternative proposal persuaded the client, but there were immediately difficulties with the work demolishing the old reinforced concrete structure of the mill, which also included large silos. While we always endeavour to be very sensitive towards the existing, in

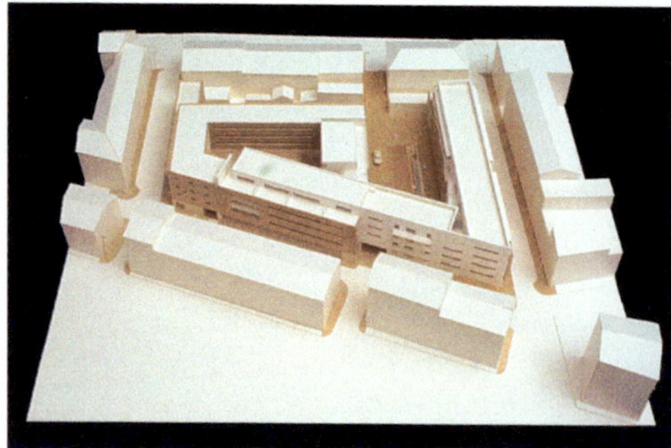

1 MODEL OF THE ISOLATO DEI RIVOCATI IN COSENZA, WITH PROVISION FOR A RESIDENTIAL BUILDING COMPLETING THE BLOCK ALONG VIA DAVIDE ANDREOTTI.

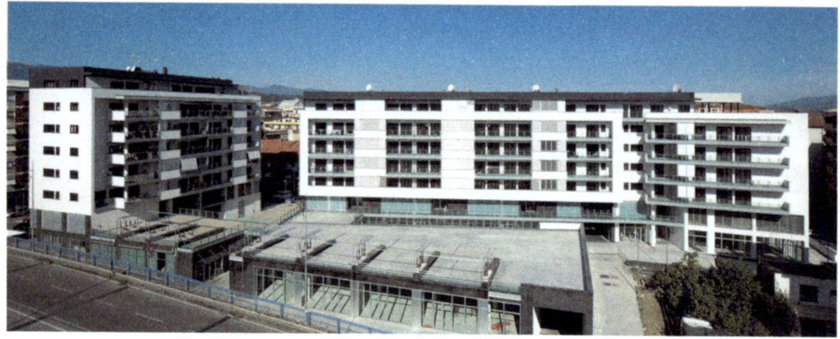

2 THE NEW PIAZZA MOLINO BLOCK IN COSENZA, WITH THE RAISED ROAD BOTTOM LEFT.

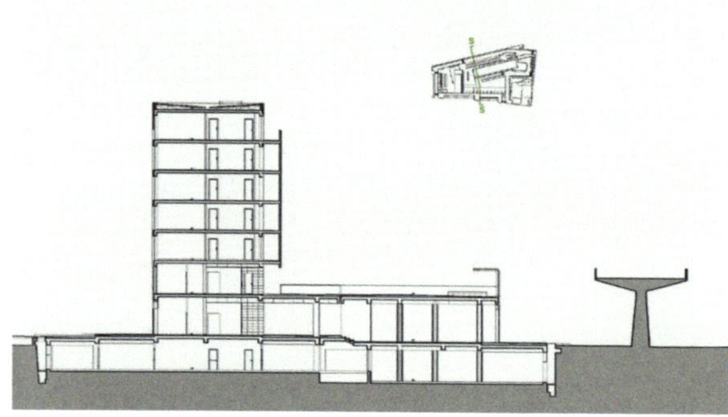

3 CROSS SECTION, WITH THE RAISED CENTRAL PIAZZA AT THE HEIGHT OF THE OVERHEAD ROAD.

4 TRIPARTITION OF THE ARCHITECTURE: STONE BASE, WHITE PLASTER RISER, ATTIC SPACE COVERED IN ZINC-TITANIUM.

this case it was not possible to convert the solid concrete industrial volumes, and twelve months were needed to complete the demolitions. The urban idea was to create a community space, complete with commercial parts and car parks, raised above the ground, putting the level of the community plaza at the height of the Sopraelevata (today Via dell'Unità d'Italia), the artery running to the south of the area **[3]**.

VC I'd like to add a more general observation. In Piazza Molino, as in other projects, and not only residential ones, we express the idea of housing in three different ways: public housing, community housing and private housing, which more specifically concerns the residence. Residence is never an isolated theme; it intersects with urban values, but also with topography, the geometry of reference and the earth connection is the device with which the project seeks forms of relationship of permeability and public use.

PAC **I also see similarities between Piazza Molino and Isolato dei Rivocati in the architectural language: you again use a stone base, in contrast with a white plaster elevation, with the addition of large loggias and balconies that characterise the building in its residential function. On this subject, can we speak of a personal interpretation of an architectural vocabulary associated with the great tradition of Mediterranean Rationalism? Are there contemporary architects who have influenced you? I'm thinking in particular of Spanish or Portuguese architects.**

VC Of course, but I'd be careful not to talk of citations as such, as our true references are the great masters of Italian Rationalism, such as Figini and Pollini, but also Terragni, architects who were also a reference point for many architects of the Spanish and Portuguese schools from the late 1980s.

GM Our architecture also takes up the Classical tripartition **[4]** between base, body and crown, also in the structuring of the functions, with the base for the shops and offices, over which are the residential floors, and with the attic floor covered with a zinc-titanium skin forming an interesting crown.

PAC **This principle of Classical tripartition immediately brings me to the next project that you realised, in L'Aquila following the 2009 earthquake. It's again a project developed for a private client, but under wholly exceptional emergency conditions, due to the need to intervene extremely quickly and with reduced construction costs. In this case the base had already been decided upon; this was the famous anti-seismic plates on which the new houses were to be assembled. Think of them as durable but not permanent houses, according to the acronym CASE (Sustainable Eco-compatible Anti-seismic Complexes).[1] We'll be talking later about the project for provisional schools that you developed that same year, under the same conditions, in L'Aquila, but now I'm interested in understanding better how this project came about.**

VC The whole thing happened rather by chance and in a great hurry. I was contacted by an entrepreneur during a football match at Avellino, who told me: 'You must lend us a hand, because we want to participate in the competition for the houses in L'Aquila.' We therefore organised ourselves together with a group of young architects from Avellino and in very few days we prepared a proposal that was then recognised as deserving the award. In the post-earthquake emergency the procedure was a kind of tendering for design-and-construct contracts, where one of the fundamental aspects was respecting the timescale. The definitive and executive project was drafted in twenty-five days and the realisation in around 90 days, with three work shifts at the construction site.

PAC **How were the rules of the game defined? Was there a single urban planning scheme that defined the positioning and the volumetric template of the individual houses? How was such a complex competition, in which companies from all over Italy could participate, coordinated?**

VC Everything was coordinated by the Civil Protection Department, which nevertheless operated on a sectorial basis, with separate competitions. First the realisation of the anti-seismic plates **[5]**, conceived by Professors Edoardo Cosenza and Gaetano Manfredi of the University of Naples Federico II, was contracted. The volumetric template was defined, and the plates were already being made when we began working. I'd dare to say that innovation could only be proposed to the façade shell, and we suggested a system of sliding panels to shade the loggias and dwellings **[6]**, an innovation that was later very much appreciated by the inhabitants. Following the allocating of the houses, they proceeded with the landscaping design **[7]**, coordinated by Andreas Kipar. There are some very beautiful photographs showing the relationship of the houses with the undulating orography of these locations, which render well the private quality of the house design.

PAC **One of the qualifying elements of your project concerns the positioning of the staircases, conceived as windows open onto the landscape** [8]. **Was it your decision to change the distribution scheme that was defined in the competition brief?**

VC It was indeed our choice to open up the staircase structures to create greater transparency for the building. This example of the staircase enables me to propose a slightly broader discussion, concerning the way in which restrictions often offer an opportunity for our work as architects. The timescale, so tight, the template and the building types imposed undoubtedly affect the outcomes, but they also form the already written sheet on which to attempt to make a contribution of quality and innovation. The managing editor of *Lotus International* magazine, Pierluigi Nicolin, moved to L'Aquila in 2010 to visit the new houses, recognising the interest of the reconstruction, with the decision to devote a significant part of the magazine to the new architectures,[2] capturing the very essence of this work. With a selection of very few projects to publish, including our own, the magazine defended the idea that the architect must 'get his hands dirty' and place himself at the service of the commu-

5 THE CONSTRUCTION SITE OF THE ANTI-SEISMIC PLATFORMS FOR THE NEW RESIDENCES IN L'AQUILA, 2009.

6 DETAIL OF THE SOLAR SCREENING IN THE NEW HOUSES.

7 THE NEW HOUSES AND PUBLIC SPACES.

8 THE OPEN STAIRCASE WITH VIEWS OF THE LANDSCAPE.

nity in times of emergency, succeeding in making a summary with only two or three rules of the game. This applies to both architects and landscape architects; under equal conditions, various design opportunities emerged for both the materials and colours.

COOPERATIVE HOUSING IN QUARTO

PAC **So far we've seen that your residential projects have been developed in temporal continuity, from the Isolato dei Rivocati to Piazza Molino and to the houses in L'Aquila. It's into this continuity that the next project, in Quarto, is inserted, beginning in 2009 immediately after the project for L'Aquila. Vincenzo was explaining earlier that restrictions become an opportunity for your work, so I'd therefore like to begin with the restrictions imposed by the special planning scheme for affordable-popular housing in Quarto, which defined the urban plan for large semi-open blocks. You therefore had to complete half a block, and this time you used bricks and plaster to differentiate the two façades clearly, towards the outside and towards the inside of the block. I've seen from the photographs that the other half of the block, conceived by another designer, also uses the same materials. Were these imposed by the neighbourhood plan, therefore?**

VC No, it was our choice, but we did indeed feel the need to coordinate with the other designer in order to have the same range of materials. Our client was the Cooperativa Edile Lavoratori Telefonici (CELT), who were building low-cost housing for their members, whereas the plot opposite had been assigned to another cooperative, who agreed to use the same materials. Our project came about from the need to go beyond the flat surface of the volume imposed by the plan and to work on the three-dimensional expression of the façade. These triangular white-plaster balconies **[9]** therefore come about and emerge from the wall mass of the external brick façades, while for the great loggias in the internal façades, we designed wooden shutters **[10]** that harken back to a Mediterranean architectural culture. Depending on the time of day and the inhabitants' choices, these shutters move continually, offering the image of a building that's transformed in relation to the various uses.

PAC **It's actually interesting to observe the powerful plasticity of these façades, which bring out the interplays of light and shade. The choice to position the staircase structures at the corners also takes on a sculptural value, which appears to be even more reinforced by the material and chromatic contrast between the plastered white volumes and the brick walls. At the level of typological choices, I've seen that you've decided to repeat an apartment type, which is quite large, without looking for greater diversification in the size of the apartments. Was that at the client's request?**

9 VIEW OF THE SOUTH FAÇADE OF THE RESIDENCES IN QUARTO, WITH THE STAIRCASE STRUCTURE ON THE LEFT AND TRIANGULAR BALCONIES.

10 VIEW OF THE EAST FAÇADE WITH FOLDING WOODEN SHUTTERS.

11 COMPETITION PROJECT FOR BIOCLIMATIC HOUSES IN JESI, BRICK NORTH FAÇADE.

12 JESI, MODEL OF A DETAIL OF THE SOUTH FAÇADE WITH LOGGIAS AND BALCONIES.

VC As this was subsidised housing for a market accessing ownership of the first home, there were not the restrictions of State social housing, and these apartments were therefore aimed at young couples, most of whom the children of the cooperative members, who were therefore comfortable with the size of these apartments, with two or three bedrooms, double bathroom, kitchen and lounge, but also with generous loggias and balconies.

PAC **You activate an interesting interplay of indentations and protrusions, enabling no less than three different types of external spaces to be obtained: a large loggia extending the lounge, a long, narrow loggia that connects the kitchen with two bedrooms, a balcony rotated by forty-five degrees that connects up two other bedrooms. I'd now like to discuss the differentiation of the façades further. This theme of the double-faced building isn't new for you, since you'd already experimented with it in a 1999 competition for bioclimatic houses in Jesi. In this case, the contrast was even stronger, with a brick north façade** [11], **with a few splayed apertures that bring out the thickness of the walls, and an open south façade, characterised by loggias and balconies** [12]. **What was the context of this competition?**

GM The competition was announced by the National Institute for Public Housing; it was a very interesting experience, which we shared with Federico Bilò, now a professor in Pescara, and with Francesco Orofino, who subsequently became general secretary of IN/Arch, the National Architecture Institute. A fine group of young architects was created between Naples and Rome, and we wanted to experiment with the principle that façades must fit the context and respond to differing climatic conditions: the north façades must protect from the cold and look out towards the countryside, while the south ones face onto the courtyard and absorb solar energy.

PAC **Whereas the first residential projects that we discussed at the start were all associated with direct commissions, offered by private operators, this project in Jesi introduces the theme of competitions, genuine laboratories of architectural innovation. Before Jesi you participated in various competitions, particularly the Europan 4 competition in Cagliari in 1996. What importance did this competition have in launching your professional activities?**

GM The competition theme was the creation of new functions for the redevelopment of the old Quarantine Hospital in the Sant'Elia district. We won second prize, while the winning project by Andrea De Eccher was subsequently realised. It was a very formative experience; we were at the beginning, in a period when we were trying out various paths, experimenting with different ways of transforming designed architecture into built architecture. A short time later we'd become protagonists of the first constructions in Cosenza.

PAC **Let's proceed with the competitions, leaping forwards and reaching 2011 with a project that interests me very much,**

the 'I Portici' competition in Frosinone. We find the theme of the double-faced building again, but also that of the redesigning of the relations between the building and the city [13] **to obtain a multifunctional block traversed by pedestrian walkways, as you'd experimented with in the previous creations in Cosenza. I find the research process to arrive at the definitive planimetric profile particularly interesting: with small volumetric models** [14] **you explore various ways of distorting and bending the building-mass of a single large edifice to create an urban system of courtyards, passageways and crossings. How did this project come about?**

GM While the previous competitions had offered above all opportunities for experimentation at the start of our career, this competition in Frosinone represents a moment of much greater maturity, because in the meantime we'd designed the residences in Piazza Molino in Cosenza, in L'Aquila and in Quarto.

VC In Frosinone we sought to interpret the typology of the courtyard building in an innovative way, with the bend in the building that's suited to solar thermal conditions, together with the desire to offer a double face and large terraces to all the dwellings: in the awareness of the references to the modern, but at the same time in the desire to invent a housing model that takes account of a whole series of relationships with the park and the city **[15]**. Of course, the theme of the porticos was also important, with an earth connection characterised by public functions.

PAC **In this project you attribute great importance to the themes of ecology and sustainability, proceeding with a line of research that had begun with the competition in Jesi. How did you define the choices regarding the materials used, which were very different in the two façades?**

VC We involved some researchers from the University of Naples Federico II on the themes of low emissions, photovoltaic cells and the skin, proposing a significant integration of photovoltaic systems and shading devices, but also certain innovations involving recycled materials. For example, we proposed using natural materials such as hemp, but also recycling materials coming from the envisaged demolition of a small building located in the area of the project.

PAC **Another very interesting aspect of the project concerns the types of apartments, conceived as modules placed side-by-side** [16]**, always with a double orientation, which allow a major variation in the size of the individual apartments. I therefore find it a definite step change compared to the much more rigid schemes that you'd previously used, and I may observe that the typological choices demonstrate great coherence with the urban profile, guaranteeing that every apartment can enjoy the double orientation, towards the park and towards the hill. Did the competition brief actually offer you greater freedom in your typological choices, or was this an achievement of your own?**

13 'I PORTICI' COMPETITION PROJECT IN FROSINONE, THE NEW BLOCK IS SITUATED BETWEEN THE VILLA COMUNALE PARK, BOTTOM LEFT, AND THE HILL, TOP RIGHT.

14 STUDY MODELS OF THE PLANIMETRIC PROFILE.

15 PERSPECTIVE VIEW OF THE BUILDING, WITH THE COMMERCIAL BASE AND THE RESIDENCES WITH SPACIOUS LOGGIAS.

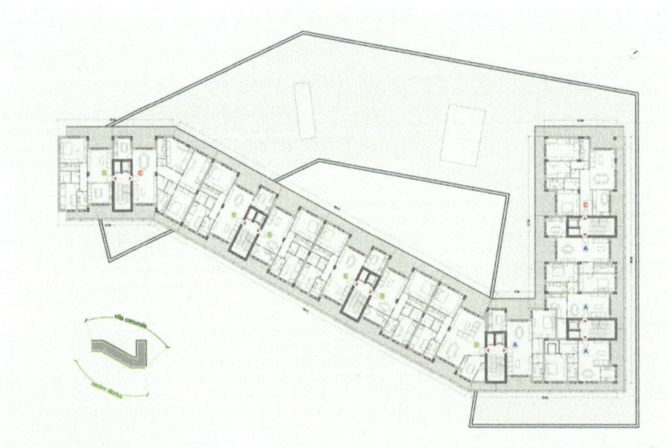

16 THE APARTMENTS CONCEIVED AS SIDE-BY-SIDE MODULES WITH DOUBLE ORIENTATION.

VC Compared to the projects for L'Aquila and for Quarto, we didn't have the restriction of an already imposed template, and so we did indeed have greater freedom for experimentation, both in defining the volumetric profile and in the typological choices.

PAC **This greater freedom was also due to the fact that the residential programme envisaged apartments for sale on the free market. I remember that the competition had been announced by a private real estate group, a rather rare event in the Italian context. Under very different conditions, you recently realised two social housing buildings in San Giovanni in Fiore, not far from Cosenza. How did that project come about?**

GM Somewhat by chance. Being Cosentino, I'm often in Sila, and one day I found myself at lunch in this small town famous for its Florense Abbey, founded in the late 12th century by Gioacchino da Fiore, who was an important abbot, theologian and philosopher, the founder of the congregation of Florense monks. During lunch the owner appeared, a building contractor, who suggested that we participate in the tender for contract that had been organised for these two social housing buildings. In reality it was tendering for design and construction contracts that required the presentation of an architectural project, which he agreed to finance. After winning we therefore continued with the drafting of the executive project. The context is interesting, because it was a matter of completing the Olivaro district, a neighbourhood of public residential buildings **[17]**, not only with the two new buildings but also with a series of small service structures for the inhabitants: wine cellars, areas for open-air activities and a shelter for the existing sports fields.

PAC **We know that social housing requires an extreme rationalisation of construction choices, so as to contain the construction costs. I am therefore intrigued by your decision to use only two types of windows** [18], **one narrow and one wider, both full height, but to arrange them with a fascinating compositional interplay, characterised by small shifts, horizontally and sometimes vertically. The façade thus becomes more inspiring, despite the repetition of the same windows, thanks to these small oscillations, but also to a breaking of the symmetry that can be read in the front portions.**

GM As you've rightly observed, we devote rigorous attention to the use of few well considered materials, in view of a very modest budget. The movement of the windows also corresponds to our desire to dissimulate the presence of the staircase structure **[19]**.

VC I may add that last summer I was in Stockholm at the Italian Cultural institute, and I had the opportunity to admire the elevation of the building designed by Gio Ponti, which reminded me of this building of ours in Sila. Every now and again these references appear, probably conceived and realised unwittingly, but indirectly influenced by these lessons.

17 LAYOUT PLAN OF THE OLIVARO NEIGHBOURHOOD IN SAN GIOVANNI IN FIORE, WITH THE TWO SOCIAL HOUSING BUILDINGS IN RED.

18 DETAIL OF THE FAÇADE WITH ONLY TWO TYPES OF WINDOWS AND BALCONIES.

19 THE MOVEMENTS OF THE WINDOWS DISSIMULATE THE PRESENCE OF THE STAIR VOLUMES.

20 VIEW OF THE HEAD WITH LARGE ROOF AND BALCONIES.

PAC **The large roof crowning the building is also a characteristic element, associated with the context of the mountain. To what extent was your choice to give a sense of heaviness to this roof dictated by a figurative desire for marked plasticity?**

GM We were in a very steep and hilly area of San Giovanni in Fiore, and so the roof became an element that was very present in the landscape **[20]**, visible from below and above. We did various tests, and at the end we wanted to characterise the roof with an almost classical entablature, even though practical reasons also apply, because in Sila it snows a great deal, so the considerable projection of the roof also serves to protect the balconies. The value of plasticity you mention is also highlighted in the use of the materials, with the intrados covered with wooden staves and the front portions closed off with zinc-titanium.

PROJECTS TO UPGRADE THE EXISTING

PAC **With this project in Sila we close the discussion of these diverse residential projects realised from scratch. Recently, on the other hand, you've associated the theme of residence with that of upgrading of the existing, in two projects that differ considerably in terms of the context in which they're included. The first project that I'd like to discuss with you concerns the upgrading of a public housing neighbourhood in Capua** [21]**, begun in 2022 and currently in the construction phase. It's a very contemporary theme, concerning an enormous quantity of buildings realised in the post-war period, particularly in the 1960s and 1970s, which are often extremely mediocre in architectural and construction terms, but which, due to many aspects, can't be demolished, requiring upgrading interventions, both in energy-saving terms and for compliance with the anti-seismic regulations. Under what conditions did you begin to work in this public housing neighbourhood in Capua?**

GM In this case too we won a competition called by the Campania Housing Authority, ACER, and the competition didn't require a project, just our CV. Subsequently, the procedure envisaged the drafting of the feasibility plan, and in this phase we began to evaluate various scenarios of intervention, because the ACER hadn't decided whether to demolish and reconstruct the buildings or to restructure them. We persuaded the client that not demolishing the buildings might have major advantages, not only in terms of the reduction in the production of CO2, but also and above all for social reasons. More than seventy families live here. Where would they go during a demolition process? With the restructuring they can remain at home during the work.

PAC **These seem to me to be very significant reasons, because it often tends to be repeated in Italy that restructuring costs more compared to demolition and reconstruction, whereas we know that the costs of demolition will become increas-**

21 OVERALL PERSPECTIVE VIEW OF THE TWO RESTRUCTURED PUBLIC HOUSING BUILDINGS IN CAPUA.

22 THE NEW EXOSKELETON SERVES AS ANTI-SEISMIC CONSOLIDATION AND AS AN EXPANSION OF THE ACCOMMODATION.

23 PERSPECTIVE OF THE NEW STRUCTURE AND THE UPGRADED OPEN SPACES.

ingly unsustainable, if we also add economic costs, energy costs and social costs. Your restructuring intervention in Capua therefore appears to be quite pioneering for Italy, whereas abroad for a few years now we've known about the exemplary interventions by Lacaton & Vassal in France, or projects in the Netherlands that have shown how convenient it is to upgrade public housing neighbourhoods.

GM As Lacaton & Vassal did, we proposed improving the quality of the dwellings with a new structure added externally, an exoskeleton **[22]**, which has the function of generating anti-seismic structural security, but which also increases the surface areas of the dwellings, some of which were decidedly undersized, with large loggias and verandas.

PAC **In the elevations of the project, what stands out is the red colour of this new exoskeleton, a very strong and distinctive colour. What type of red were you thinking of?**

GM It's a social, political red that's reminiscent of the working-class neighbourhood, in harmony with the nature of these locations. It's not the red of Pompeian painting or Capodimonte.

VC We're returning to these themes that we've considered a few times, to the idea of the total design that Alberto Izzo had taught us, to the fact that *firmitas* becomes *venustas*, to the need to associate the project with a continuous comparison between the disciplines of architecture, engineering and landscaping. Every project makes us express a value judgment on the existing first of all. This choice by us to act in Capua within the existing **[23]** instead of demolishing and reconstructing is the result of following a path of getting to know and evaluating the alternatives and the opportunities, which are always specific because they're devised for specific locations.

PAC **This reflection by you brings us to a discussion on the latest project, this too the restructuring of an existing building, but in a totally different context, in the historic centre of Taranto, where you intervened to transform Palazzo Frisini into residences for students. This project seems to me to be particularly interesting, due to the fact that it proposes a synthesis between two themes of work that you had previously explored in parallel, associating housing research with the theme of monumental restoration and adaptive reuse in historical contexts. Palazzo Frisini has a complex and highly unusual history. Its owner, Gaetano Frisini, had donated it to the city of Taranto in 1912 to have it turned into an orphanage, a care home for abandoned babies, but then the building was decommissioned and transformed into a middle school, and then a high school. With your project, the building will in some ways return to its origins, with both a residential and a welfare function, for students and no longer for newborn babies. The fact also seems interesting to me that these are innovative apartments in terms of the ways of life that you pro-**

24 PERSPECTIVE OF THE COURTYARD OF PALAZZO FRISINI IN TARANTO, REDEVELOPED AS A GARDEN.

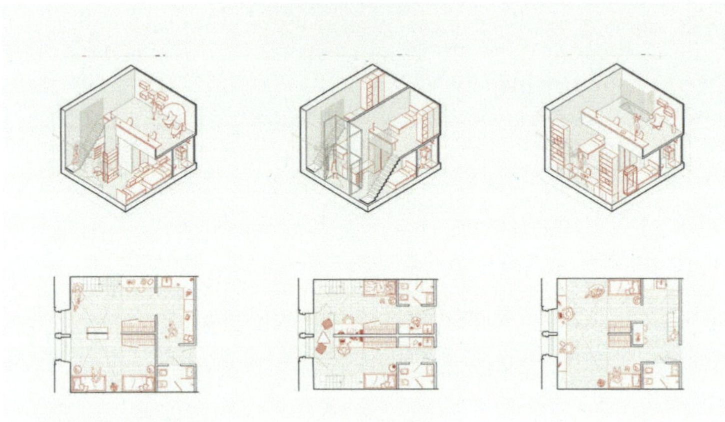

25 DIAGRAMS OF TYPOLOGICAL VARIATIONS OF THE DOUBLE BEDROOMS WITH MEZZANINE FLOORS.

26 PERSPECTIVE VIEW OF A DOUBLE BEDROOM WITH SHARED LOGGIA AND INDIVIDUAL MEZZANINE FLOOR.

27 FAÇADE OF PALAZZO FRISINI FACING ONTO THE STREET WITH THE TYPICAL TWO-ARCH WINDOWS.

pose, based on principles of cohousing. I'd like to discuss with you the way in which the architectural project was developed, and if in certain respects it was a shared design process that involved the future users.

GM The project came about with the 'Puglia university region' programme, deliberated on by the Regional Council of Puglia in 2019, following which three architecture competitions were announced, for the cities of Taranto, Brindisi and Lecce. We won the competition in two phases for Palazzo Frisini in Taranto, and the entire procedure was managed very well by the Agency for the Right to University Study of the Puglia Regional Authority, leading to the three construction sites being opened in 2025. It was a very important initiative by the Puglia Regional Authority to propose to install the new university residences in restructured historical buildings. The project has the ambition of forming the place of reference for this new community, the community of students, in a reasonably central district in the city of Taranto: not on the oldest part of the island, but in the new districts of 19th–20th-century expansion, not far away from the waterfront and from the historical gardens. The building has a beautiful internal courtyard, which will become a garden **[24]**, and a very interesting distribution system. We exploit the significant heights of the floors and the terrace on the top, which we'll make usable for community purposes. There are all the ingredients, therefore, to achieve an excellent quality of life for the students. After all, it's a public asset that returns to being a place that performs a service, through a community in dialogue with the neighbourhood.

PAC **I may observe that you've cleverly exploited the significant height of the storeys to create mezzanine floors, so as to obtain a certain flexibility in the types of residence** [25]**, but also to define a clear hierarchy between the community spaces, looking out onto the courtyard, and the private spaces facing towards the street. Is this variation in the size of the residences the result of discussions with the clients, or even a design process shared with the students' representatives?**

GM We were the ones who proposed these variations in types. I remember a brilliant event in Taranto, when we came to present the project to the city. There are not many students in Taranto currently, because the university was new, dependent on Bari and Lecce, but the youngsters were enthusiastic, they participated in the event and they can't wait to be able to use the new hall of residence.

PAC **The perspective views that you produced in the studio represent very well the various lifestyles** [26] **that you imagine in this small community of students. I found the way in which you also represent the typical disorder that characterises students' accommodation very amusing.**

GM It was a kind of game with the collaborators of the studio, who had initially made views that were too precise and orderly. In effect we did significant work on the interiors, on the furniture, the materials and the colours, but also to showcase the bifora windows on the streetside façade **[27]**, which become micro-loggias in some types.

SCHOOLS AS LANDSCAPE, SCHOOLS IN THE LANDSCAPE

PAC **Now we'll discuss the theme of schools, which you tackled at the start of your career with some internal restructuring work. I remember in particular the restructuring of the 'Fermi–Gadda' Technical Industrial Institute in Naples** [28], **completed in 2004, inside an interesting building from the 1930s. Nevertheless, I'd like to begin with the projects and realisations of new buildings. As we saw previously with the residential projects, you participated in many competitions and tenders for design work, which offered you the opportunity to experiment with innovative approaches. I propose beginning with the competition project for a school in the Casal Monastero district in Rome, an interesting project in an unusual landscape context, on the boundary between residential suburbs and countryside. In this project we find the theme of a large roof that folds to form an artificial topography** [29], **a theme that we'd already discussed about the project for Pontecagnano, illustrated in the previous chapter. In what context had this competition been announced?**

VC It was announced in 2005 at an extraordinary time for the city of Rome, which, first with Francesco Rutelli and then with Walter Veltroni, had established a Competition Office, run by Francesco Ghio, coordinating an intense season of architecture competitions. This was a very significant opportunity for us. The project sought to combine urban and rural, and to find a cohesion between the building and its landscape context, transforming the countryside to make it become an element welcoming architecture.

PAC **In this project, you've given prominence to the design of the open spaces, which form a threshold between inside and outside. In particular, the classrooms are projected towards the countryside and are prolonged with sloping gardens** [30]. **All this work deforming the topography also enables the belt that habitually encloses schools, also for reasons for privacy and security, to be eliminated. Instead of an enclosure, you create a kind of moat, a difference in height that separates the countryside from the interior of the school: in this way you create a spatial and visual continuity between the space of the classroom and the open landscape.**

VC I agree with your observations, but I may add that this theme of spatial continuity had already been explored in previous urban projects, particularly in the Isolato dei Rivocati and the Molino Bruno in Cosenza, where we also find this idea of permeability and strong interaction with the context. The school at Casal Monastero presents elements of typological innovation in becoming a kind of building-landscape.

PAC **Let's now proceed with the provisional schools that you realised in L'Aquila,[3] returning to the context of the**

28 RESTRUCTURING OF THE 'FERMI–GADDA' TECHNICAL INDUSTRIAL INSTITUTE IN NAPLES.

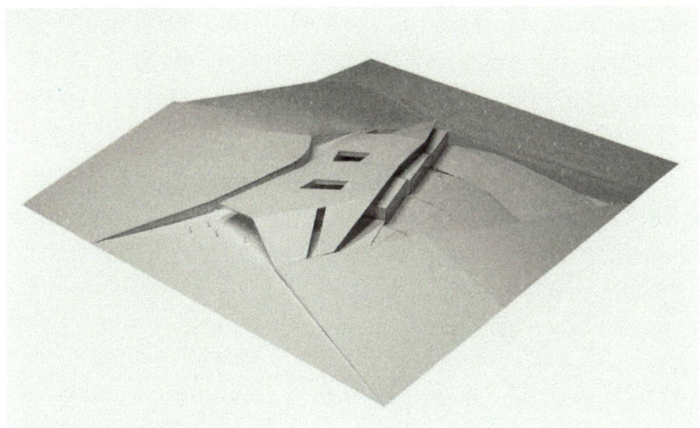

29 COMPETITION PROJECT FOR THE SCHOOL IN CASAL MONASTERO IN ROME, MODEL WITH LARGE FOLDED ROOF.

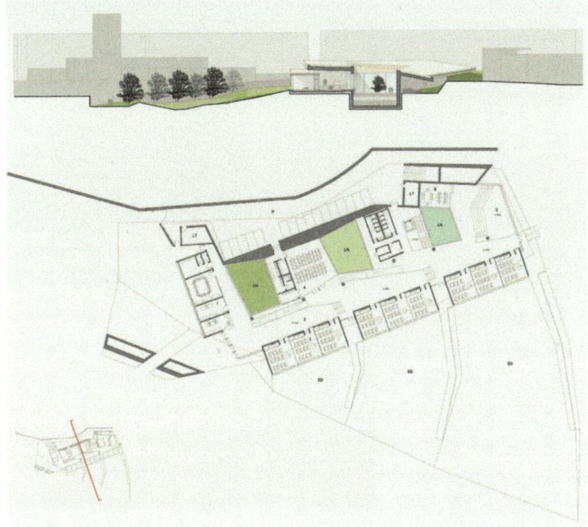

30 PLAN AND CROSS SECTION OF THE SCHOOL.

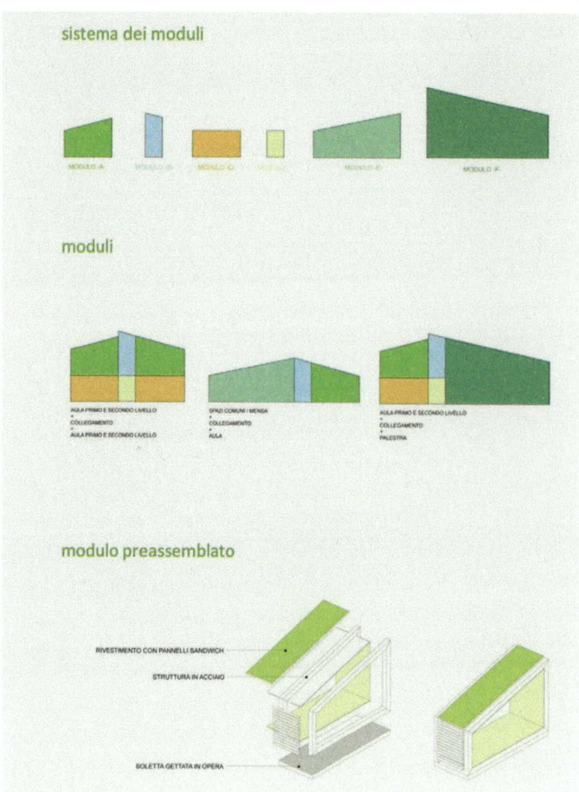

31 MODULES FOR PROVISIONAL SCHOOL USE (MUSP) IN L'AQUILA, DIAGRAMS OF THE COMPOSITION OF THE MODULES.

32 COMPOSITION OF THE PREFABRICATED PANELS WITH TWO COLOURS.

post-earthquake emergency in 2009, which we discussed previously on the subject of anti-seismic houses. Although they were different competitions, in this case too you had to act very quickly. What conditions did you have to face for this project?

GM The project for the schools in L'Aquila came about under extremely difficult conditions, due to the great speed of the design and construction process. The competition briefs had been released in the month of July, and the project was drafted in the first two weeks of August, because the winners then had to begin construction immediately after Ferragosto, 15th August, in order to inaugurate the school year by the end of September. As the basis of competition there was a very clearly defined functional programme, because it was necessary to welcome the students of the schools rendered uninhabitable, so respecting the classroom numbers, even though with the new schools we sought to improve some spaces and some functions of the pre-existing buildings. As this was a prefabricated construction, the builder gave us precise indications on the technological system they used, and the use of prefabricated panels, which were therefore the basic elements from which to depart. We therefore worked on the form of these panels and on the way of placing them together, on spatiality, on three-dimensionality **[31]**.

PAC **A significant aspect of your project concerns the use of colour. We discussed your relationship with artists previously, and I therefore wanted to understand if this use of colour corresponds to a desire to highlight a plastic—we could almost say painterly—dimension of the architectural object. In installing the two colours of the prefabricated panels, white and green, did you think of specific artists that may have influenced you?**

GM This question of colour came about rather by chance, as had happened with the competition brief for Piazza dei Bruzi, which required presenting with an artist. Once the need to use prefabricated elements had been recognised, the building firm informed us that it was only able to deliver the white panels and the green panels **[32]** by the end of August. It was therefore the firm that provided us with the palette of colours, to tell the truth, reduced to just these two, as there were no other possible choices! From that moment on, the design theme had become that of how to combine the panels in an interesting way.

PAC **On balance, it may be said that you were lucky to find yourselves with green and white panels, and not orange and blue, because the former are pleasant colours in the relationship between building and mountain landscape.**

GM We were indeed lucky, and this experience of colour was useful when we designed the school in Carate Brianza. The plan was very simple, with a linear volume for the classrooms and two other constructions for the canteen and the gymnasium **[33]**. We remembered the experience in L'Aquila, yet modulating the colours differently. The linear volume is white, while the other two con-

33 PRIMARY SCHOOL IN CARATE BRIANZA, WITH THE WHITE LINEAR VOLUME OF THE CLASSROOMS TO THE LEFT AND THE ROUNDED GREEN VOLUME OF THE GYMNASIUM TO THE RIGHT.

34 SPACES OF DISTRIBUTION OF THE CLASSROOMS.

35 VIEW OF ONE OF THE TWO SCHOOLS BUILT IN L'AQUILA, WITH THE VOLUME OF THE 'LITTLE HOUSE' THAT FORMS THE ENTRANCE THRESHOLD OF THE SCHOOL.

structions are covered with green and white metal panels. We also used colour in the interiors [34], orange specifically, after long discussions with the teachers, the head teacher and the school manager, who explained to us that lively colours are useful in primary schools.

PAC **This use of coloured prefabricated panels reminds me of the famous schools designed by Gino Valle in the 1970s with the Valdadige company, a Veronese prefabricated systems manufacturer. The idea of modularity and the assembly of elements was also central in these schools by Valle, to allow for various arrangements depending on the various functional programmes. When you began your project, did you look at these previous examples?**

GM This example that you mention is very interesting, and we undoubtedly had many other projects in mind relating to the idea of modularity, associated with the use of specific construction systems. I'm delighted to point out that we find ourselves today, purely by coincidence, needing to take on a project for new schools in Foligno, and the idea is therefore returning to us of working on a school concept designed as an aggregation of forms, starting from a single project, capable of adapting to meet all the requirements of the various school complexes, but also to the different contexts. In Foligno we have to reconstruct schools that have become obsolete and uninhabitable from the perspective of anti-seismic safety, a situation that therefore has similarities with that post-earthquake in L'Aquila.

PAC **Returning to L'Aquila, I've seen that many schools have been criticised by citizens because they'd been realised with excessively reduced volumes, essential, simple containers, while in your project you've used the pitches of roofs to enrich the volumetric expression. How was this idea for the roofs accepted by the builder, knowing that any innovation risks increasing the construction costs?**

GM There were no difficulties, because from the outset the economic aspect was shared with the company, who didn't consider the increase in the internal volume of the classrooms problematic compared to a solution with flat roofs. Another important innovation, willingly accepted by the users, was the 'little house' that we placed at the entrance **[35]**, which forms a space of transition and threshold: a place where parents and children say goodbye before the latter enter school. It's as if to say that the school is a small house that welcomes children.

VC I'd like to add a memory of my own from a few years ago, when I found myself in L'Aquila, for another reason, and I went to see one of the schools. I went to see the school manager, explaining that I was one of the architects and that we'd endeavoured to do our best. She hugged me, telling me that she'd never had such a beautiful school! It needs to be remembered that these schools, like the anti-seismic houses, had been created as provisional modules, with the idea of dismantling them after a few years, whereas they're still here after fifteen years of use. Finding out years later that this provisional aspect can satis-

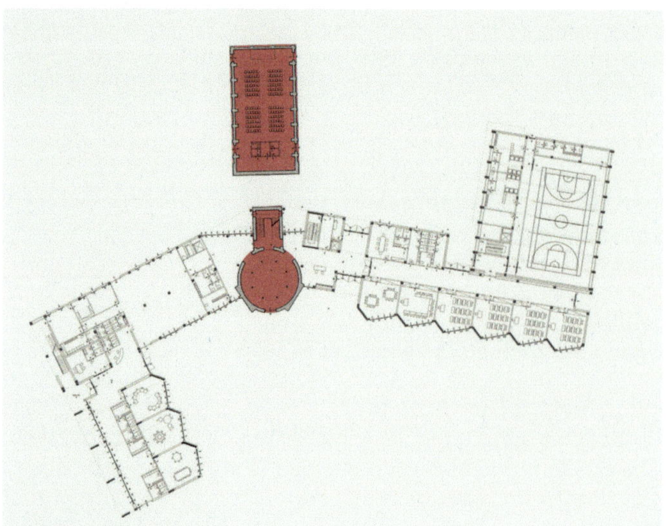

36 PLAN OF THE NEW SCHOOL IN PAOLISI, WITH THE CONSERVED PARTS OF THE PRE-EXISTING SCHOOL (ROTUNDA AND GYMNASIUM) IN RED. AROUND THE ROTUNDA, RESTRUCTURED AS A LIBRARY, THE PRESCHOOL ON THE LEFT AND THE ELEMENTARY AND MIDDLE SCHOOLS ON THE RIGHT, TOGETHER WITH THE NEW GYMNASIUM.

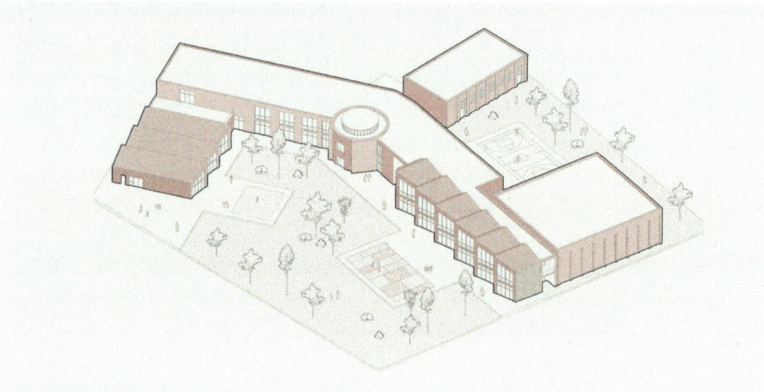

37 AXONOMETRY OF THE SCHOOL.

38 PERSPECTIVE VIEW OF THE GARDEN, WITH THE PRESCHOOL ON THE LEFT AND THE ELEMENTARY AND MIDDLE SCHOOLS ON THE RIGHT.

fy the community so clearly undoubtedly comforted us, because we think that architecture must always be conceived with this ethic.

PAC **To finish, I'd like to discuss the latest school project that you currently have under construction, in the municipality of Paolisi, between Caserta and Benevento. In this case too you won a competition to rebuild a school that had become obsolete as regards energy saving and anti-seismic safety regulations. We'd previously discussed the case of the public housing neighbourhood in Capua, with your decision to restructure instead of demolishing and reconstructing. How did you tackle this theme of memory in Paolisi?**

GM Demolition was envisaged, but our critical evaluations led us to propose the conservation of certain elements **[36]** that could remind the community of fragments of life lived inside this building. These were not pure formal choices, because these elements are not very significant as architecture, but they are part of the collective imagination, shared by many generations. We therefore proposed conserving the large cylindrical volume, which becomes the library and the formal pivot of the composition, and the gymnasium, which will be transformed into an auditorium **[37]**.

PAC **Your project fundamentally takes up the arrangement of the classrooms in two wings, added to which are the volumes of the new gymnasium and preschool. I nevertheless see your intention to structure the volumes of the classrooms into small units on two floors, like little houses** [38], **with a slight rotation accentuating this decomposition of volumes. Could you explain this compositional idea better?**

GM We in fact wanted to have separate volumes to describe the various parts of the programme, as we'd already done with the school in Carate Brianza; for this reason we had also differentiated the volume of the maternal school. The project was envisaged with realisation in phases, and for financing reasons the preschool part was removed, and later allocated to another designer with his own financing. Even though this preschool was moved to a position at the centre of the plot, overall the logic of separate volumes that find the element of union between the various parts in the central drum was respected.

1 **The CASE project envisaged the realisation of 4,500 apartments in just 7 months, for 14,000 citizens of L'Aquila evacuated from houses either destroyed or considered uninhabitable. Cf. https://www.protezionecivile.gov.it/it/approfondimento/le-vostre-domande-sul-progetto-c-a-s-e-/ e https://www.abitare.it/it/architettura/2009/08/10/laquila-progetto-case/.**

2 ***Lotus International*, 144 (2010), cf. also the essay by Nina Bassoli in the same issue: Nina Bassoli, '2010. L'Aquila un anno dopo il terremoto'.**

3 **The schools reconstruction programme was called MUSP (Modules for Provisional School Use), the two schools designed by the Corvino + Multari studio were the Amiternum Primary School and the Santa Maria degli Angeli Institute (kindergarten, pre-school, primary and secondary school), both located in Via Ficara.**

PIAZZA MOLINO RESIDENTIAL AND COMMERCIAL REDEVELOPMENT
COSENZA, 2002–8

The project for the upgrading of the area of the former Molino Bruno SpA factory represents, in the urban context, a private programme of strategic intervention for the upgrading of a central zone of the northern expansion of Cosenza.

The project, in an area of around 8,500 square metres, came about from the reading of four elements: the presence of the overhead bypass, the large residential building to the west of the area, the oblique line along the northern edge and the landscape of La Sila in the distance, which dominates the whole city. The geometry of the project forms a large central space for use for commerce, sports and leisure time, contained between two buildings that form a visual angle towards the Sila Mountains.

The three-dimensional development organisation is based on the study of the heliothermic axis in order to ensure good exposure, ventilation and sunlight to the two buildings, one tower-shaped, the other linear. The building type envisages a commercial use for the ground floor, offices and professional studios on the first floor and residences with dimensions of between 70 and 120 square metres on the upper floors. The area of intervention is endowed with a basement car park floor, which is accessed via three vehicle ramps and several stairways, which connect the car park with the outdoor spaces and with the entrance halls of the buildings.

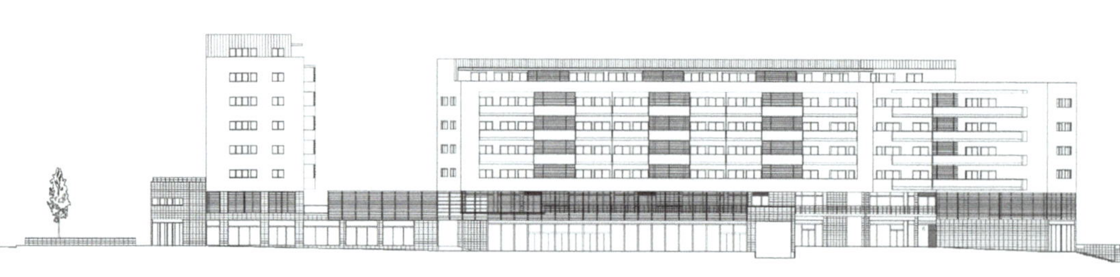

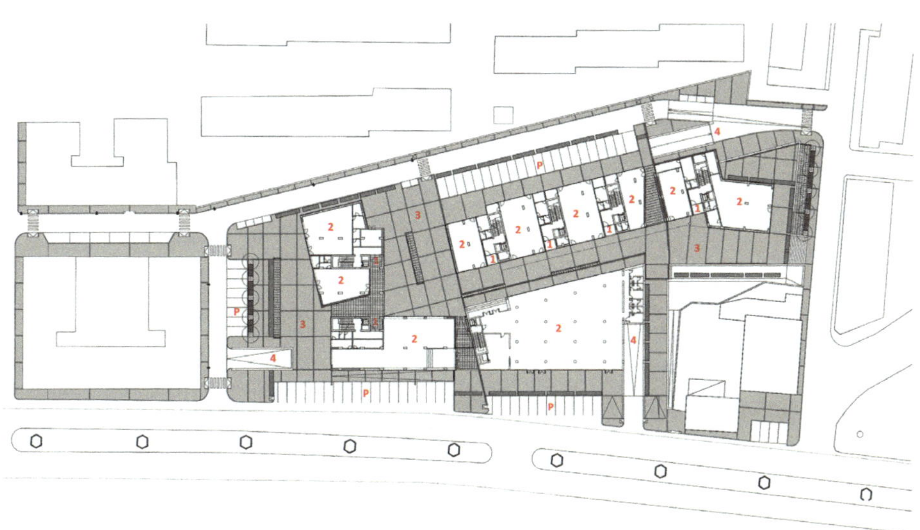

RESIDENTIAL BUILDINGS ON SEISMICALLY ISOLATED PLATFORMS
L'AQUILA, 2009

The project has been developed with a multidisciplinary approach, respecting the regulations of the CASE project (Sustainable Eco-Compatible Anti-Seismic Complexes), in response to the housing emergency following the 2009 earthquake. The new structure has been devised to guarantee durability, speed of construction and architectural recognisability. With a rectangular plan of 55.6 × 13.06 metres and a total gross surface area of 2,078 square metres, the building includes twenty-six dwellings, divided over three levels and distributed along the main north–south axis through two staircases with lifts, also guaranteeing full accessibility to people with disabilities. The dwellings are structured into various types, from studio apartments to three-roomed flats, to respond to the various housing requirements, all with continuous terraces.
The building is characterised by the subdivision between fixed elements—the compact, modular blocks of the dwellings—and mobile elements—the shading devices running horizontally to improve the climate control and adaptability of the project. From the architectural point of view, the rhythm of the façades is marked by an alternation of solid walls and transparent surfaces with shading devices, contributing to the aesthetic identity and light regulation. The materials selected guarantee durability and speed of assembly, responding to the need for construction efficiency and environmental sustainability.

The use of prefabrication enables the building shell to be separated from the bearing structure, made using rigid frames and one-dimensional concrete pillars. The components are produced in the factory, guaranteeing precision and quality of construction, and are subsequently assembled at the construction site with bolted connections. This system enables construction times and wastage of materials to be reduced, as required for emergency interventions with very strict timescales, as in the case of the post-earthquake reconstruction in L'Aquila. The walls are made using insulating sandwich panels, while the floors are aerated concrete. The window frames are thermal aluminium and the roof is steel with thermal isolation and waterproofing. The centralised systems guarantee energy efficiency with underfloor heating and solar captors for the production of hot water.

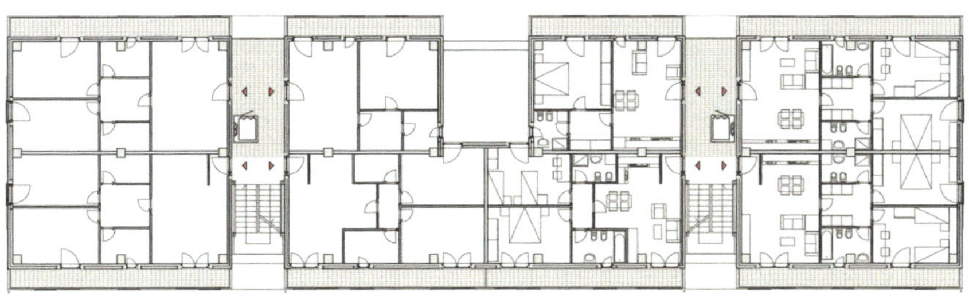

TWENTY-FOUR CO-OPERATIVE HOUSING DWELLINGS
QUARTO, 2009–14

Included in a property development plan in the PEEP zone of Quarto, in the middle of the largest extinguished crater in Campi Flegrei, the building forms a 'C'-shape around a courtyard.

The rhythmic sequence of the volumes is characterised by the compactness of the exposed brick wall towards the outside and by the diaphragm of wooden shading devices towards the courtyard. The unifying element of the whole complex is its lava stone base, a reminder of the volcanic activity of Campi Flegrei. The choice of all the materials has been based on elements characterised by durability. From a typological perspective, the complex is composed of twenty-four dwellings arranged in a line along the main north–south axis and served by three staircase–lift volumes. The dwellings are organised on four levels, added to which is the basement floor, for use as garages with twenty-four car spaces. The dwellings located on the ground floor are endowed with private gardens that are accessible from the courtyard. The interior spaces are distributed so as to give precedence to the arrangement of the most used locations to the west, such as lounge–dining room and main bedrooms, while kitchens, toilets and bathrooms and secondary rooms are positioned to the east according to the logic of being spaces for passing through. Consequently the surfaces of the elevations have various characteristics. The east elevation has a predominance of transparent surfaces, in order to better exploit the sunlight, but also a system of integrated solar chimneys and wooden shading devices, while the west elevation is characterised by a measured relationship between opaque and transparent surfaces with the aim of limiting energy dissipation. The typical dwelling consists of: lounge–dining room, kitchen, three bedrooms, closet, box-room, multi-use room, two bathrooms, a balcony and two loggias.

P

TWO SOCIAL HOUSING BUILDINGS IN LA SILA
SAN GIOVANNI IN FIORE
2016–21

For the new social housing in San Giovanni in Fiore in the province of Cosenza, in the vast territory of Sila Grande, the project introduces a strategy capable of realising a community location made of public and private facilities and services, a place without fences and enclosures, a space for the existing that looks after a community, its traditions, its everyday life.

The design strategy for the new houses identifies the Sila landscape as a structuring element for the process of transformation, into its main components: the woodland and the community. The woodland gives rise to dynamic, rediscovered environments and regulates the rainwater and surface water under conditions of hydro-geological and hydrographic sustainability. The community finds itself around the most authentic values of the mountain that were so dear to Abbot Gioacchino da Fiore, who had identified these landscapes of La Sila as the perfect place for the creation of a historic community project, as the Florense Abbey, founded in 1190, was and still is today. The theme of the home is organised between two different conditions: the first is delineated between architectural choices and effectiveness of management, generating a high standard of use of the spaces, public and domestic, albeit with limited construction costs for easy maintenance; the second consists in finding a reliable relationship between an internal spatiality and an outdoors capable of giving the locations the atmospheres of the Sila plateau.

These are places to live, areas without barriers, in which people have the possibility of recognising themselves in a simple, comfortable, safe environment. The locations between the houses are open, permeable spaces, directly perceivable, with clear visual lines, marked by recognisable elements, where it is easy to get your bearings, where it proves simple to keep watch, where barriers do not exist between public spaces, shared spaces and domestic spaces. The spatial translation corresponds to a highly prized equilibrium between the functionality of everyday life and the calmness of the natural landscape, paying great attention to the quality and continuity of the community spaces. The conditions are created to take care of a community, who live in the present of these thousand-year-old locations.

MODULES FOR PROVISIONAL SCHOOL USE
L'AQUILA, 2009

The building consists of a steel structural grid and self-bearing modular panels that define its shell. The entire constructed organism is made entirely in the workshop and assembled dry on the construction site. This construction system produces measured spatial and functional articulations generated by prefabrication, an essential condition for the realisation of interventions to support a territorial emergency and capable of containing building construction times. At the same time, the prefabrication system conceived and selected has favoured architectural solutions capable of adapting to suit the various places of intended use, but also the different functional programmes, which vary from pre-school to secondary school.

The central theme is that of flexibility as a project construction methodology: an organism composed of modules, combinable both horizontally and in space, in several possible types, also on two levels if necessary, and with the possibility of adapting if necessary to terrains structured with terracing. The school, as a whole, welcomes the functional programme respecting the demands of residence and use, with architectural and distribution choices that guarantee the clear recognisability of the elements that compose it.

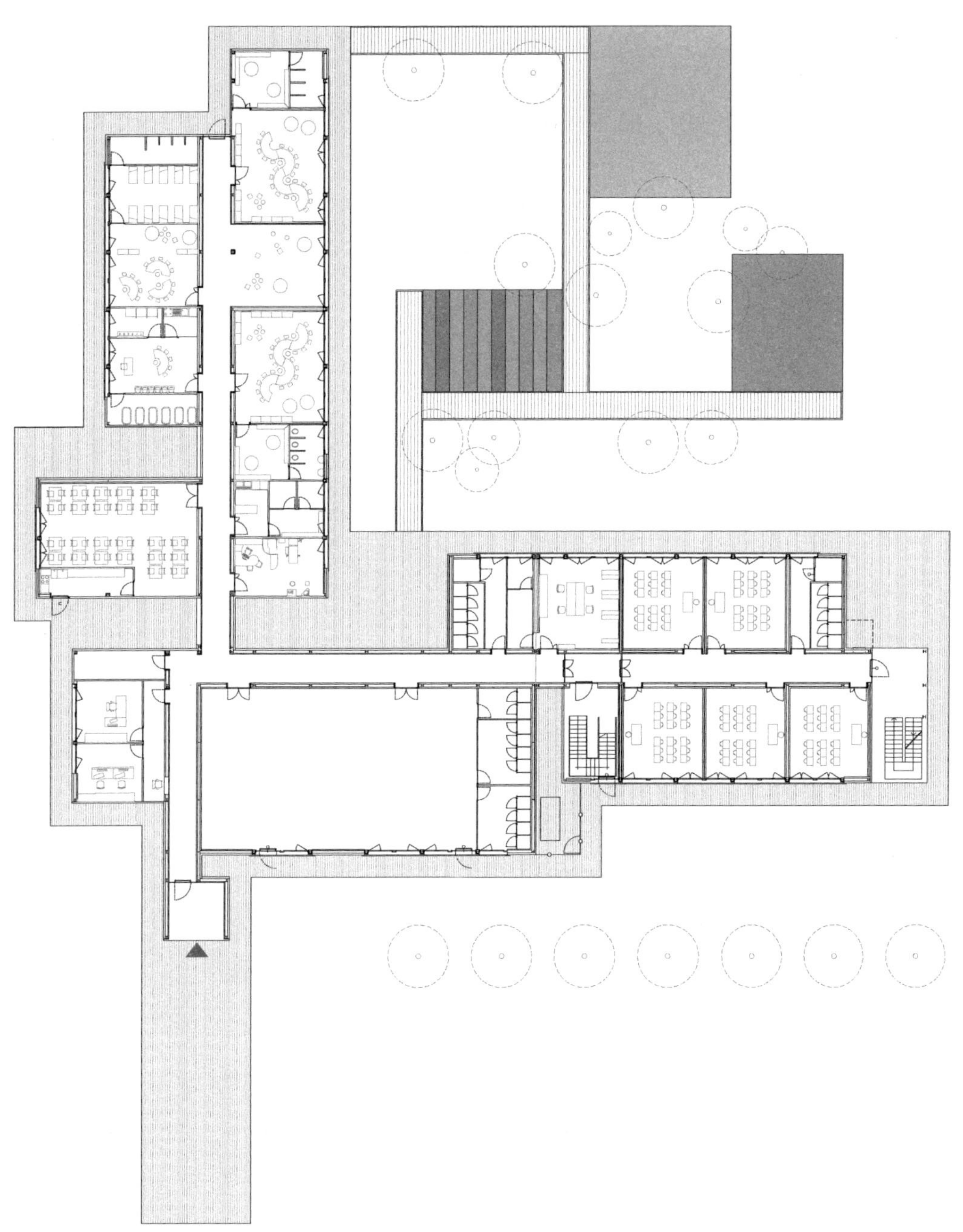

NEW PRIMARY SCHOOL
CARATE BRIANZA
2011–14

The architectural layout of the new school building is structured into three main volumes: two intended for shared functions, and a third, in a line, for use for classrooms. The project takes the programme as the rule for the construction of architecture. The space intended for teaching is oriented so as to best exploit the sunlight for the classrooms. The entrance atrium is wide and adequately lit thanks to the full-height glass walls rendering it open and permeable to the outdoor space. The atrium continues inside the school with a large double-height hall, facing onto which is the reception and inserted into which is an open staircase for access to the upper floor. A large central corridor provides distribution to all the classrooms on the two long sides of the architectural volume. On the ground floor permeability with outside is guaranteed by an aperture on the south side and two apertures on the short sides. The two constructions that are detached from the building in a line, which house the canteen and the gymnasium, have a similar distribution of the interior spaces, that is, a services zone developed along the west side of the construction, so as to guarantee an indoor space that is as free as possible to serve the functions to be hosted there. The canteen occupies a privileged position with respect to the other volumes due to its direct contact with the transport system serving it. The structure of the canteen and gymnasium buildings is characterised by a covering with plate panels, their rhythm marked by tall, narrow fenestrations. The classroom building, on the other hand, a traditional triple volume in a line, is characterised by a stereometric plastered shell, also marked by a long sequence of vertical cuts corresponding to the façade apertures.

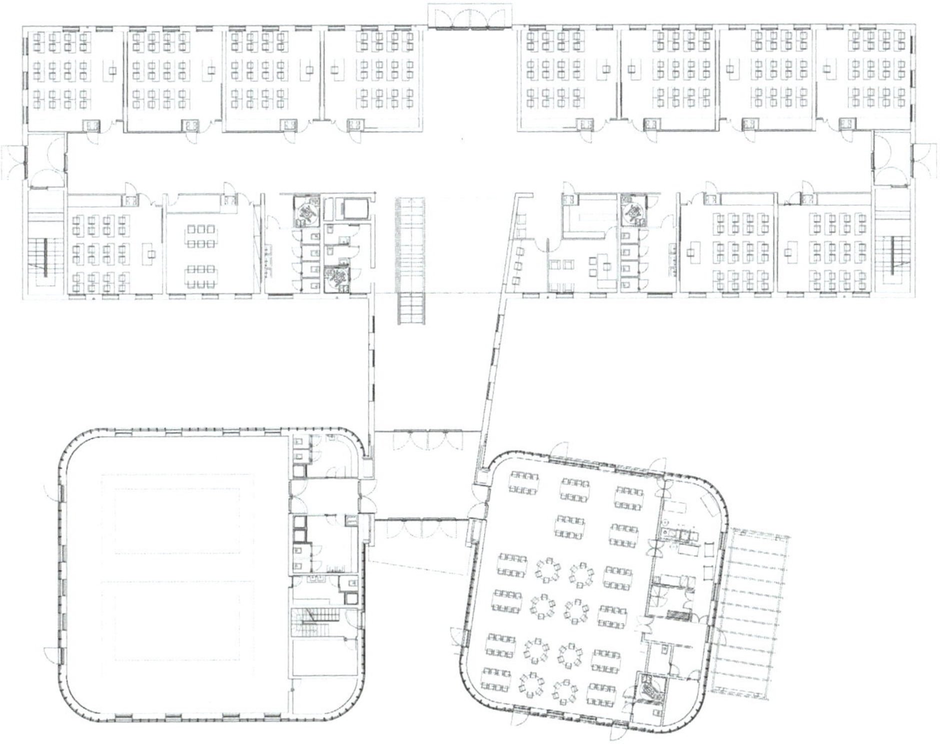

6
DECOMMISSIONED LOCATIONS

PAC **A significant number of your projects involve abandoned buildings and urban sites. I therefore propose entitling this chapter 'Decommissioned locations', and in it we'll discuss the various ways in which you've intervened to bring them back to life. One of your first projects in this field concerned the regeneration of an important monumental complex, the so-called 'Bourbon military quarter' in Casagiove** [1]. **How did the project come about?**

VC The Municipality of Casagiove owned the former military quarter and wanted to transform it into a centre for meetings between different cultures, organising a national design competition. Our project was subsequently partially financed, ending up the winner in 2002 of the third edition of the Centocittà Prize, conceived by Renzo Piano and held by the Fondazione Compagnia di San Paolo. We were in a season of virtuous competitions and highly qualified juries; in this specific case the president of the jury was Margherita Guccione, at the time Superintendent in Caserta.

PAC **Your project was based on the idea of public routes through the courtyards** [2], **radically transforming the closed and introverted character of the military buildings to highlight the urban dimension of the complex, which is in a pivotal situation between the historic centre and the new city. How was this urban dimension of the intervention managed by the Municipality of Casagiove?**

GM In effect our idea was to bring new life to a space, an architecture, a location associated with the city and its memory. The monumental complex had always been a closed-off space, created as a hospital, then a quarantine hospital for plague victims, and finally a military barracks; it was therefore recognised by the community as a non-penetrable location, a place of refuge and pain. The front of the buildings along Via Quartiere Nuovo was fully constructed, and one of our first actions was to have a modern concrete building demolished in order to open up the enclosure. This demolition was greeted with great enthusiasm by the community of Casagiove, because it was then possible to begin to recognise the elements that had been put in place over time. We recognise ourselves very much in this idea of subtraction, even before imagining any possible addition.

PAC **As in other restoration projects, however, where necessary you've intervened with new elements, declaredly contemporary ones in the use of materials, such as the insertion of a new light iron staircase** [3], **or the new lift in the main courtyard of the complex, which you configure as an abstract blind volume. Where did this idea come from?**

GM In reality, there was already a small volume in this position, and we rebuilt it with a particular design: there's this blind wall, very silent, but at the same time the glazing highlights the staircase that leads to the upper floor **[4]**. As often happens with us, the project followed a process of small interventions that reverberate in more significant actions involving entire parts of buildings, shared spaces and relations with the city.

PAC **At a distance of more than twenty years, how do you judge this project experience, which unfortunately couldn't be realised in its entirety? We know of many cases where the theme of the unfinished leads to interesting developments, because actually the regeneration of historic buildings is a process of continuous transformation.**

VC Imagining a multicultural centre in a context such as the Caserta area, burdened by the need to play host to a large number of people coming from other countries, had seemed a very interesting idea. Now the building hosts offices of the Municipality and play and recreation activities, spaces for the elderly and temporary cultural events, because the courtyards are of such dimensions as to be able to lend themselves to uses that may change, modify, adapt with time. To conclude on this theme of the unfinished, I'd say that for many small municipalities this season of competitions has resulted in major difficulties in management. In particular, in the South, the municipalities are no longer capable of carrying forward such ambitious competitions, firstly because no clear managerial model exists: functions are often identified without then having the actors capable of managing the work realised. These are complex works that require huge financing, often much greater than that identified at the time of the competition, and so at a certain point the municipalities alone were no longer capable of carrying procedures forward: hence the State's need to identify subjects such as the State Property Agency to finance and identify management models for the regeneration of abandoned buildings and urban sites.

UTILISING DECOMMISSIONED MILITARY COMPLEXES

PAC **In Casagiove you intervened for the first time on the theme of the restoration and restructuring of a large decommissioned military complex, a theme that you've tackled subsequently on various other occasions, particularly with the new Public Prosecutor's Office in the former military hospital in Catanzaro. In both cases, you intervened in very central urban locations and in monumental complexes that were subject to restrictions, where the historical value of the architecture strongly conditions the intervention in terms of restoration. In recent times, on the other hand, you've developed projects for decommissioned military complexes in urban fringe contexts, or else those characterised by a more recent architecture, sometimes even without significant quality. The decommissioning of these military complexes therefore created the opportunity for interventions where the definition of a project strategy based on the opposition between conservation and dem-**

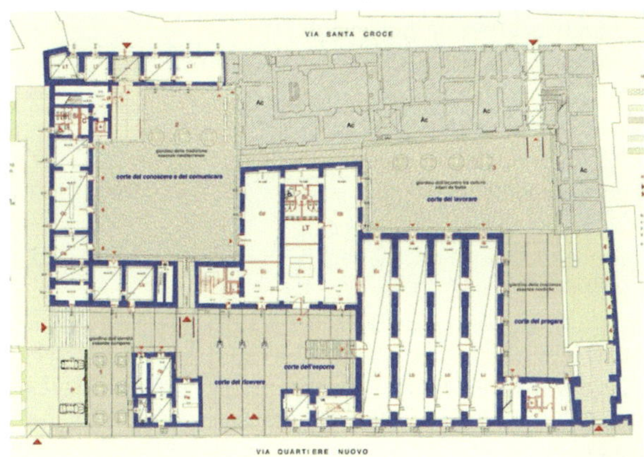

1 RESTORATION OF THE BOURBON MILITARY QUARTER IN CASAGIOVE, 2001–9, PLAN OF THE GROUND FLOOR WITH THE VARIOUS INTERNAL COURTYARDS CONNECTED BY THE NEW PEDESTRIAN WALKWAYS.

2 THE PEDESTRIAN WALKWAY CROSSING BETWEEN THE ‘COURTYARD OF RECEIVING’ AND THE ‘COURTYARD OF KNOWING AND COMMUNICATING’.

3 NEW LIGHT STAIRCASE MADE OF IRON AND STEEL GRID.

4 THE NEW LIFT IN THE ‘COURTYARD OF KNOWING AND COMMUNICATING’.

olition appears decisive. I'd like to begin with your project for the new headquarters for the Revenue Agency in the area of the former Air Force warehouses in Via Simeto in Cagliari, in a very impressive landscape context [5], **near to the airport to the north of the city. How was the design competition that you won in 2018 conducted?**

VC The international competition had been called in conjunction with a 'Piano Periferie', (urban fringe plan) concerning the entire area of the neighbourhood of Sant'Avendrace. The siting of the sole headquarters of the Regional Revenue Agency therefore corresponds to the intention to create a new polarity of attraction on an urban and territorial scale, so that this peripheral area may aspire to becoming a town. We were the competitors who proposed partially contradicting the planning orientation document attached to the competition brief, which envisaged realising a multi-storey car park to replace the large warehouse at the back of the headquarter building; this was an interesting building that we proposed upgrading and restoring, allocating it for office use and creating a formal and compositional unity for the entire complex. The new car park is located in a new construction on the northwest side of the plot.

PAC **An interesting aspect of your project concerns the respecting of the shape of the pre-existing buildings, most of which restored and others reconstructed, and the creation of a system of piazzas and public gardens** [6], **relating to a hypothesis of showcasing possible archaeological finds. Can you explain this relationship with archaeology better?**

VC We found ourselves in a context abounding in archaeological finds in the immediate proximity, and so we worked with the landscapist João Nunes on the hypothesis of future finds that could be showcased inside the system of public gardens. For this reason we remained within the shape of the pre-existing buildings and connected the main restructured building with its extension by means of bridges, so as to leave the open space free.

PAC **In a similar way to what happened in Casagiove, you propose demolishing the boundary wall to remove from this decommissioned complex its status as a place of isolation and segregation. This type of proposal often poses problems of security and control for public bodies, and so I'll ask you if the Revenue Agency will actually allow the public to cross the site freely.**

VC We arrived at a compromise in the programme agreement between Municipality, Revenue Agency, State Property Agency and Procurement and Supply Department for Public Works, which envisaged that this park could only be used by the public during office opening hours. I may add that the urban planning offices of the Municipality of Cagliari supported us considerably in this idea of valuing the urban character of the building and the whole area.

5 THE LANDSCAPE IN THE AREA OF SANT'AVENDRACE IN CAGLIARI.

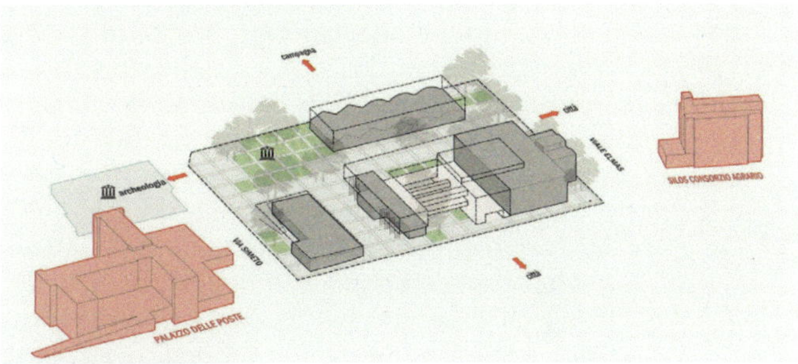

6 SCHEMATIC AXONOMETRY OF THE PROJECT WITH THE ALTERNATION BETWEEN VOLUMES FOR OFFICES AND PUBLIC SPACES. THE RESTORED BUILDINGS IN DARK GREY, THE EXTENSIONS IN PALE GREY.

7 THE NEW FAÇADE WITH SHADING DEVICES ENVELOPING THE UPGRADED VOLUME OF THE LARGE WAREHOUSE.

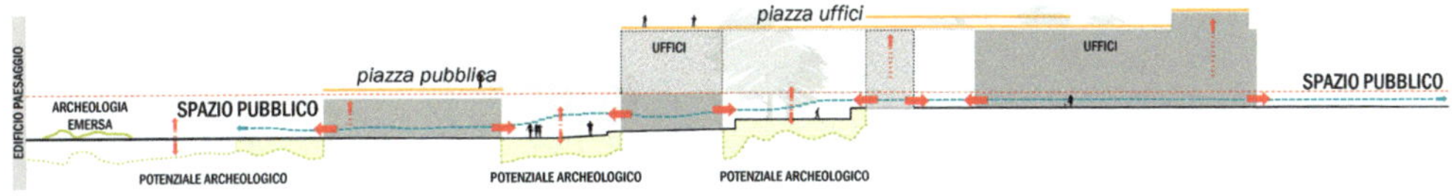

8 LONGITUDINAL SECTION THROUGH THE WAREHOUSES, ON THE RIGHT, WITH THE ALTERNATION BETWEEN CONSTRUCTIONS AND COURTYARDS.

PAC **The most significant intervention clearly concerns the central volume of the offices, obtained with the upgrading and enlargement of the large warehouse. You maintain the beautiful structure of this attractive building, characterised by mighty beams and reinforced concrete pillars, but you propose a contemporary language for the façades that is reminiscent of previous interventions, particularly the Public Prosecutor's Office in Catanzaro, with a series of vertical shading devices that create a sort of giant order** [7], **suspended above the high porticoed base, with a bipartite division in clear contrast with the internal structuring into three floors of offices. I was also interested to see that, though maintaining the original structures, you succeeded in breaking the compactness and uniqueness of the volume of warehouses, so as to obtain, together with the added construction, a fascinating profile of a 'palazzo' with two internal courtyards** [8], **or two cloisters. Therefore there is a return of these classical figures of the cloister and the palazzo that we already discussed on the subject of your other previous projects.**

VC Perhaps the most synthetic image of the philosophy of our intervention is the internal perspective of the central hall, a full-height space, lit from above, in which there coexist beams and pillars from the old warehouse, with the original floors removed, and new parts connected by walkways cast in the middle of this void. This central space sums up well the idea of unity between existing and new, a unity that can also be perceived by climbing up onto the roof-garden to observe the landscape and the large stretches of water, as happens when you climb up onto the Saint Remy Bastion in the historic city.

PAC **Let's proceed now with other projects, again in the context of abandoned military complexes, moving to Brescia, to the area of the Caserma Papa, the former barracks that has the peculiarity of presenting a significant discontinuity between the representation building, constructed in 1932, which marks the corner of the plot, and a series of industrial buildings from the same period. I'm interested in finding out how the discussion was conducted with the Municipality, the Superintendence and the bodies that will use the site of the former barracks, on the question of what to conserve and what to demolish.**

VC I can't conceal that we suffered a small defeat on this issue, which, as always, obstinately, we'll seek to limit with good quality of realisation. The reasons can well be understood if you observe the model of what was our original idea **[9]**, shared with the architect Anna Maria Basso Bert of the Superintendence of Brescia. Following the first on-site inspections, we had admired those beautiful industrial sheds as extraordinary monuments **[10]**, recognising the true typological and morphological value of this area **[11]** in their oblong shape. We'd therefore proposed to maintain them and for this reason we'd introduced a series of variants to the Urban Planning Scheme,

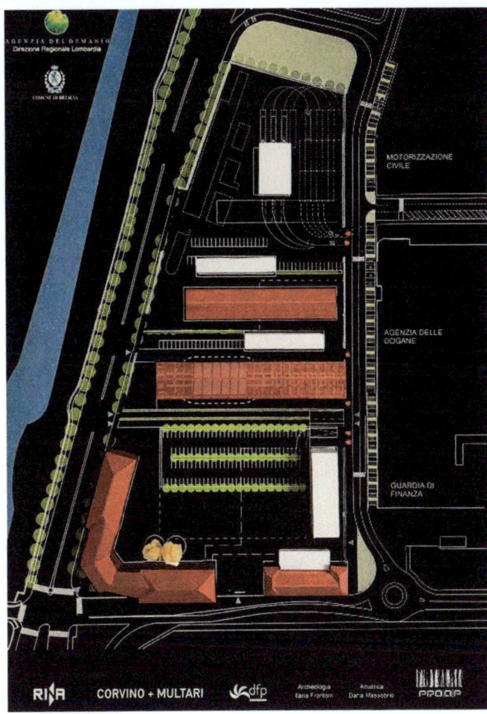

9 URBAN REGENERATION OF THE PAPA BARRACKS IN BRESCIA, THE MODEL OF THE FIRST DESIGN PROPOSAL, 2022, WITH THE BUILDINGS TO BE CONSERVED IN RED.

10 PAPA BARRACKS, BRESCIA, INTERNAL VIEW OF THE INDUSTRIAL BUILDING THAT WILL BE RESTRUCTURED.

11 AERIAL VIEW OF THE COMPLEX OF THE PAPA BARRACKS.

12 VIEW OF A NEW VOLUME, LEFT, CONNECTED WITH A GLASS BRIDGE TO THE RESTRUCTURED INDUSTRIAL BUILDING.

already approved by the Municipality, but unfortunately we encountered in our path an official of the Department of Motor Vehicles, who completely rejected the idea of revising the Urban Planning Scheme, due to a potential risk of wasting time. While all the other parties had proved favourable, we unfortunately lost this battle due solely to the opposition of this gentleman, when, for example, the officials of the Finance Police had proven to be sensitive and attentive, and also in favour of this revisiting. For this reason, in the end only one of these industrial monuments could be conserved in full, others were partially conserved, others demolished.

GM This question of procedure was decisive in this case. These are complex procedures in which it's hard to disentangle ourselves as architects, because we find ourselves in the middle of discussions between the bodies that manage the buildings, the owners and the bodies that will then have to use them, and often each one already has their own pre-established idea. Unfortunately, then architecture succeeds in doing little in these conflictual contexts, even though, after all, it was right to attempt to reshape the Plan that preceded our intervention.

PAC **It can be perfectly understood that your first proposal to maintain a number of sheds could have led to a more interesting project, and it's a pity that it wasn't welcomed by everybody. Nevertheless, it can clearly be ascertained from the perspective views that you managed to value the pre-existing elements with a very calm** [12]**, almost silent architecture, which emits an image of lightness through the steel grid skin, so as not to overpower the existing elements. Let's go further and now discuss your project for the 'Citadel of Security' in Naples, again in a decommissioned military area** [13]**. Once more in this case you propose breaking the enclosure to form a new urban composition, with a grid of new buildings and a genuine urban boulevard on the edge of the plot. What were the planning rules on the basis of which the competition brief had been drafted?**

VC Unlike the Brescia project, we were lucky enough to be able to develop the overall form of settlement of this Police Town, the largest in Italy, based on the idea of a public through-route between Miano and Scampia and on the setting back of the part that will remain enclosed, so as to create a true public square along Via Miano, utilising the existing low building and a group of beautiful pines **[14]**. The new buildings are organised as a system of communicating courtyards that concludes with the high tower, which becomes a totemic element, in a relationship with the high buildings of Scampia. The Mayor Gaetano Manfredi likes this project very much, because creating a place for security and justice in a location such as Scampia, where the police are sometimes viewed as an enemy to be fought, will offer a major opportunity for upgrading the district. The work we're doing is also to create a sort of 'architectural empathy'.

PAC **The pre-existing Boscariello barracks was characterised by the almost obsessive repetition of low buildings without**

13 AERIAL PHOTOGRAPH OF THE BOSCARIELLO BARRACKS, ON THE LEFT, AND CARETTO BARRACKS, ON THE RIGHT, POSITIONED ON THE AXIS OF VIA MIANO IN NAPLES.

14 PERSPECTIVE OF THE NEW PIAZZA ALONG VIA MIANO, WITH THE PRESERVED HISTORIC BUILDING ON THE LEFT AND THE NEW AUDITORIUM ON THE RIGHT.

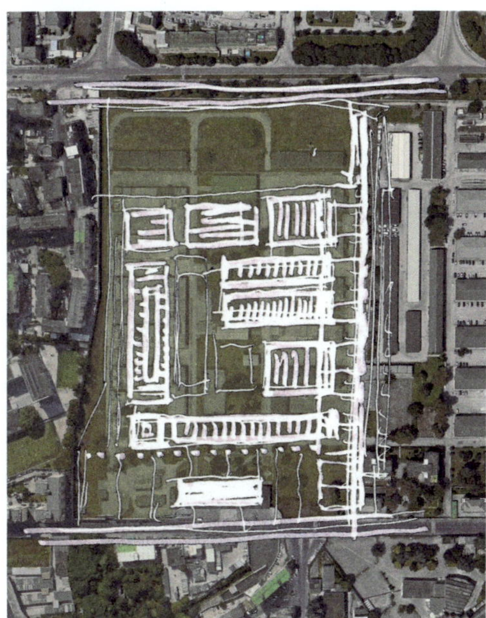

15 PROJECT SKETCH WITH THE NEW URBAN GRID AND THE NEW BOULEVARD ON THE BOUNDARY WITH THE CARETTO BARRACKS (RIGHT).

16 PERSPECTIVE OF THE NEW PIAZZA AND THE TREE-LINED STREET, ON THE RIGHT, BETWEEN THE FORMER BOSCARIELLO AND CARETTO BARRACKS.

architectural quality, constructed in the 1940s and grouped into six 'U'-shaped courtyards. Your project is based on a new settlement pattern with different sizes and rhythms, and also with a decidedly higher density, when enables a more urban character to be obtained, to all intents and purposes a small town consisting of streets, squares and buildings with courtyards forming mini-blocks. I'm interested in understanding better how you came to define the sizes and rhythms of this new urban grid.

GM This project undoubtedly represents a rather rare opportunity to work with the new in such an intensive way. Relying on a grid **[15]** helps find forms that are compatible with the programme and with the territory, to regulate the contours and the internal elements, to consider different ways of organising the individual modules. In the case of the Boscariello barracks, in view of the strong volumetric and dimensional impact of this project, I believe it was certainly useful to trust in a traditional urban form, recurring, capable of generating various volumetric dimensions, making some elements porous, giving density and fluidity to the entire system. At the same time, one of the most significant aspects of our project is the conservation of the small pre-existing building along Via Miano, which is in dialogue with the similar building in front of the nearby Caretto barracks. These are two very small, very delicate constructions, but they play a fundamental urban role because they recall the old relationship of these barracks with the street.

PAC **On the boundary between the areas of the two barracks, Boscariello and Caretto, you've proposed a new tree-lined street** [16]**, the size of a genuine boulevard, but for security reasons this urban space will remain inside the belt and be used as a car park for employees. Isn't this fact in open contradiction with the principles of openness and urbanity that are at the basis of your project?**

VC It does indeed remain inside the enclosure, but the Police imagine that in some circumstances, for example on Sunday mornings, this boulevard can exceptionally open up to the neighbourhood for walks. In reality, a programme agreement was recently signed between Police, Municipality and the Carabinieri who occupy the area alongside, envisaging widening the interior road with a new connecting linear park. We've therefore just begun to design this green space with the landscape architect João Nunes, who's also developing a very interesting project for the internal gardens in the courtyards of the buildings.

PAC **This demonstrates once again how important the creation of a void is as a founding and irreversible element of the urban form, irrespective of the problems of management, which remain contingent, because the new architecture and the new town will have to last over time.**

MANTUA AS SYNTHESIS

PAC **A significant number of your projects developed for decommissioned buildings and sites have concerned State-owned properties, starting with the project for the new Public Prosecutor's Office in the former military hospital in Catanzaro. How did your relationship with the State Property Agency develop in the years that followed?**

VC In effect a consistent number of design competitions in which we participated were called by the State Property Agency, because we recognised that for a few years this client was beginning to run a significant part of the financial flows of the country on the subject of urban regeneration. In a similar way to what happens in France, it's the State that runs processes of these dimensions.

PAC **Have you always participated in these numerous design competitions with the same team?**

VC Over the years we've consolidated our relationship with Rina, Italy's largest engineering company, because we recognised that our 'artisan' work as architects could be accompanied by a major organisation of process, also with important economic-financial capabilities. Added to this combination are various engineering companies of small dimensions, which enable us to conceive and control the project better.

PAC **The fact seems important to me that Rina Consulting recognises this need to work with architects to achieve actual architectural quality, while many other engineering firms are self-referential and do everything by themselves, often with disastrous results in terms of the quality of their interventions.**

GM I'd like to return for a moment to the role of the State Property Agency, which has a very precise mission, that of utilising public assets in relation to the needs of the municipalities and users. The State Property Agency has understood the importance of competitions; it's therefore attempting to imagine a more dynamic mission with regard to the city and the territory. In the specific case of Mantua, it understood the advantages that granting in concession to them the transformation and use of totally abandoned military sheds could represent for the Municipality. I believe that the Mantua project is in some ways the most complete synthesis of our way of working on the existing, which has characterised our research for thirty years now. I have no doubts in this regard, but more than referring to the quality of the architecture, and therefore to the result, I'm referring precisely to the process, to the fact of having succeeded in developing a series of actions with the Municipality to the advantage of the existing, to the advantage of the city, the territory and its citizens. These are precise individual actions, but connected together, so as to achieve an overall upgrading in the end. This way of proceeding should be carried out more or less everywhere, also knowing how to adapt, not beginning with a closed and concluded project, but rather with a project that's still open to various possibilities and is also capable of welcoming and attracting new actors and new users. The quality of this open process will probably only be registered in ten years, when all the transformations have been completed, and their history acquired as collective memory.

PAC **When you talk about this project strategy, consisting of precise interventions that are connected and coordinated together, for me this evokes what at one time was the fundamental mission of the technical offices inside the public administrations. I know the case of the city of Brescia very well; in the 1970s they'd invited Leonardo Benevolo to inaugurate a season of visionary urban planning, with the role of a planning office inside the Municipality at the centre, with a function not only of analysis and control, but also and above all of programming and active coordination. This role of a 'Projects office' that coordinates and promotes a series of interventions over the territory, subsequently entrusted to public or private interventions, has almost entirely disappeared in Italy, whereas it remains active in countries such as France, Spain and Switzerland, which have maintained a strong tradition of quality urban planning. I'm interested in knowing if in the case of Mantua, after winning a planning competition, your role shifted from that of designers of buildings to that of a kind of 'public architect' who doesn't work inside the public administration, but rather as a consultant for the administration, in some ways replacing a technical apparatus of the administration that is in dire straits, or else has been totally retired. How did your relationship with the municipal administration of Mantua develop?**

VC The project for Mantua came about within the sphere of the financing of the so-called Piano Periferie, the urban fringe plan, a programme launched with the Renzi government, which generated major and virtuous opportunities for various municipal administrations. To apply, the Municipality of Mantua used Stefano Boeri as an urban planning consultant, and he identified various themes for intervention **[17]** over a very extensive area. The competition that we won didn't require design proposals as such, but only the submitting of our CV, the dossiers of similar design services already realised, and a methodological report. We participated with Rina as group leader, and I think the Municipality was very interested in identifying a group of professionals to guarantee it clear architectural thought, but at the same time the capacity to manage an order of this complexity. Even though financed by the Piano Periferie, in reality the project concerned an area inside the historical fabric of the city. We were able to engage in dialogue with a very far-sighted administration, with very young mayors and councillors, some thirty years old at the time, such as Mattia Palazzi and Andrea Murari, who had a strong desire to win this challenge.

PAC **Were there moments of exchange with the Milan Politecnico's Mantua site?**

VC The request arrived from the Politecnico to design the upgrading of the abandoned part of the former ceramics factory to create a students' hall of residence **[18]**. Our project was granted financing by the Ministry of the University and Research, but unfortunately to date no contributions have arrived, and it isn't known whether this function will be maintained.

PAC **Clearly it's a great pity, because the restoration of the former ceramics factory appears today to be unfinished, with the east part already operational as the 'Andrea Mantegna Technical Institute', and the west part in ruins** [19], **facing out onto the new public space. I'd now like to go into the subject of your architectural intervention, starting with the school in the former ceramics factory. There are some fascinating photographs by Marco Introini that document certain phases of the construction site, when they were beginning to assemble the new staircases and walkways inside the large void of the industrial building** [20]. **In this phase of the worksite your strategy of grafting a new steel architecture inside the historical container, characterised by mighty reinforced concrete pillars, was therefore clearly visible. In visiting the completed building, I can't deny a certain disappointment, compared to the major poetic force of the worksite photographs, because my feeling is that of a space that is excessively shiny, apparently entirely new** [21]. **The patina of time and the poetics of the tension between existing and new that characterised your other interventions, I'm thinking in particular of the castle in Baia with the presence of the Roman walls, seem to have disappeared.**

VC All this is true, but the need to entirely cover all the new elements comes from the fire regulations for school buildings; if the building had been used as a museum, we'd probably not have had to be subject to such stringent regulations. I had proposed leaving exposed at least the beautiful rust-coloured structural consolidations that you see in Introini's photographs at the base of the columns **[22]**, but not even that was possible. We nevertheless considered it necessary to leave a trace of how our project was conceived and then realised, and for this reason we had Marco Introini's beautiful photos displayed on the walls of the corridors, on all the floors, because it's important for the students to be aware of this memory to which you're referring. Our decision to use plasterboard to achieve a uniformity of colour ultimately corresponds to the desire to showcase the plasticity of the interior space.

GM It's a delicate subject; these black-and-white photographs depicting the transparency of the structural frames produce a sensation of a very strong building, which is reminiscent of the Palais de Tokyo in Paris with the exemplary restoration by Lacaton & Vassal. All in all, what's important is having been able to conserve the significant height of the central distribution space, introducing a different spatial order with respect to the classic central corridor. This school in the former ceramics factory remains one of the cornerstones of this work that we're carrying forward in Mantua; I nevertheless con-

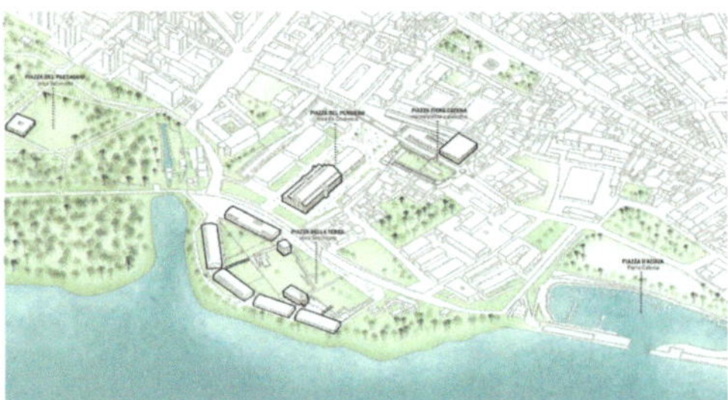

17 SCHEMATIC AXONOMETRY OF THE MANTOVA HUB WITH THE FOUR AREAS OF INTERVENTION.

18 PERSPECTIVE VIEW OF THE CENTRAL SPACE OF THE PROJECT FOR UNIVERSITY RESIDENCES INSIDE THE FORMER CERAMICS FACTORY.

19 VIEW OF THE FORMER CERAMICS FACTORY BEFORE THE RESTRUCTURING INTERVENTION, WITH THE PART ENVISAGED FOR UNIVERSITY RESIDENCES ON THE LEFT.

20 PHOTOGRAPH BY MARCO INTROINI AT THE CONSTRUCTION SITE OF THE SCHOOL IN THE FORMER CERAMICS FACTORY.

21 VIEW OF THE CENTRAL SPACE OF THE SCHOOL AT THE FORMER CERAMICS FACTORY.

sider it one of the most interesting projects, since it represents very well the idea of a design that comes about from strategic aspects, with precise interventions that we made subsequently with the gymnasium in Piazza Fiera Catena and the redevelopment of the old military buildings in the area of San Nicolò, and with widespread use of the public space that becomes the element relating the various interventions together.

PAC **I've noted some interventions by artists inside the school, and this reminds me of our discussions on street art on the subject of the action of the artist Zilda in the Tempio della Scorziata in Naples. I'm therefore interested in finding out how you involved artists in Mantua.**

VC We were indeed able to do that in Mantua inside the school, whereas other artists such as Fabio Tellas will soon also be involved in Cagliari for the project for the headquarters of the Revenue Agency. At the moment street art is a rather misunderstood art form; there's extensive debate on its status as provisional decoration, to discuss whether in the future it will become an art form that can last over time. There's a street art festival that takes place in Mantua, which came about in 2016 for Mantua Italian Capital of Culture: it's entitled *Without Frontiers*, and it's a festival of urban upgrading and the showcasing of cultural phenomena through interventions by artists coming from all over the world, who in particular have realised a series of murals on social housing buildings. Our idea was to engage these artists to participate directly in the designs, instead of inviting them to decorate a blank wall. Everything came about from a very simple observation by the head teacher, who informed us that he was afraid that, after the inauguration, the white columns inside the entrance hall would be defaced by the students' scribblings. To prevent this potential damage, we thought, together with the mayor and the curator Simona Gavioli, of identifying two well-known artists, Aris and Ceres, and inviting them to decorate these columns **[23]** with their own graffiti on the theme of green nature and the earth, in this way preserving them from possible defacing.

PAC **Now let's talk about the new gymnasium, which is in the basement, so as to lower the height of the building above ground and offer those walking by views of the sport field from above. This decision led to the need for an archaeological dig, which proved very rich in finds, yet without having consequences for the realisation of the gymnasium. How was the dialogue conducted with the Superintendence and the archaeologists?**

VC Before answering, I'd like to recall that the Municipality had planned to build the gymnasium on the site opposite, demolishing the skeleton of an unfinished building **[24]**, whereas later we shared with them, on the basis of an overall vision, the idea of changing location in order to create a small green park and reinforce the opposite corner with the new gymnasium **[25]**, which thus becomes a kind of access gate to the whole area for those arriving from the historic centre. We therefore proceeded to conduct an archaeological excavation campaign, in accordance with the legal obligation of so-called

22 PHOTOGRAPH BY MARCO INTROINI AT THE CONSTRUCTION SITE OF THE SCHOOL IN THE FORMER CERAMICS FACTORY, WITH THE STRUCTURAL CONSOLIDATIONS AT THE BASE OF THE REINFORCED CONCRETE COLUMNS ON THE RIGHT.

23 THE WORK OF THE STREET ARTISTS ARIS AND CERES ON THE COLUMNS IN THE ATRIUM OF THE SCHOOL.

24 THE SKELETON OF THE INCOMPLETE BUILDING, DEMOLISHED TO CREATE THE NEW PIAZZA FIERA CATENA. OPPOSITE, ON THE RIGHT, THE SITE OF THE NEW GYMNASIUM.

'preventive archaeology', and good fortune willed the discovery of the most precious finds from the Bronze Age in the city of Mantua. The Superintendent Gabriele Barucca told us that the building finds were of little interest from the point of view of architecture, being little more than old workshops, whereas the objects were very interesting and precious, particularly the bronze kitchenware and pottery, which were numbered, catalogued and restored for subsequent display in the Archaeological Museum inside Palazzo Ducale. Once these finds had been surveyed, it was possible to proceed with the excavation and then with the construction of the gymnasium.

PAC **Similarly in the area of San Nicolò, occupied by the abandoned military buildings, the archaeology profoundly conditioned your way of operating, and you had to modify your project on account of the need to commemorate the presence of a Jewish cemetery. Can you tell us this story, which is fascinating in many ways?**

VC While we were developing our project, some representatives of the international Jewish community **[26]** began to contest the fact that the area of San Nicolò could be regenerated, because there was a Jewish cemetery of 15th-century origin in the area, in which some of the most important cabalists had been buried up to the 17th century. After an edict from the end of the 18th century ordering the whole area not to be built upon, subsequently this edict was probably forgotten at the end of the 19th century, when the area became the property of the army, who then built a series of industrial sheds. In the first version of the project, the upgrading of these sheds envisaged the realisation of a mezzanine floor, with an increase in surface area, but with the financial resources not being sufficient, provision was therefore made to only restructure two sheds. This solution made it necessary to create a new structure with foundation piles sunk sixteen metres deep, and this provoked a debate and an intervention by the Jewish community against this project hypothesis, with an application to the Chamber of Deputies, following which we were summoned as designers, together with the mayor of Mantua, to discuss a solution with the representatives of the Jewish community. The debate involved not only Italian Jewish associations, but also and above all an international association, with its headquarters in New York, whose role was the safeguarding of Jewish cemeteries all over the world.[1] Rabbi Chizkiya Kalmanowitz, who is director of this association, came from New York to discuss our project, explaining to us that in order to give consent to the construction of the new structure on an area previously occupied by a Jewish cemetery, it was necessary to respect a Jewish concept that we may sum up with the expression 'void on void'. According to this concept, vertical structures cannot stand directly as struts on the ground, but rather must be distanced from the earth using intermediary struts, in a form of respect towards the sacredness of this terrain. Rabbi Kalmanowitz came a number of times from New York to Mantua, to sign the executive drawings with us and the structural engineer. It was therefore a very unusual experience, because an even better project came about from these restrictions during the course of development.

PAC **So what was the concrete outcome of this discussion?**

25 VIEW OF THE NEW PIAZZA FIERA CATENA, WITH THE CONSTRUCTION SITE OF THE NEW GYMNASIUM ON THE LEFT.

26 THE AREA OF SAN NICOLÒ WITH THE VISIT BY REPRESENTATIVES OF THE JEWISH COMMUNITY.

27 INDUSTRIAL BUILDING IN THE AREA OF SAN NICOLÒ, WITH ITS LARGE VAULTS.

VC The mayor was very good in this crisis in taking the opportunity to regenerate all the sheds, eliminating the mezzanine floors, and obtaining further financing from the Prime Minister's Office in order to complete the intervention. From the point of view of architecture, the project has therefore been improved by leaving the spatiality of the large vaults unchanged **[27]**, the only true element of architectural quality of these 20th-century industrial buildings, recognised as such by Ministry of Culture official Anna Maria Basso Bert before assigning the monumental restriction to these sheds. Subsequently, with the regional reorganisation of the Superintendences, the new Superintendent of Mantua Gabriele Barucca consistently proved to be very collaborative in bringing this long process of reworking of the project to a conclusion. Consequently, new excavations should also be avoided for the building systems project, so as not to further offend the historical memory, remaining inside the plot of the buildings, but out of necessity some further excavations were carried out, always under the control of the Jewish community. Some finds from the abbey of San Nicolò therefore emerged, resulting in an in-depth archaeological study, but in view of this almost excessive wealth of finds, the superintendent proposed to cover everything, agreeing with the need to engrave the pattern of wall traces on the pavement: a great opportunity, through a unitary project, to be able to transmit both the Jewish and the Christian memory of the area. Other discussions came about when human remains were found inside the former gatekeeper's house; these were entirely unexpected finds, as happens with archaeological excavations, meaning the project had to be continually modified. In any event, the very orthodox positions of the Jewish community deserve great respect, making us do wholly unprecedented work to ensure that the monumental restrictions, together with the restrictions of a theological nature, were adopted by the project. Rabbi Kalmanowitz continues to tell us that this is the only case in the world where buildings are restructured above a Jewish cemetery. So he too sees our project as a major challenge, a sort of 'derogation' of Jewish precepts, to which to respond with purely technical indications. Even though he's neither an engineer nor an architect, he's demonstrated that he knows how to have an excellent dialogue with us, but also with Alessandro Aliotta for the construction management, the structural engineer Nuccio Sangiuliano and the service engineer Angelo Puorto.

URBAN REGENERATION AND COLLECTIVE MEMORY

PAC **We'll now discuss some recent projects where this theme of collective memory, already very present in Mantua, appears to be central in the activation of urban regeneration processes. The first project that you're now realising in Messina concerns the regeneration of the so-called 'Città del Ragazzo', (the Boy's City), a complex of buildings constructed between 1951 and the 1980s by Padre Nino Trovato** [28] **for the care and education of orphans. The context is that of a hill with an extraordinary military building on the top, the so-called 'Castellaccio', dating back to 1500 but profoundly transformed and damaged over the subse-**

quent centuries. The project is very interesting on account of its social dimension, because it's a matter of transforming an orphanage into a very different welfare institution. What does the functional programme envisage?

VC This private structure founded by Padre Nino has become public property of the Metropolitan City of Messina, who wanted to convert it into a new type of welfare organisation: the 'After us' location, in the sense of imagining care to disabled people whose parents are the guardians of their lives. What will happen to these people when they lose their parents, or they're abandoned, for a thousand different reasons? 'After us' is the city that becomes the guarantor of this social vocation. For us as architects, it was very interesting to meet the entire disability association sector of Messina, and subsequently to introduce new types of buildings to respond to this need to design spaces to cater for the necessary functions.

PAC **As this is a very heterogeneous building complex, how do you define a precise project strategy in order to decide what to conserve and what to demolish?**

VC The project came about with the Metropolitan City of Messina administration's desire to conserve most of the buildings, while after the first investigations it was immediately clear that many buildings, often also of limited architectural value, were completely impossible to recover as regards compliance with the anti-seismic regulations, which are particularly strict in Messina. For this reason, we identified the Castellaccio and the house of Padre Nino as the cornerstones of the memory of this location.

PAC **It's interesting to observe that this need for demolitions has led you to propose an apparently undersized plan, with a total disposition of masses fourteen thousand cubic metres less than the pre-existing volume. This appears to be a rather rare case in Italy, where as a tendency the public administrations never want to forego consolidated volumes. How did you succeed in convincing the administration of the need for a significant contraction of the construction?**

VC One of the first things the mayor told me, when we met for the first time, was that we had to do everything respecting the financing allocated, and I replied to him that I could only promise that to him provided we could agree on the need to reduce the existing disposition of masses. Reducing the heights of the volumes from six floors to three or four also offered a great opportunity to mitigate the speculative building consumption that had invaded the hill, and the Superintendence was a great help in convincing the client of the good quality of the proposal. We used two different lines of argument: the first concerned the budget and the construction costs, and we demonstrated that with the sums available it was only possible to realise works of quality for a more limited quantity of buildings. The second line of argument consisted of the workshop organised in Messina with all the associations, during which it clearly emerged that the new institution's functional programme had to be reduced compared to the previous institution.

PAC **How will the Castellaccio be restored?**

VC The building was in very poor static condition and had been rendered unrecognisable by the numerous additions made by Padre Nino, who'd built a school beside it **[29]**. We persuaded the mayor of the need to demolish all the building additions and to restore the Castellaccio, returning to its original profile of a fort with four bastions. The only innovation is the creation of a low steel and glass volume forming a kind of continuous cloister, open for various uses. This is the only building that will be managed directly by the Municipality and not by the associations.

PAC **The only other building that will be maintained and restored is the 'House of Padre Nino Trovato', a four-storey residential property with a decent standard of architecture, characterised by round columns and balconies. What will this building become?**

VC That was the building in the best condition, which Padre Nino built for himself, and it will become a building of memory. An inventory is being drafted, along with a survey of all the furnishings and artistic objects made by the boys in the various workshops, which are currently held in the buildings that will be demolished. Before the demolition, the photographer Mario Ferrara will conduct a photographic survey campaign. Objects and furniture will therefore be kept inside this building of memory.

PAC **I observe with interest that the demolished volumes will be replaced by three compact buildings, three or four storeys high, which also create an interesting dialogue with the restored house of Padre Nino** [30]**, of which they take up the theme of the continuous balconies. What materials do you intend to use?**

VC Our architectural idea is to enhance the tectonics of the buildings with a prefabricated concrete panel covering, coloured with pigments, and to create a system of terracing and plazas, for which the landscape architect Michelangelo Pugliese is doing very interesting work.

PAC **The theme of collective memory that we're discussing sometimes takes on a tragic connotation, as in the case of the project for the Polcevera Park in Genoa, drafted in response to a competition called in 2019 in remembrance of the victims of the collapse of the Ponte Morandi and to regenerate the whole area located at the foot of the new viaduct designed by Renzo Piano. What were the salient elements of your proposal?**

GM It was necessary to combine actions on several levels, associating the idea of a park with that of a memorial, but also considering the overall regeneration of a large and complex area, which the Torrente Polcevera passes through and therefore with rather significant hydro-geological risks. We participated in the first phase with a multidisciplinary group, including the

28 PADRE NINO TROVATO IN FRONT OF THE ENTRANCE TO THE 'CITTÀ DEL RAGAZZO' (THE BOY'S CITY), IN MESSINA. ARCHIVE PHOTO.

29 AERIAL VIEW OF THE CASTELLACCIO WITH THE BUILDING ADDITIONS THAT WILL BE REMOVED.

30 HISTORIC PHOTO OF THE 'CITTÀ DEL RAGAZZO' (THE BOY'S CITY), WITH THE HOUSE OF PADRE NINO IN THE CENTRE.

landscape architect Michelangelo Pugliese, while in the second phase we proposed investing the sum made available with the reimbursement of expenses to organise a three-day workshop in Genoa, with a work group extended to include a whole series of associations and personalities capable of telling us the lived history of this location. I remember in particular the Committee of inhabitants, a number of engineers and workers from Ansaldo, which was already established in the late 19th century in the Val Polcevera, but also the head teacher of a school, who introduced us to the very important theme of the relationship between schools and neighbourhoods. We understood that only an approach starting from the bottom up, from the people and from the community, could in some way compensate for what happened, with the decision taken from above to build the new viaduct. In this circumstance, following a spirit of service to the community, we imagined a series of possibilities, with few elements and small, measured interventions, capable of being integrated and enabling the existing to survive. The experience of the workshop was decisive in enabling us to come into direct contact with the inhabitants, the true actors of this very dramatic reality. Among the founding elements of our project, I remember the creation of a pedestrian viaduct **[31]**, a kind of transept connecting the various levels, and the idea suggested by Michelangelo Pugliese to plant forty-three Ginkgo Bilobas together with the inhabitants, one for each victim; this is a tree that withstood the bomb in Hiroshima, and that possesses this evocative power of resistance to grief and tragedy. To represent this particular process of participation of inhabitants, we imagined a comic strip story **[32]** describing certain moments of the participatory workshop.

VC This theme of participation in architecture projects is one that's very dear to us, and that we find in some of our more recent projects, particularly that for the Creative Hangars in Livorno. We imagined a participatory path with the municipal administration on the theme of decommissioning, offering the community the possibility of reappropriating certain decommissioned buildings, also in a first transition phase, to use them as sites for entertainment and social gatherings. I think the architecture of our time must increasingly become the interpreter of the needs of the community.

PAC **On the theme of memory, however, I don't think the competition brief had been very clear regarding the possibility of maintaining some fragments of Ponte Morandi. How did you deal with this issue?**

GM In the on-site inspection in the first phase, there were still some pieces of the stayed structure of the bridge **[33]**, whereas when we returned for the second phase, there was no longer anything, and we experienced this as a major absence, because the Ponte Morandi designed something important in that space. Our feeling was that the sky had changed shape. Renzo Piano probably did the right thing with his viaduct, so simple and essential; he didn't want to be in competition with Morandi's work, but now in Genoa the sky has changed when you walk down along the Polcevera. We can state that on the theme of memory a fragment of the bridge could have been maintained, there were too many polemics and the whole operation was probably done in too much of a hurry. There also remains the regret that Morandi

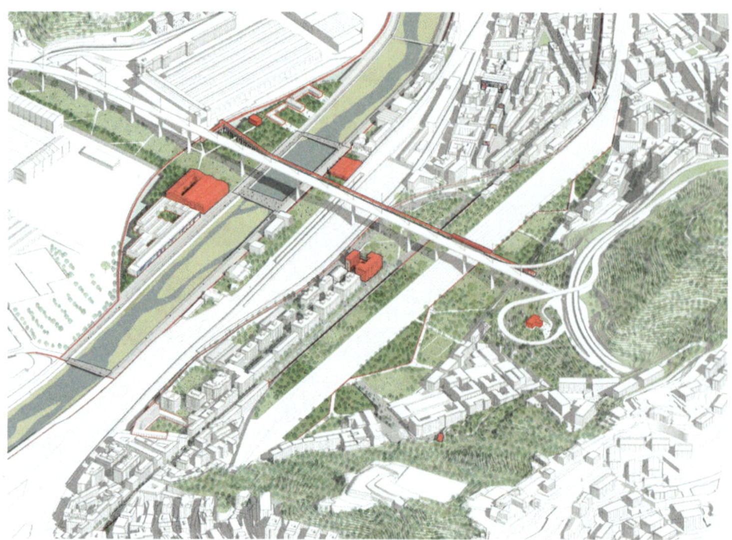

31 AXONOMETRY OF THE COMPETITION PROJECT FOR THE POLCEVERA PARK IN GENOA, 2019, WITH THE PROJECT INTERVENTIONS IN RED.

32 COMIC-STRIP STORY OF THE PARTICIPATORY WORKSHOP FOR THE POLCEVERA PARK, DRAWINGS BY LORENZO PALADINO.

33 FRAGMENTS OF THE STAYED STRUCTURE OF THE MORANDI BRIDGE AFTER THE COLLAPSE IN 2018.

himself had clearly written that it was necessary to guarantee careful maintenance over time. In Milan too there were those who wanted to cancel out the memory by eliminating the original aluminium façade of the Pirelli Skyscraper and making a new one; we maintained and restored it. In Genoa an opportunity to maintain an element of memory has been lost.

PAC **Even though you didn't win the competition for the Polcevera Park, was what you experimented with therefore reinvested in Livorno?**

VC Competitions are the biggest investment, also economic, that we make at our studio, but they're undoubtedly the best instruments and opportunities for doing research, which is often transformed into a useful advance for our experimentation. For the competition in Genoa we invited Luisa Fatigati to collaborate with us; she's excellent as a cultural and social mediator, so she helped us to build this participation, succeeding in defining subjects and ways of posing questions that persuaded the inhabitants to welcome us and talk to us. Our desire is always to develop the demand through the response of the project, a client's demand that may originate from a competition, an institution or a private individual. This characterises our way of working, to cultivate an ever more extensive demand, hence the idea that the city is our true client.

PAC **So let's talk now about this latest project for the Creative Hangars in Livorno, which envisages the conversion of the former warehouses and bus depots** [34] **into a cultural programme and for the associations. You cited this project earlier in relation to the theme of participatory design. How are citizens and associations involved in the public debate on this project?**

VC Before the design competition the Municipality of Livorno had done some very interesting preparatory work, and the various possible intended uses had emerged through participatory workshops **[35]**. This process of participation is now continuing, after we developed our design proposals; the citizens are continually updated on the intended uses and the Municipality is working directly with the associations that will handle the management of the spaces. It's starting from users' real needs that we're designing the individual architectures.

PAC **What are the relations between the hangars that are upgraded and the small volumes that you're adding in front of the multi-storey car park** [36]**, which evoke the typical shed template of the historical warehouses?**

VC Our winning idea was not to consider this multi-storey car park solely for its function; it seemed to us, in fact, to be a waste to construct such a large building when, in its 2030–50 Plan, the Municipality of Livorno has already envisaged reducing car use and developing the pedestrianisation of the city. Our idea, very simple and inspired by very interesting contemporary experiences such as the car park built in Miami by Herzog & De Meuron, was that a

34 PHOTORENDERING OF THE PROJECT FOR THE CREATIVE HANGARS IN LIVORNO, 2024.

35 PARTICIPATORY WORKSHOP ORGANIZED BY THE MUNICIPAL AUTHORITY OF LIVORNO INSIDE THE FORMER BUS DEPOSIT ON 15 DECEMBER 2022, AS A PRELIMINARY TO THE PLANNING PHASE.

36 PERSPECTIVE OF THE MULTI-STOREY CAR PARK WITH THE VOLUMES FOR CREATIVE ACTIVITIES.

37 PERSPECTIVE OF THE PEDESTRIAN WALKWAY BETWEEN VIA MEYER AND THE NEW PIAZZA, WITH THE PROJECTING VOLUME OF THE RESIDENCES FOR ARTISTS ON THE LEFT.

car park can also become a public place, with a hanging garden on the roof that can be hired for events. The small volumes at the base of the car park on the ground floor, covered in stretched plate, are designed to offer further creative spaces.

PAC **Do they therefore form an urban threshold between car park and piazza?**

VC They do indeed create a transition, but they also define an interesting frontage facing onto the green piazza designed by João Nunes and Andrea Menegotto for PROAP, this too devised as a space for music and creative activities **[37]**.

PAC **Shall we conclude this chapter here, which is the one that also closes the book?**

GM I'd like to add a final consideration. All these recent projects are the result of design competitions and framework agreements that take on a major public value, because they attempt to resolve problems for communities and for territories, also through State institutions such as the Police, the Finance Police or the State Property Agency. The procedures count a great deal, but I believe that there's a capacity of Corvino + Multari that must be recognised, our capacity to endeavour on each occasion to transcend the framework imposed by the procedures, not in the sense of distorting them, but rather in always taking a step forward to make the project more interesting, also for the profiles of the architecture that it must propose. Will we succeed? All being projects still in progress, it's a topic that's yet to be proven. What I do feel I can talk about are the works accomplished to date, because the proof of the construction is everything in architecture, because it's in the construction that all that aspects that are also the result of compromises reside. And in the end, as always, what you build can't have subtitles.

PAC **This seems an excellent conclusion to me. What has characterised your work as architects over these thirty years, from the first projects to the latest ones, is precisely this fact of always working critically inside the frameworks of reality, adapting yourselves innovatively to procedures and conditions of production of architecture that have changed a great deal in these last thirty years. I think that the strongly ethical dimension of your work, in your relations with your clients, with the cities, and in your defence of the public value of every architecture, emerges very clearly from our dialogues.**

1 Heritage Foundation for Preservation of Jewish Cemeteries (HFPJC), with headquarters in Brooklyn, NYC. Cf. https://hfpjc.com/.

NEW HEADQUARTERS OF THE REVENUE AGENCY
CAGLIARI, 2019–27

The project, part of the programme for the urban upgrading of the Sant'Avendrace district promoted by the Municipality of Cagliari, will transform the former Simeto barracks into the new pole of the Ministry of the Economy and Finances, showcasing the historical and archaeological context with an approach combining past and present. The area of around 29,000 square metres, once used by the Italian Air Force for warehousing, is characterised by the presence of numerous buildings, some of historical interest, and falls within an urban fabric abounding in archaeological artefacts. The project presents itself as a developing landscape, where green spaces and archaeology define the transformation of the public spaces along Via Elmas and Via Simeto, creating a strong bond with the existing urban fabric and favouring connections with the neighbourhood. The public space is conceived as a neutral matrix, which interacts autonomously with the architectural system and is reminiscent of the organisation of an archaeological site.

The project is structured into three main levels: an underground level, associated with the presence of potential archaeological finds, an intermediary level, on which the project is developed as land conceived as space for crossing and use, and a raised level, devoted to buildings to be repurposed and the new constructions. Some buildings of no value or that are non-functional to the new intended use will be demolished, while the headquarter building, of historical value, will be conserved after structural adaptations. A new building will be built in continuity with the former headquarter warehouse, defining a new volumetric order. All the buildings are characterised by an architectural language enabling their clear identification and use, aiming at transparency as an aesthetic and functional value, favouring the entry of natural light into the internal spaces and referencing the concept of the openness and accessibility of public institutions. The entire complex is designed in accordance with high building quality and energy efficiency standards with the aim of achieving LEED certification.

DIREZIONE
PROVINCIALE

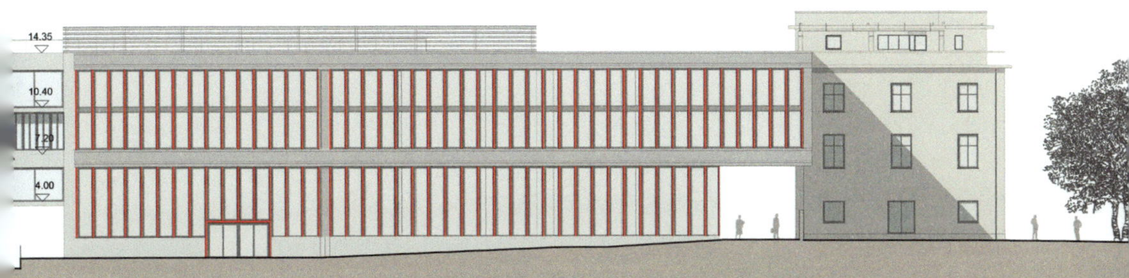
14.35
10.40
7.20
4.00

CITADEL OF SECURITY
NAPLES, 2018–30

The project concerns the redevelopment of the former Boscariello barracks in Naples with the realisation of a coordinated system of buildings that will host all the police's functions: offices, shared and individual accommodation, canteen, bar and multipurpose room, shooting range, storerooms, garages, gymnasium, auditorium, gatehouse and security services, plus technological services of control and management. The area of around 80,000 square metres fits within a landscape context consisting of the protected areas of Campi Flegrei and the Parco delle Colline in Naples. Starting from a value judgment on the context, the project configures the new Citadel of Security as a new centrality in the urban system, with public spaces, green areas and a historical building upgraded for exhibition uses.

The main objective of the project has been to characterise the new citadel as a series of buildings the structuring of which takes account of the functions to be combined according to type of activity. From the point of view of the recognisability and identity of the urban plan, the aim was mainly to characterise the frontage facing onto Via Miano, where a public area is envisaged for facilities (tree-lined car parks, a green area and a piazza), which has its fulcrum in the upgrading of the building that formed the original entrance to the Boscariello barracks, with a new use as a popular exhibition space on the theme of legality. At the back of the upgraded building, a curtain of buildings is formed for offices that are open to the public, at the top of which is the volume of the auditorium. The second area consists of a sequence of three buildings for offices with courtyards along the axis that develops transversally from Via Miano to Via Ciccotti and terminates with the tall building that marks a point of reference of the urban plan on a territorial scale. The third area that forms the heart of the internal activity of the complex consists of the central plaza, facing onto which are the building for the main common services along with the building for shared accommodation and changing rooms. The central plaza also forms the main outdoor area for exercises. The last area, directly served by vehicle access along Via Ciccotti, is intended to contain the garages and the refuelling zone.

Polizia di Stato

MANTOVA HUB
MANTUA, 2018–26

The Mantova Hub project implements a strategy to stitch back together the city of Mantua in urbanistic and socioeconomic terms thanks to the upgrading of underused and deteriorating spaces, creating a new system of public plazas with specific urban functions that utilise the relationship between the city and Lago Inferiore. With a total surface of intervention of 90,000 square metres, the different areas are connected together by a system of vehicle, pedestrian and cycle routes, being organised around four new plazas. These four new plazas sum up some of the main characteristics and values of the Mantuan territory: its relationship with water, with land, the presence of nature and culture, in a relationship with the daily life of the city and with its cultural and production routes.

Piazza della Terra in the area of San Nicolò showcases the historic buildings of the Gradaro military complex, including a munitions store from 1739, through the realisation of a covered portico and optimisation of the functional distribution, with the function of a centre for work and research (offices, training centres, municipal infopoint and centre for people with disabilities). Particular attention has been devoted to the need to respect and value the grounds of the old Jewish cemetery in the middle of the area. Piazza del Pensiero is structured around the decommissioned industrial area of the historic former Ceramic Factory, an example of 20th-century industrial archaeology that has been regenerated to host the Mantegna Technical Institute, with seismic adaptation and energy sustainability interventions. After the demolition of the pre-existing reinforced concrete structure on Via Grayson, the area of Piazza Fiera Catena has been transformed into a large public green space designed for sports, leisure and social gatherings, facing onto which is the new gymnasium conceived to enable various sports activities to be practised, complete with a grandstand with seating for around a hundred and spaces for the various neighbourhood activities. Located near the Bosco Virgiliano and the Parco del Mincio, the Valletta Valsecchi area will be transformed into Piazza del Paesaggio, a large green space with educational and play functions. The project envisages an urban forestation intervention to mitigate the urban heat islands and a park with facilities for residents and visitors, together with the redevelopment of the former school building in order to welcome around a thousand students.

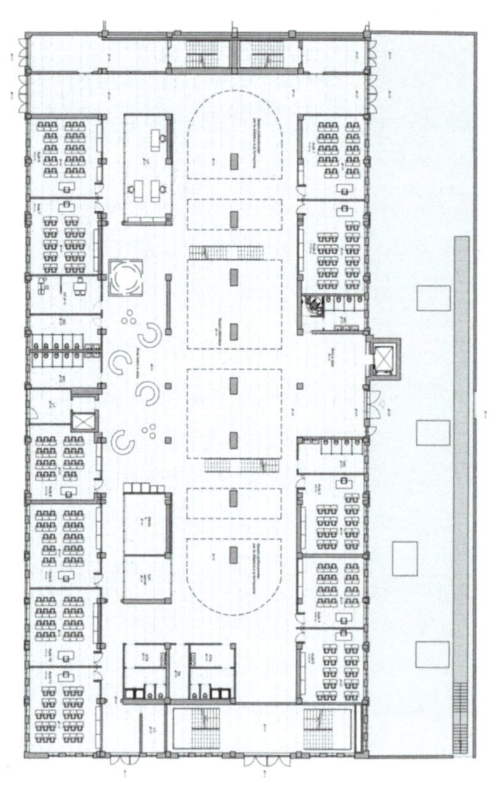

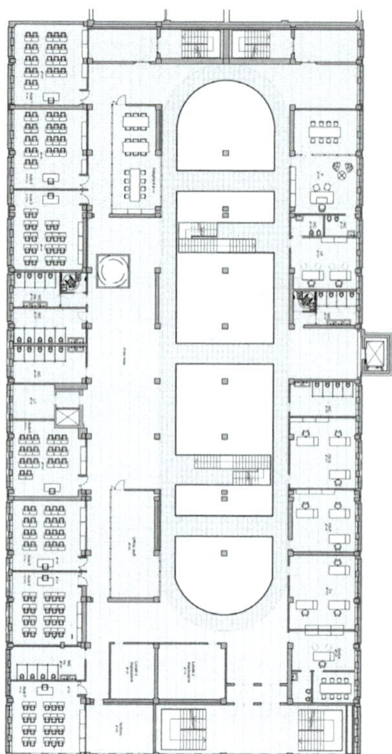

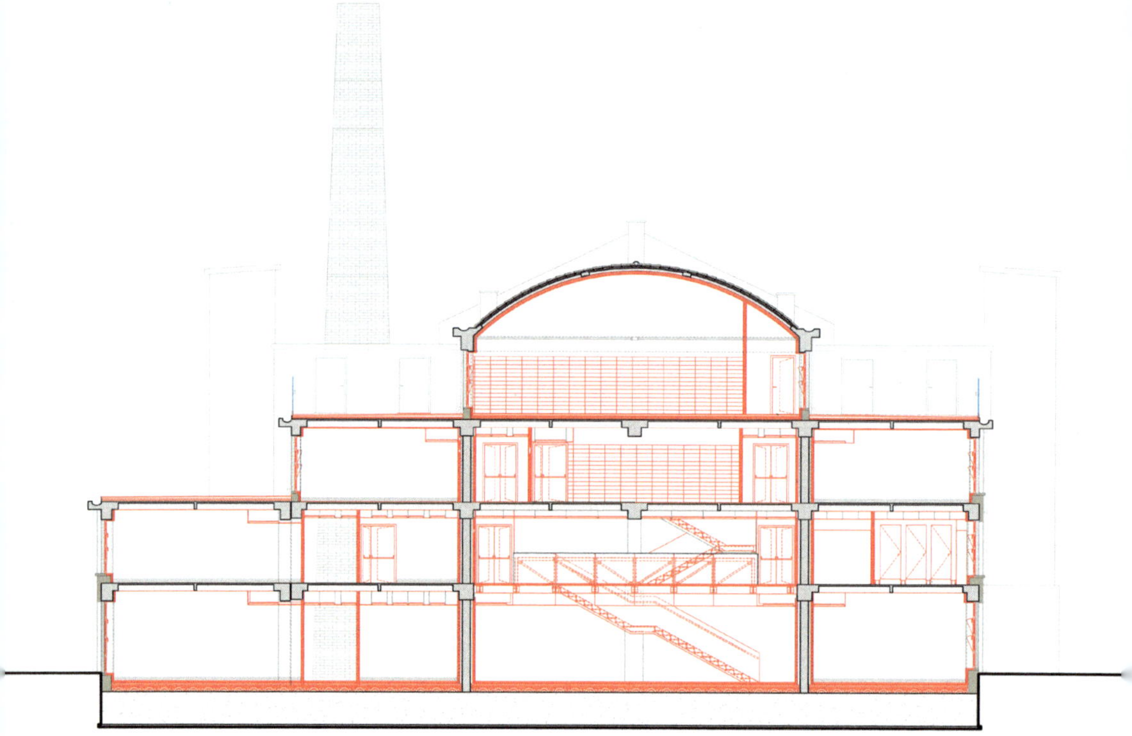

Santa Maria del Gradaro
Viale Salvador Allende
Vicolo Maestro
Vicolo San Nicolò
Vicolo Maestro

'AFTER US' WELFARE CENTRE
MESSINA, 2023–28

The project concerns the upgrading of an area of around 43,000 square metres on the hillsides of the Gravitelli district in Messina, where between the 1950s and 1980s the 'Città del Ragazzo' (the Boy's City) was created at the wishes of neighbourhood parish priest Padre Nino Trovato. The area is characterised by a significant presence of vegetation extending along the slopes, at the top of which stands the Castellaccio, the city of Messina's oldest castle. Consistent with the original welfare mission, the project will enable a new pole of reception, training and assistance for social integration to be created, the 'Dopo di Noi' (After us) Welfare Centre, which will offer social inclusion, training and autonomy services for people with disabilities. The Castellaccio will have the various building additions removed, be restored and restructured with the addition of a glazed portico around the central courtyard, to earmark it for use by the public, together with green spaces and sports facilities.

While many buildings will be demolished as they have seriously deteriorated and no longer comply with the current anti-seismic regulations, the new centre will be developed around the restructured building that was Padre Nino Trovato's House and three new buildings for training and support in working towards autonomy for people with disabilities. The new buildings located at the foot of the hill are delicately inserted into the surrounding housing context, respecting the natural monumentality through a system of squares and terracing structures. All the functional arrangements envisaged are contained inside the three new buildings, which are organised according to the typology with courtyard, which is preferable from the structural and housing comfort points of view. Gathering around a central courtyard forms the typological basis of the project and the meaning of the entire intervention: the courtyard is gathering, meeting and relating, turning the gaze towards a future of social inclusion through support, welfare and coexistence with individuals with disorders of the physical–sensory type or coming from difficult family contexts.

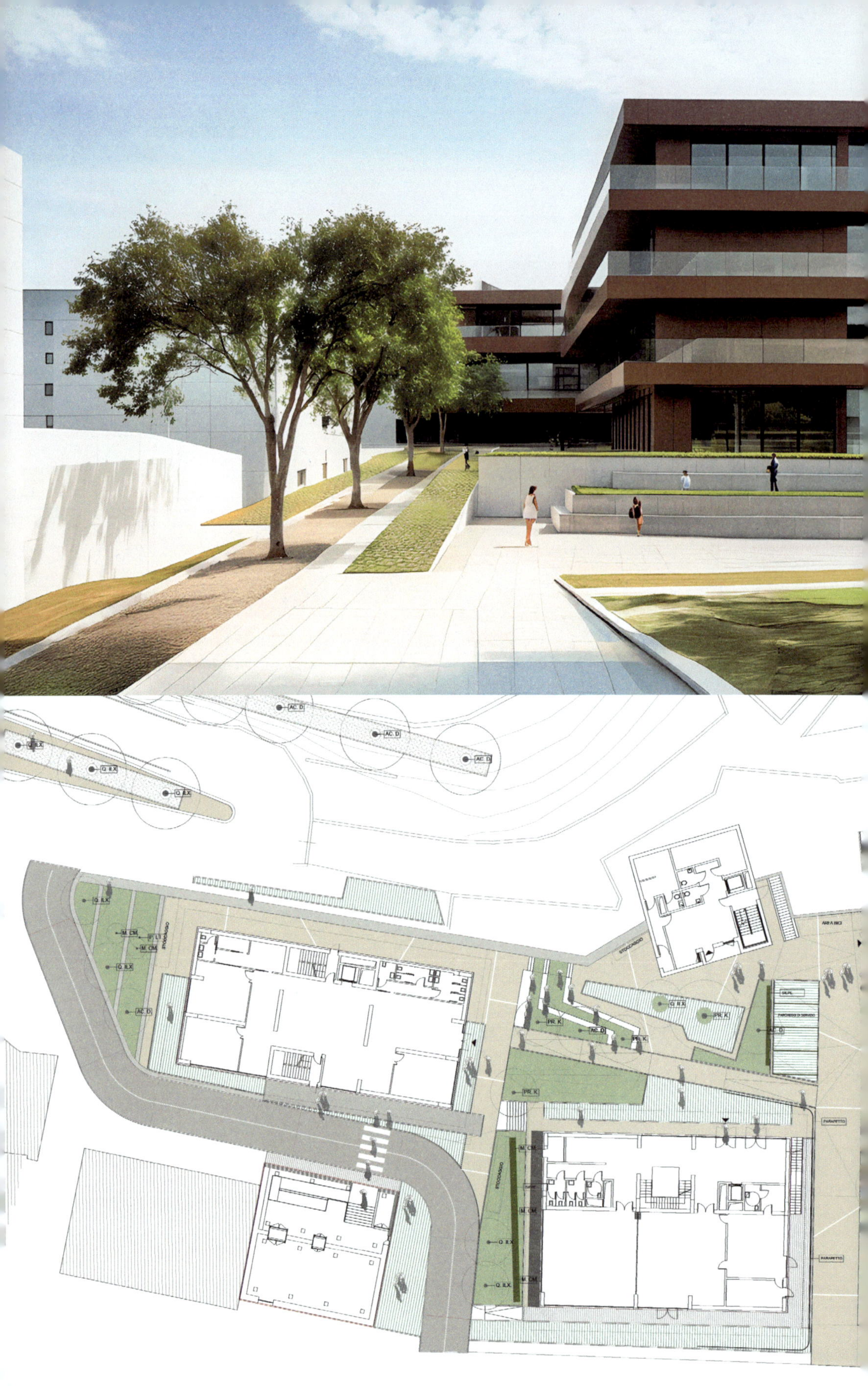

AC. D
Q. ILX
M. CM
PR. K
STOCCAGGIO
AREA BICI
PARCHEGGI DI SERVIZIO
PARAPETTO
PARAPETTO

PIAZZALE DON NINO
STRADA CARRABILE DI SERVIZIO
PARAPETTO
SIEPE
AREA BICI

POLCEVERA PARK
GENOA, 2019

The competition project is based on the conviction that memory cannot refer solely to a location—a square, a street, a monument—but to the entire sphere of intervention. It is proposed, therefore, to conceive the future Parco del Ponte as a widespread, multi-scale intervention involving the construction of the park, the public space and the existing buildings of the neighbourhoods of the Val Polcevera. The territory of Genoa, in particular the Val Polcevera, presents fragilities due to the interweaving of basic geo-morphological conditions, artificialisation of the surface hydrographic network and a high level of soil-sealing of the urban and peri-urban terrain. The project proposal aims to trigger a process of upgrading of the neighbourhood, stitching the urban spaces together with the rural and natural ones and favouring a better interaction between citizens and ecosystem, and to create the conditions for an aware reappropriation of the spaces beneath the bridge, marked by a strong symbolic value that characterises them as a natural memorial.

The primary act of regeneration will be the planting of around five thousand trees and bushes, which, in clusters and parts, will build up the new spatiality of the valley over time. Among these, forty-three monumental ginkgo biloba trees will be planted in memory of the victims of the bridge collapse. In this reconfiguration of trees and plants, a fundamental role is played by the transept, a central void beneath the new motorway viaduct, defined by thick vegetation along the north and south edges. The transept is the place where absence becomes memory, it is the structure of the park and the beginning of the Square of Memory, which is configured as an active, social space, but also as a symbolic element, with long ridges of green stone of the Val Polcevera that will bear inscriptions of the stories of the victims of the collapse, in collaboration with the committee of relatives. The horizontal Gymnasium, a long, red-painted steel cycle path and pedestrian walkway, will connect up all the longitudinal filaments of the valley, and will run alongside the transept to the north, in the shadow of the new viaduct designed by Renzo Piano. This walkway will become an artistic and narrative itinerary, with murals that will tell of the historical and social memory of the territory, the naturalistic and landscape context and the historical and cultural values of the community.

APPENDIX

VINCENZO CORVINO AND GIOVANNI MULTARI'S WRITINGS

G. Multari, Il fiume e la città, *Progettazione urbana*, 1 (1994), 17–8.

V. Corvino, 'Abitazioni alla Giudecca di Gino Valle: riflessioni su un metodo', *Progettazione urbana*, 2 (1994), 14–5.

V. Corvino, 'Architettura religiosa: tipologia di un simbolo', in C. M. De Feo (ed.), *Pietrelcina. Memoria, tradizione, identità* (Naples, 1995), 91–101.

G. Multari, 'Il disegno dello spazio urbano', in C. M. De Feo (ed.), *Pietrelcina. Memoria, tradizione, identità* (Naples, 1995), 115–39.

G. Multari, 'Cosenza, il risveglio di una città. Sei progetti di riqualificazione urbana', *Edilizia popolare*, 259 (1998), 18–41.

G. Multari, 'Trasformazione ed aree dismesse: il progetto per la nuova Tate Gallery a Londra', in A. Izzo (ed.), *Berlino/Londra/Madrid. Un'esperienza di progettazione triennale* (Naples, 1999), 48–53.

V. Corvino, E. S. Glückstein, *Klaus Kada. Un concorso di architettura dall'idea alla costruzione* (Naples, 2000).

V. Corvino, G. Multari, *I rivocati: programma integrato di interventi a Cosenza* (Castellammare di Stabia, 2002).

V. Corvino, G. Multari, 'Working lunch', *Ottagono*, 156 (2002), 178.

V. Corvino, G. Multari, C. Falci, 'Gio Ponti. Il grattacielo Pirelli. Il restauro delle Facciate: Estratto dalla relazione di progetto del restauro delle facciate', *Recupero e Conservazione*, 52 (2003), 47–55.

G. Multari, 'La biblioteca, luogo della città contemporanea', in A. Izzo (ed.), *Napoli, didattica e progetto: due casi studio* (Naples, 2004), 101–9.

V. Corvino, 'Berlino: riflessioni sul futuro delle aree centrali', in A. Izzo (ed.), *Berlino/Londra/Madrid. Un'esperienza di progettazione triennale* (Naples, 2004), 10–26.

V. Corvino, 'Il Museo nella condizione urbana contemporanea', in A. Izzo (ed.), *Napoli: didattica e progetto*, i (Naples, 2004), 84–99.

V. Corvino, G. Multari, 'Esperienze di acclimatazione', in VV.AA., *Spazi per l'acclimatazione. 11 progetti a confronto per un'area dismessa* (Naples, 2004), 15–6.

V. Corvino, G. Multari, 'I progetti del Laboratorio – Gruppo 2', in V. Cappiello (ed.), *Alla ricerca dell'urbano. Scritti e progetti sul recupero della periferia*, ii (Naples, 2005), 193–5.

V. Corvino, G. Multari, 'Beyond the box', in L. Affuso (ed.), *Frame & mutations: visioni di architettura* (Rome, 2005), 94–101.

V. Corvino, G. Multari, R. Vanacore, G. F. Frascino, G. Moliterni, *Alberto Izzo: Insegnare l'architettura. 16+1 tesi in mostra* (Naples, 2005).

V. Corvino, G. Multari, 'Bacoli', in M. Casamonti (ed.), *20.06 overview sull'architettura italiana. Sud: learning from south. Paesaggi urbani del Mediterraneo* (Milan, 2006), 184–5.

G. Catoggio (interview edited by), 'Il progetto come luogo della conoscenza', *Progettare*, 28 (2006), 82–5.

V. Corvino, G. Multari, G. Leoni, 'I Grattacieli della Romagna', in A. Trentin (ed.), *I Grattacieli della Romagna* (Bologna, 2006) 120–71.

A. Izzo, F. Izzo, V. Corvino, G. Multari, R. Vanacore, 'Genealogie. Il magistero della prassi', *D'A. D'Architettura*, 34 (2007), 142–51.

'CORVINO+MULTARI', in A. Alessi, *Italy now? Country Positions in Architecture* (New York: Cornell University, 2007), i, 54–7.

V. Corvino, G. Multari, E. Vasumi Roveri, 'Laboratorio e Restauro. Percorsi nuovi di ricerca alla Facoltà di Architettura Aldo Rossi di Cesena', *Progetti*, 12 (2007), 150–5.

V. Fisichella, C. De Simone, 'Intervista a Corvino + Multari', in M. A. Crippa (ed.), *Il restauro del grattacielo Pirelli* (Milano, 2007), 55–8.

V. Corvino, G. Multari, 'Il progetto come conoscenza', in A. Cavani, A. Zamboni (eds.), *Il progetto come conoscenza: laboratorio di restauro architettonico B* (Bologna, 2008), 27–35.

V. Corvino, G. Multari, 'Schizzi di Architettura', in F. Serrazanetti, M. Schubert (eds.), *La mano dell'architetto* (Milan, 2009), i, 96–7.

V. Corvino, G. Multari, 'I colori delle idee. Progetti come conoscenza di storie, contesti e luoghi', in M. Balzani, F. Maietti (eds.), *Colore e materia* (Rimini, 2010), 221–6.

V. Corvino, 'Memorie di futuro', *Architetti Napoletani* (2011), 14.

G. Multari, 'La residenza da modello tipo-morfologico a nuovo paesaggio', in VV.AA., *Abitare il nuovo/abitare di nuovo ai tempi della crisi* (Naples, 2012), 1101–10.

G. Multari, *La città e il fiume. Tra geografia e architettura* (Cosenza, 2013).

G. Multari, 'Giovanni Multari. Architetto', in A. Calderoni (ed.), *Existenzmaximum. Il necessario* (Naples, 2013), 69.

G. Multari, F. Izzo, V. Corvino, *Yearbook 2010/2011. Master di II livello Progettazione di Eccellenza per la Città Storica* (Naples, 2013).

G. Multari, *Alberto Izzo e la Facoltà Teologica di Napoli* (Naples, 2013).

G. Multari, 'Architettura della città: Napoli lo spazio della città che cambia', *EDA – Esempi di architettura*, July 2013, online edition.

G. Multari, 'Il restauro del grattacielo Pirelli', in A. Caruso di Spaccaforno, S. Caprio, C. Santoro (eds.), *Il grattacielo / La città per l'uomo: Il Grattacielo. Dove? Per chi?* (Como, 2013), 12–21.

G. Multari, 'Campania Felix, Smaller Towns, Vernacular and Sustainability', in C. Mileto, F. Vegas, L. Garcia Soriano, V. Cristini (eds.), *VERSUS 2014. International Conference on Vernacular Heritage, Sustainability and Earthen Architecture* (Valencia, 2014), 527–30.

G. Multari (ed.), 'The cloister of Monteoliveto in Naples', *Esempi di architettura*, 1 (2014), 27–44.

G. Multari, 'I progetti' and 'Il restauro del grattacielo Pirelli', in A. Picone (ed.), *Progetti per Via Nuova Marina* (Naples, 2014), 60–3, 92–9.

V. Corvino, G. Multari, 'Via Cenni, Milano', in G. Ferri, L. Pacucci, E. Pero (eds.), *Nuove forme per l'abitare sociale* (Milano, 2014), 99.

G. Multari, R. Capozzi, F. Visconti, 'Imparare facendo, fare insegnando. Progetti per l'area FS-Sistemi Urbani a San Giovanni a Teduccio – Napoli', in M. Raitano (ed.), *La formazione dell'architetto. Problemi e prospettive* (Rome, 2015), 66–8.

G. Multari, 'Introduzione' and 'Misura e strategie di densificazione', in G. Multari (ed.), *La grande dimensione in architettura. Il Centro Direzionale di Napoli* (Rome, 2015), 18–22, 25–34.

G. Multari, 'Recensione a: Gio Ponti. Amate l'Architettura', *Op. Cit.*, 153 (2015), 50–3.

G. Multari, G. Cafiero (eds.), *Architetture resistenti. Progetti per la musica nel Rione sanità / Resistant Architectures* (Rome, 2016).

V. Corvino, G. Multari, 'Il valore del progetto', *L'Architetto*, February 2016.

V. Corvino, G. Multari, 'Imparare da Napoli. Da Nea-Polis a Metro-Polis', *The Plan*, 94 (2016), 16–9.

V. Corvino, 'Il ruolo dello spazio pubblico nella città storica', in G.M. Cennamo (ed.), *Processi di analisi per strategie di valorizzazione dei paesaggi urbani* (Rome, 2016).

G. Multari, 'The Architecture of the City Contended Between History and Contemporary', in G. Strappa, A. R. D. Amato, A. Camporeale (eds.), *City as organism new visions for urban life* (Rome, 2016), 145–54.

G. Multari, 'L'esperienza della costruzione', in *Corvino + Multari. Esperienze dell'architettura / Architecture Experiences 2007–2017* (Rovereto, 2017), 28–37.

V. Corvino, 'I progetti e le città / The projects and the cities', in *Corvino + Multari, Esperienze dell'architettura / Architecture Experiences 2007–2017* (Rovereto, 2017), 18–27.

G. P. Scaglione, 'Conversazione con Vincenzo Corvino e Giovanni Multari', in *Corvino + Multari. Esperienze dell'architettura / Architecture Experiences 2007–2017* (Rovereto, 2017), 139–55.

G. Multari, 'Living as a student', *The Plan*, 103 (2017), 99–102.

G. Multari, 'Il Centro Direzionale di Napoli. L'esperienza del Laboratorio di Progettazione', in A. Antoniciello, M. Russo (eds.), *Meridiani paralleli* (Florence, 2017), 50–3.

G. Multari, 'Alberto Calderoni. Appunti dal Visibile', *Firenze Architettura* (2017), 207.

G. Multari, 'Misura e dimensione dello spazio pubblico nell'antica Neapolis', in M. Losasso, *Principi insediativi e progetto ambientale* (Naples, 2017), 37–49.

L. Cupelloni, 'Il Grattacielo Pirelli. Conversazione con Vincenzo Corvino e Giovanni Multari', in L. Cupelloni, *Materiali del Moderno* (Rome, 2017), 265–8.

G. Multari, 'Design Strategies and Non-Standard Territories. The Resilience of the Domitian Coastline', *The Plan Journal*, 2 (2017), 669–83.

V. Corvino, G. Multari, *The Strategy of Order* (Divisare Books n. 149; Rome, 2018).

G. Multari, 'I grattacieli balneari della Romagna', *ANANKE*, 83 (2018), 137–40.

G. Multari (ed.), *Living as a student. Nuove residenze per studenti nel centro antico di Napoli* (Naples, 2018).

G. Multari, 'Misura e dimensione dello spazio pubblico dell'antica Neapolis', in M. Losasso (ed.), *Principi insediativi e progetto ambientale. Conoscenza e indirizzi per la valorizzazione del sistema dei vuoti del Centro Antico di Napoli* (Naples, 2018), 37–49.

G. Multari, 'La Piccola America. Rosarno, realtà territoriale non-standard', in P. Scaglione, *Città incompiute. Orti, paesaggi, nature negate e disegnate* (Catanzaro, 2018), 182–5.

G. Multari, O. Niglio (eds.), *The Resistance of Architecture* (Rome, 2018).

G. Multari, 'Ascoltare l'edificio. L'eredità del Grattacielo Pirelli', *Abitare la terra*, 50 (2019), 128–9.

G. Multari, 'The Large scale in Architecture. Il centro direzionale di Napoli', in M. Falsetti, *Paesaggi oltre il paesaggio* (Syracuse, 2019), 199–203.

G. Multari, 'Medma', in F. Messina, L. Zerella, *La città dell'inclusione* (Spoleto, 2019), 74–5.

G. Multari, 'Prefazione', in F. Pelma, *Interpretare l'ambiente rurale. Il caso della Cascina Palma nel Parco Agricolo Sud Milano* (Ariccia, 2019), 10–3.

G. Multari, 'Decumano maximus, Neapolis urban shape', in C. Fontaine, R. Valente, V. D'Ambrosio, *NAPLES lab*, (Louvain, 2019), 74–5.

M. A. Perletti (interview edited by), 'V. Corvino: The City as a Client', *Il giornale dell'Architettura*, 12 May 2019, online edition.

G. Multari, F. Izzo, C. Didonna, 'Abitare l'antica Neapolis', in C. Didonna, *Attraversamenti. Il complesso di Donnaromita e vico Orilia, Napoli* (Canterano, 2019), 12–5.

G. Multari (ed.), *Architettura Alto Adige. Bergmeisterwolf – MoDusArchitects* (exhibition catalogue; Rome, 2020).

G. Multari, G. De Martino, 'Introduzione', in F. Cinque, *Interpretare l'architettura del Novecento. La Mostra d'Oltremare di Napoli* (Canterano, 2020), 10–2.

G. Multari, 'Abitare il presente', in P. Scaglione, *'ArteSila': Ecological Urban Design – Quaderno di metodo, progetto, strategia, didattica* (Rovereto, 2021), 56–7.

G. Multari, 'Banchi di Prova: spazi della formazione per il polo dell'infanzia di Bari', in Apulia Region, *Spazi per crescere. I concorsi di progettazione dei Poli per l'infanzia Zerosei in Puglia* (Bari, 2021), 91–2.

A. Calatroni (interview edited by), 'Corvino + Multari. L'architettura dialoga con Sant'Agostino', *Luce*, 335 (March 2021), 76–9.

V. Corvino, 'La Città nella Città', *AND*, 39 (2021), 66–9.
G. Multari, I. Cortesi (eds.), *Abitare e interpretare l'esistente. Case Nuove, Rosarno* (Naples, 2022).

G. Multari, M. Pugliese, 'Strategie e luoghi possibili per il parco fluviale di Rignano sull'Arno', in A. Iacomoni, *Paesaggi d'acqua* (Milan, 2022), 220–33.

V. Corvino, G. Multari, 'Involucro non è solo epidermide', *Domus*, 1070 (2022), 39.

G. Multari, 'Ascoltare l'edificio. L'eredità del Grattacielo Pirelli', in S. Acciai, D. Buonanno, B. Di Palma, C. Orfeo, *Per una nuova cura dell'abitare* (Naples, 2022), 38–9.

G. Multari, D. Ciaravolo, *Architetture d'acqua* (Rome, 2022).

G. Multari (ed.), *Italian Foreign Architecture – Baukuh e Onsitestudio* (exhibition catalogue; Rome, 2022).

G. Multari, M. Pugliese, *MEDMA. Architettura e paesaggio per l'esistente* (Rome, 2022).

G. Multari, *La Facoltà Teologica di Napoli* (Naples, 2022).

G. Multari, 'Strategie di progetto e realtà territoriali non standard', in M. Annese, L. Chiapperino, N. Martinelli, *Territori interni. Dilatazioni e interferenze nel periurbano* (Syracuse, 2023), 34–45.

G. Multari, R. Picone, 'L'Accademia Aeronautica di Pozzuoli: un paradigma della sperimentazione architettonica del secondo Novecento', in M. Caporusso, E. D. Cortese, N. D'Avino (eds.), *1923 | 2023. 100 anni di Accademia aeronautica* (Naples, 2023), 173–87.

G. Multari, A. D'Agostino, 'Un catalogo delle possibilità', in A. D'Agostino (ed.), *Across the Giant. Dal progetto di una ricerca alla ricerca di un progetto* (Naples, 2023), 78–83.

G. Multari, 'Interpretare l'esistente. Strategie e luoghi possibili', in M. Annese, L. Chiapperino, N. Martinelli, *Territori interni. Dilatazioni e interferenze nel periurbano* (Syracuse, 2023), 136–42.

G. Multari, C. Didonna, F. Montalto, 'Non finito da abitare. La porta del lago', in M. Annese, L. Chiapperino, N. Martinelli, *Territori interni. Dilatazioni e interferenze nel periurbano*, (Syracuse, 2023), 156–72.

V. Corvino, G. Multari, 'Imparare dalle città / Learning from Cities', in M. Mulazzani (ed.), *Costruire nella città / Building in the City. La Procura della Repubblica di Catanzaro /The Catanzaro Public Prosecutor's Office* (Milan, 2023), 63–8.

G. Multari, 'Prefazione', in F. Iuliano, M. Maurea, *Progettare nella città antica* (Naples, 2023), 7–9.

G. Multari, 'Prefazione', in L. Renzullo, *Il tempo sospeso del progetto: The New Mies Memorial Library* (Naples, 2023), 7–8.

G. Multari, M. Maurea, P. Ascione, V. Gioffrè, 'Living the Spaces of Post-Production: Design Scenarios for Bagnoli', in M. Capone, N. Galván Desvaux, L. Agustin-Hernandez, L. Fernández-Trapa (eds.), *Industrial Archaeology European Approach to Recovery Productive Memory* (Naples, 2024), 139–69.

G. Multari, F. Romeo, 'Concrete Long-Span Buildings' Adaptive Reuse: Sustainable Rethinking of Public Architecture and Industrial Heritage', in H. Torrent (ed.), *Modern Futures: Sustainable Development and Cultural Diversity* (Santiago de Chile, 2024), 337–44.

G. Multari, *La cultura del progetto* (Rome, 2024).

G. Multari (ed.), *Architettura pro esistente. Labics – Zamboni Associati* (exhibition catalogue; Rome, 2024).

G. Multari, F. Iuliano, 'Over-Modern Inhabiting: Different Scales of Densifications in the Casanova Building, Naples', *Rzut*, 37 (Warsaw 2024), 6–14.

G. Multari, 'Architettura come modificazione', *Architettura e città*, (*La cura dei luoghi*, 19; Milan, 2024), 31–4.

G. Multari, 'Il Progetto di Paesaggio come "opera aperta"', in V. Gioffrè, *Rigenerare naturale. Nuovi paesaggi postindustriali per Bagnoli tra didattica, ricerca, terza missione* (Syracuse, 2024), 145–7.

PUBLICATIONS ON CORVINO + MULTARI

A. Ferlenga, 'Progetto di restauro della Torre delle Nazioni a Napoli', *L'industria delle costruzioni*, 283 (1995), 46–8.

C. Del Grosso, 'Risultati in Italia: Cagliari', [Europan 4 Competition], *Edilizia popolare*, 246–7 (1996), 92–3.

F. Bilò, 'La nuova Piazza dei Bruzi', *Edilizia Popolare*, 259 (1998), 42–7.

M. G. Zunino, 'Piazza dei Bruzi, Cosenza', *Abitare*, 389, (1999), 160.

M. Pisani, 'Sistemazione di Piazza dei Bruzi a Cosenza', *L'industria delle costruzioni*, 335 (1999), 52–7.

'Il grattacielo Pirelli di Gio Ponti: il concorso per la realizzazione del Centro Congressi', *L'industria delle costruzioni* (Rome, 1999), 44–7.

'Piazza dei Bruzi, in Cosenza', in A. M. Cafiero Cosenza (ed.), *Giovani Architetti Europei* (Naples, 2000), 126–9.

F. Bilò, F. Orofino, 'Bioarchitettura per l'edilizia sociale', *Edilizia Popolare*, 266 (2000), 86–7.

'Gruppo Progetti: Piazza dei Bruzi a Cosenza', *Area*, 54 (2001), 14–5.

'Piazza dei Bruzi', in A. Acocella, P. C. Pellegrini, M. Casamonti (eds.), *Lo spazio pubblico in Spagna 1990–2000, lo spazio pubblico in Italia 1998–2000* (Florence, 2001), 154–7.

N. Flora, 'Palazzo per uffici, Cosenza', Area, 59 (2001), 106–13.

'Programma Integrato di Interventi', in M. Mulazzani (ed.), *Almanacco di Casabella. Giovani Architetti Italiani 2000–2001* (Milan, 2001), 63–7.

A. Izzo, 'Prefazione', in V. Corvino, G. Multari, *I rivocati: programma integrato di interventi a Cosenza* (Castellammare di Stabia, 2002), 12–3.

B. Gravagnuolo, 'Introduzione, Leggere geometrie', in V. Corvino, G. Multari, *I rivocati: programma integrato di interventi a Cosenza* (Castellammare di Stabia, 2002), 14–7.

'Sede degli uffici dell'Azienda Ospedaliera di Cosenza, 1997', in M. Falsitta (ed.), *50/50 Nuova generazione architettura italiana. Due generazioni a confronto* (Milan 2002), 66–9.

S. Volpi, 'Piazza Gabrio Rosa', in Municipal Authority of Milan (ed.), *Piazze per Milano* (Milan, 2002), 44–51.

'Piazza Ohm', in Municipal Authority of Milan (ed.), *Piazze per Milano* (Milan, 2002), 118–23.

'Sede Uffici Azienda Ospedaliera', in A. M. Cafiero Cosenza (ed.), *Giovani Architetti Europei 2002* (Naples, 2003), 186–9.

Regional Council of Campania, *Il Ristorante* (Castellamare di Stabia, 2003).

M. A. Crippa, 'Restauro e recupero del Grattacielo Pirelli a Milano', *D'A. D'Architettura*, 20 (2003), 88–97.

'Restauro della Torre delle Nazioni alla Mostra d'Oltremare di Napoli', *D'A. D'Architettura*, 22 (2003), 72–5.

'Sistemazione di viale Omero e piazzale Gabrio Rosa, Milano', in M. Mulazzani (ed.), *Almanacco di Casabella. Giovani Architetti Italiani 2002–2003* (Milan, 2003), 54–9.

'Edificio per uffici a Casoria, Napoli', in M. Mulazzani (ed.), *Almanacco di Casabella. Giovani Architetti Italiani 2003–2004* (Milan, 2004), 42–7.

F. Beltrami Gadola, 'Creatività emergenti', *L'Arca*, 191 (2004), 68–71.

P. Righetti, 'Il Pirelli', *Modulo*, 297 (2004), 1108–13.

M. V. Capitanucci, 'Il ristorante del Consiglio Regionale della Campania', *Abitare*, 441 (2004), 68–71.

C. Golbi, 'Profumi lontani', *Presenza tecnica in edilizia*, 198 (2004), 16–9.

'Sede dell'Azienda Ospedaliera di Cosenza', in E. Burroni (ed.), *Laterizio. Costruire italiano sostenibile* (exhibition catalogue; Florence, 2004), 58–9.

G. Bonelli, *Corvino + Multari 1995–2005* (Naples, 2005).

'Restauro del Grattacielo Pirelli', in S. Brandolini (ed.), *Milano. Nuova architettura* (Milan, 2005), 64–7.

'Sede dell'Azienda Ospedaliera di Cosenza', in A. Piva, P. Galliani (eds.), *Ricerca Formazione Progetto di Architettura. Architetti italiani under 50*, national conference proceedings, 4 May 2005 (exhibition catalogue, 5 May–12 June 2005; Venice, 2005), 122–3.

'Restauro Auditorium Grattacielo Pirelli', in A. M. Cafiero Cosenza (ed.), *Giovani Architetti Europei 2004* (exhibition catalogue, Naples, 1 July–30 September 2005; Naples, 2005), 216.

'Centro Europeo per le Creatività Emergenti a Pontecagnano Faiano; Il restauro del Grattacielo Pirelli a Milano', in I. Olszanska, R. Chionne (eds.), *Architettura, Architektura, Architecture* (exhibition catalogue, Rome, Milan, Padova, and Krakow, from 2005 to 2007; Rome 2005), 27–33.

A. P. Lusardi, 'Nuovi uffici nel quartiere dei Rivocati a Cosenza', *Costruire in laterizio*, 103 (2005), 4–9.

R. Sacchetti, 'Auditorium al Grattacielo Pirelli', *D'A. D'Architettura*, 27 (2005), 84–5.

'European Centre for the Emerging Creativities in the Tabacco Factory Centola, 2004–2007, Auditorium at the Pirelli Skyscraper, Milan Italy', *World Architecture* (SHIJIE JIANZHU), 10 (2005), 42–7.

'ASL Offices, Cosenza Italy; Pirelli Skyscraper restoration, Milan Italy; l'Altrareggia Casagiove, Italy', in G. Scaglione (ed.), *Net.it: a snapshot of contemporary architecture, design and photography in Italy* (Barcelona, 2005), 294–304.

'Progetti in concorso: San Martino', in VV.AA. *Concorso internazionale di progettazione: tre punti di ristoro per tre musei napoletani* (Naples, 2005), 80–3.

P. Scaglione, 'Cosenza, oltre il piano verso la strategia', *D'A. D'Architettura*, 24 (2005), 40–7.

'2000–2001 Programma Integrato di Interventi a Cosenza; 2002–2003 Sistemazione di Viale Omero e Piazzale Gabrio Rosa a Milano; 2003–2004 Edificio per uffici a Casoria (Napoli)', in M. Mulazzani (ed.), *Architetti Italiani. Le nuove generazioni* (Milan, 2006), i, 575–9.

'"Vino nuovo in otri nuovi": il Tempio Duomo di Pozzuoli', in A. Gianfrano (ed.), *Tempio–Duomo di Pozzuoli. Progettazione e Restauro* (Naples, 2006), 109–19.

A. Isozaki, 'Corvino + Multari e Renato Sarno, Restauro del Grattacielo Pirelli. Premio Speciale per il Restauro', in F. Irace (ed.), *Medaglia d'Oro all'Architettura Italiana 2006* (Milan, 2006), 49–55.

'Il Restauro del Grattacielo Pirelli', *AI*, 11 (2006), 8–13.

'Auditorium del Grattacielo Pirelli', *Ottagono*, 186 (2006), 191.

'Restauro del grattacielo Pirelli a Milano', *The Plan*, 15 (2006), 111–4.

'Che cosa è un superluogo? Proposte per una nuova definizione: Corvino+Multari', in M. Agnoletto, A. Delpiano, M. Guerzoni (eds.), *La civiltà dei superluoghi* (Bologna, 2007), 168.

'Il Centro storico, metamorfosi per interni: Mercato Coperto', in L. Molinari (ed.), *Reggio Emilia: scenari di qualità urbana* (Milan, 2007), 52–3.

M. A. Crippa, *Il Restauro del Grattacielo Pirelli* (Milan, 2007).

'Corvino + Multari', in A. De Poli (ed.), *Enciclopedia dell'architettura – Vol. 1* (Milan, 2007), 488.

G. Leoni (ed.), 'Il magistero della prassi. Alberto e Ferruccio Izzo, Corvino + Multari, Roberto Vanacore', *D'A. D'Architettura*, 34 (2007), 142–51.

E. Di Meo, 'Tra arte e architettura', *Of Arch*, 101 (2008), 76–85.

J. C. Montero, 'Una forma acabada, aberta aos usos, como un monumento', *Arquitectura e Vida*, 93 (2008), 22–31.

'Integrated Centre for Handicrafts and Trade, Pompei, Napoli', in L. Molinari, A. D'Onofrio (ed.), *Sustainab.Italy–Contemporary Ecologies–Energies for Italian Architecture* (Rome, 2008), 96–7.

L. Cupelloni, 'Il restauro della facciata di Gio Ponti', *Docomomo Italia Giornale*, 22 (2008), 9.

F. Pacifico, 'Topografia del lavoro', *Abitare*, 482 (2008), 112–23.

B. Gravagnuolo, 'Un recupero esemplare. "L'AltraReggia": un centro di incontro tra culture diverse', *Il giornale dell'architettura*, 64 (2008), 16–8.

'Nuovi tessuti urbani', *Presenza tecnica in edilizia*, 239 (2008), 14–22.

'Corvino+Multari: recent works', in A. Mangiarotti, I. Paoletti (eds.), *Dall'idea al cantiere: progettare, produrre e costruire forme complesse* (Milan, 2008), 27–41.

'Recupero del Quartiere Militare Borbonico', in M. Mulazzani, P. Desideri, C. Zucchi (eds.), *Almanacco di Casabella. Architetti Italiani 2008* (Milan, 2008), 60–5.

'Uffici Griec-Am, Palazzo Aronne', in A. Castagnaro, A. Lavaggi, A. Picone (eds.), *Piccolo e Bello* (Naples, 2009), 92–5.

'Riqualificazione di Piazza Ohm', in F. D'Amico (ed.), *Urban solutions / building solutions, green solutions, culture & research* (Milan, 2009), 164–9.

L. Tozzi, 'L'Aquila – progetto C.A.S.E.', *Abitare*, 10 August 2009, online edition.

'Edificio per uffici', in A. Baldini, L. Prestinenza Puglisi (eds.), *Press/Tmag* (Rome, 2009), 36–9.

'Sede dell'Azienda Ospedaliera di Cosenza', in A. Campolongo (ed.), *Architettura e metodiche costruttive a Cosenza Nuova. Un'indagine per il recupero dell'edilizia del Novecento* (Rome, 2009), 335–8.

'Nasce Led, il nuovo spazio per il tempo libero', *Presenza tecnica in edilizia*, 252 (2010), 27–30.

G. De Siena, *Corvino + Multari: Vesuvius* (DVD; Naples, 2010).

'Corvino+Multari (Opere e progetti in Campania)', in C. Gambardella, M. D. Morelli (eds.), *Architettura per oggi e per domani. La ricerca a Napoli e in Campania* (Naples, 2010), 84–7.

'Corvino+Multari', in A. Bittner, A. Kądziela-Grubman, U. Kwiatkowska (eds.), *Museum of the Second World War. International architectural competition* (2010), 65.

'N. Bassoli, 2010. L'Aquila un anno dopo', *Lotus International*, 144 (2010), 46–59.

'Progetto C.A.S.E.', *Lotus International*, 144 (2010), 62–3.

'Nuovo Complesso Parrocchiale Madonna delle Grazie, Parrocchia S. Giorgio Martire in Dresano', *Casabella*, 785 (2010), 10–6.

'Edifici–tipologia 12', in R. Turino (ed.), *L'Aquila: Il progetto C.A.S.E., Complessi Antisismici ed Ecocompatibili* (Pavia, 2010), 68–71.
Grattacielo Pirelli a Milano, in L. Prestinenza Puglisi (ed.), *ItaliArchitettura*, iii (Turin, 2010), 92–9.

'Une restauration exemplaire', in *Le Moniteur Architecture*, 210 (2011), 96–8.

M. Aprile, 'Residenze in Piazza Molino a Cosenza', *L'Industria delle Costruzioni*, 421 (2011), 92–9.

L. Prestinenza Puglisi, 'Made in Italy: Corvino+Multari', *The Plan*, 49 (2011), 39–48.

'Centro Integrato per l'Artigianato e il Commercio a Pompei', in L. Zevi (ed.), *Le Quattro Stagioni: Architetture del Made in Italy da Adriano Olivetti alla Green Economy* (Milan, 2012), 193.

D. Lama, 'Produceva carta per sigarette, ora è diventata centro commerciale', *Il Giornale dell'Architettura*, 108 (August–September 2012), 2, online edition 25 September 2012.

'Un Luogo di Incontro', *Presenza tecnica in edilizia*, September 2012, 19–23.

'Sede dell'Azienda Ospedaliera di Cosenza', in F. Berlingieri, L. Thermes (eds.), *Guida alle Architetture del Novecento in Calabria* (Reggio Calabria, 2012), 130–1.

F. Maietti, 'Urban regeneration: layer by layer', *Paesaggio Urbano*, 3 (2012), 42–9.

'Complesso immobiliare in Piazza Molino', *Ottagono*, 262 (2013), 122–3.

P. Daverio, 'Disegni d'autore, Razionalismo e lirismo. Il nuovo Centro Parocchiale di Dresano', *L'Architetto*, July–August 2014.

E. Di Meo, 'La logica della funzionalità', *Of Arch*, 135 (2015), 92–5.

G. P. Scaglione (ed.), *Corvino + Multari Esperienze dell'architettura / Architecture Experiences 2007–2017* (Milan, 2017).

G. Menna, 'La Chiesa degli uomini, Complesso Parrocchiale della Diocesi di Lodi', *The Plan* (2017), pp. 34–42.

'La chiesa che raccoglie la Comunità. Nuovo Complesso Parrocchiale della Diocesi di Lodi a Dresano, Milano', *Chiesa Oggi*, 109 (2018), 56–65.

'Sede dell'Azienda Ospedaliera di Cosenza', in F. Martorano, *L'Architettura in Calabria dal 1945 ad oggi* (Reggio Calabria, 2020), 208–9.

'Un caso esemplare: il progetto "Mantova HUB"', in M. A. Perletti (ed.), *Costruire sostenibile con la canapa* (Santarcangelo di Romagna, 2020), 315–33.

'Il progetto di restauro e di rivitalizzazione della Torre delle Nazioni alla Mostra d'Oltremare di Napoli', in A. Aveta, A. Castagnaro, F. Mangone, *La Mostra d'Oltremare nella Napoli occidentale. Ricerche storiche e restauro del moderno* (Naples, 2021), 503–11.

'Complesso Parrocchiale Diocesano', in V. P. Mosco, *Viaggio in Italia. Architetture e città* (Santarcangelo di Romagna, 2021), 31.

'Corvino + Multari – Mantova Hub', in *Renaissance. 4a biennale di Architettura di Pisa. Spazio Collettivo Spazio Individuale* (Pisa, 2021), 26–9.

'Istituto tecnico Mantegna, Mantova', *Modulo* (2023), 46–9.

M. Mulazzani, 'Progettare nella città / Designing in the city', *Casabella*, 944 (2023), 28–37.

M. L. Crupi, 'Sila Social Housing, San Giovanni in Fiore, Cosenza', *Domus*, 1085 (2023), 22–5.

M. Mulazzani (ed.), *Costruire nella città / Building in the City. La Procura della Repubblica di Catanzaro / The Catanzaro Public Prosecutor's Office* (Milan, 2023).

'L'Esperienza del Sacro, il nuovo complesso parrocchiale a Dresano', in M. Pisani, *Spazio Sacro* (Foligno, 2023), 85–92.

A. Calderoni, 'Memoria e innovazione: il futuro del Museo di Capodimonte', *Rassegna ANIAI Campania*, 2 (2024), 36–9.

D. Lama, 'Capodimonte. La grande transizione ecologica, digitale e sociale', *ArkedaMagazine*, 11 (2024), 20–7.

P. Solomita, 'Corvino + Multari. Social Housing. Quarto Napoli', *Costruire in laterizio*, 196 (ottobre 2024), 38–45.

M. Vercelloni, 'Complesso parrocchiale Madonna delle Grazie. Diocesi di Lodi, Dresano (Milano)', *Percorsi in Ceramica*, 49 (2024), 24–9.

LIST OF PROJECTS

Piazza dei Bruzi
Cosenza
Competition project: 1995
First prize
Realisation: 1997–98

Banking agency
Capaccio, Salerno
Project and realisation: 1995–96

Council Chamber and restaurant
Naples
Competition project: 1995
First prize
Realisation: 1996–2003

Restoration of Lazzaretto Vecchio
Cagliari
Competition project (Europan 4): 1996
Running-up project

Residences and sports area
Pozzuoli, Naples
Project and realisation: 1996–99

Isolato dei Rivocati
Cosenza
Competition project: 1997
First prize
Realisation: 1998–2001

Restoration of Palazzo Cosentini
Cosenza
Project: 1998–2000

Disused railway and industrial areas
Pomigliano d'Arco, Naples
Competition project: 1998
First prize
Executive project: 2000–2

Restoration of the Pirelli Skyscraper
Milan
Competition project (auditorium and belvedere): 1998
First prize
Realisation: 2001–5
With Renato Sarno

Bioclimatic residences
Jesi
Competition project: 1999
With Federico Bilò and Francesco Orofino

Concert hall
Sarajevo
Competition project: 1999

Department of Motor Vehicles headquarters
Avellino
Project: 1999–2001

Renovation of Piazza Gabrio Rosa, Viale Martini and Viale Omero
Milan
Competition project: 2000
First prize
Realisation: 2001–3

University multipurpose centre
Naples
Project: 2000–2
Realisation: 2003

Museo del Novecento in the Arengario
Milan
Competition project: 2001
With Klaus Kada

Restoration of the Bourbon military quarter
Casagiove, Caserta
Competition project: 2001
First prize
Executive project: 2003–5
Realisation: 2006–8

Inarcassa headquarters
Rome
Competition project: 2002
Second prize

Renovation of Piazza Ohm
Milan
Competition project: 2002
First prize
Realisation: 2004–6

Piazza Molino residential and commercial redevelopment
Cosenza
Project: 2002–4
Realisation: 2005–8

Restoration of Palazzo Aronne
Catanzaro
Project and realisation: 2002–3

Technical school 'Enrico Fermi'
Naples
Project and realisation: 2002–4

Office building
Casoria, Naples
Project: 2002
Realisation: 2003–4

Secondary school in Casal Monastero
Rome
Competition project: 2003
Second prize

European Centre for Emerging Creativities
Pontecagnano Faiano, Salerno
Competition project: 2003
First prize
Realisation: 2005–7

Restoration of the Temple–Cathedral in the Rione Terra
Pozzuoli, Naples
Competition project: 2004
Selected project

Residential and commercial towers
Lampugnano, Milan
Project: 2004–9

Restoration of Torre delle Nazioni
Naples
Project: 2004–12

Landscape renovation of disused road 'Salerno–Reggio Calabria'
Campagna, Salerno
Competition project: 2005
Second prize

College extension for Milan universities
Milan
Competition project: 2006
Second prize

Upteam Holding office
Naples
Project and realisation: 2006–7

Palaponticelli auditorium
Naples
Project: 2006–12

Restoration of the Benedictine Abbey of Tyniec
Krakow
Competition project: 2007
Running-up project

Conference centre
Krakow
Competition project: 2007
Running-up project

La Cartiera shopping and crafts centre
Pompeii, Naples
Project and realisation: 2007–12

Physical activity workshops and childcare
Naples
Project: 2008
Realisation: 2010

Implementation urban plan of the ex Breglia area
Ponticelli, Naples
Project: 2008–12

Residential buildings on seismically isolated platforms
L'Aquila
Project and realisation: 2009

Modules for provisional school use
L'Aquila
Project and realisation: 2009

Extension of the Regional Council of Calabria
Reggio Calabria
First prize

High-speed train station upstream of Vesuvius
Striano, Naples
Competition project: 2009
Running-up project

Restoration of the Covered Market
Reggio Emilia
Project and realisation: 2009–12

Urban redevelopment of the brownfields ex Salamini
Parma
Competition project: 2009
First prize

Twenty-four co-operative housing dwellings
Quarto, Naples
Project and realisation: 2009–14

Restoration of the headquarters of the Campania Regional Government
Naples
Project: 2009–12
Realisation: 2024–26

Urban recovery program in Rione Traiano
Quartiere Soccavo, Naples
Project: 2009–18

Renovation of the seacoast and new marina
Massa Carrara
Project: 2010

Parish complex Madonna delle Grazie
Dresano, Milan
Competition project: 2009
First prize
Executive project: 2010–12
Realisation: 2013–17

Residences and stores 'I Portici'
Frosinone
Competition project: 2011

New primary school
Carate Brianza, Monza and Brianza
Project and realisation: 2011–14

Restoration of San Paolo Stadium and new stadium at Ponticelli
Naples
Project: 2012

Masterplan of the Italian Creative Design Centre
Shanghai
Competition project: 2012
Running-up project

Water Park Santa Chiara
Rende, Cosenza
Project and realisation: 2012–15

Directional tower of new Municipal offices
Casoria, Naples
Competition project: 2013
First prize

Renovation of the Manifattura Tabacchi
Naples
Project: 2013–15

Renovation of Piazza della Repubblica
Varese
Competition project: 2015
Fifth prize

Residential building in Via Formicola
Casoria, Naples
Project and realisation: 2015–17

Renovation of Intesa San Paolo buildings
Naples
Project: 2016

Restoration of Banca di Credito Popolare
Torre del Greco, Naples
Project: 2016–17
Realisation: 2019

New Public Prosecutor's Office in the former military hospital
Catanzaro
Project: 2017–18
Realisation: 2019–22

Restoration of Sacred Tempio della Scorziata
Naples
Project: 2017–24
Realisation: 2025–26

Mantova Hub
Mantua
Project: 2018–19
Realisation ex Ceramica and Fiera Catena: 2020–23
Realisation area San Nicolò: 2024–26

Station 'Castellammare centro' of Circumvesuviana train line
Castellammare di Stabia, Naples
Project: 2018–20

New Cardarelli hospital emergency room
Naples
Project: 2018–20

New primary and secondary school
Paolisi, Benevento
Project: 2018–23
Realisation: 2025–26

Citadel of Security
Naples
Project: 2018–25
Realisation: 2026–30

Student service building, University of Calabria
Arcavacata, Cosenza
Project: 2019
Realisation: 2020

Two social housing buildings in La Sila
San Giovanni in Fiore, Cosenza
Project and realisation: 2016–21

Aragonese Castle of Baia Restoration of Cavaliere pavilion
Bacoli, Naples
Project: 2019–22
Realisation: 2023–25

New headquarters of the Revenue Agency
Cagliari
Competition project: 2019
First prize
Executive project: 2019–22
Realisation: 2024–27

New headquarters for the State Archives Restoration of the former Monastery of Sant'Agostino
Piacenza
Project: 2019–22

Polcevera Park
Genoa
Competition project: 2019
Third prize

Renovation of former Papa barracks
Brescia
Project: 2020–24
Realisation: 2024–26

Italian Embassy in Kenya
Nairobi
Competition project: 2021
First prize
Executive project: 2022–25
Realisation: 2026–28

Renovation of Palazzo Frisini for students' residence
Taranto
Competition project: 2021
First prize
Executive project: 2021–23
Realisation: 2025–26

Restoration of the Casa d'Italia
Zurich
Project: 2021–22
Realisation: 2024–26

Restructuring of the Municipal Stadium
Florence
Competition project: 2021–22
Second prize
With Kengo Kuma

Justice Park
Bari
Competition project: 2022

Renovation of the DEMM Department, Sannio University
Benevento
Project: 2022–23
Realisation: 2024–26

Restoration of the Central State Archives
Rome
Project: 2022–23
Realisation: 2024–26

Renovation of public housing
Capua, Naples
Project: 2022–24
Realisation: 2024–26

Restoration and energy upgrading of the Capodimonte Museum
Naples
Project: 2020–22
Realisation: 2023–25

Third tower of the Tuscany Regional Authority
Florence
Competition project: 2022
Second prize

Renovation of United Nations Building E
Geneva
Competition project: 2022

Restoration and upgrading of the old Customs House
Avellino
Project: 2022
Realisation: 2023–26

Regeneration former base camp TAV
Novara
Project: 2023

Prosecutor's Office in the former women's prison
Perugia
Project: 2023–24
Realisation: 2025–27

'After us' welfare centre
Messina
Project: 2023–24
Realisation: 2025–28

Renovation of the former Ricovero dei Cappuccini
Altamura
Project: 2023–24

University residences in the former San Francesco complex Completion of the Civic Library Francesco Calvo
Alessandria
Project: 2023–24
Realisation: 2025–27

Restoration of the regional headquarters of the State Property Agency
Milan
Project: 2024–25
Realisation: 2026–28

Creative Hangars
Livorno
Competition project: 2024
First prize
Executive project: 2024–25
Realisation: 2026–29

Restoration and renovation of Villa Caetani
Fogliano, Latina
Project: 2024–25
Realisation: 2026–28

Renovation of Municipal school facilities
Abruzzo, Lazio, Marche and Umbria
Project: 2024–25

Urban redevelopment of the railway yard
Naples
Project: 2024–25
Realisation: 2025–27

Enhancement of the archaeological parks of Paestum–Velia New archaeological museum of Velia
Paestum–Velia, Salerno
Project: 2024–25
Realisation 2026–28

Parking Calata Piliero
Naples
Project: 2024–25
Realisation: 2025–26

CREDITS

1 PUBLIC SPACES AND URBAN CONNECTIONS

PIAZZA DEI BRUZI

Place Cosenza
Client Cosenza Municipality
Architects Corvino + Multari
with Roberto Serino
and Carmen Del Grosso
Sculpture Mimmo Paladino
Construction management
Alessandro Adriano
Artistic management
Giovanni Multari–
Corvino + Multari
Building company
Costruire coop. a.r.l., Matera
Functional programme
Public spaces
Chronology
1995—Competition
1997—Executive project
1998—Realisation

ISOLATO DEI RIVOCATI

Place Cosenza
Client Cosenza Municipality
Architects Corvino + Multari
Structures A. Bonsanti
Installations Tecnica Ingegneri
Associati–A. Iaconanni, M. Curcio
Geology G. Calia, F. Baldassarre
Urban planning R. Lanini
Applied economics P. Rostirolla
Safety coordinator
A. Iaconanni, M. Curcio
Construction management
Giovanni Multari–
Corvino + Multari
Building companies
Consorzio Nazionale Cooperative
di produzione e lavoro Ciro
Menotti, Ravenna–Costruire
Coop. s.r.l., Matera
Technical direction
N. Olivieri, G. Dionisi
Functional programme
(First and second phases)
Administrative headquarters
of Cosenza Hospital Company,
telematics and multimedia
centre of Cosenza Municipality,
science and technology
exhibition centre, I.T.I.S. 'A.
Monaco', underground parking,
residences, private offices
(Third phase) Residences
Chronology
1997—Competition
1998—Executive project
1999–2001—Realisation

RESTORATION OF THE COVERED MARKET

Place Reggio Emilia
Client La Galleria s.p.a.
(Coopsette Soc. Coop. e Tecton
Soc. Coop.–Reggio Emilia)
Promoting office
Reggio Emilia Municipality
Person in charge of the process
Massimo Magnani
Design and Artistic management
Corvino + Multari
High supervision of the Superintendence for Architectural and Landscape Heritage for the provinces of Bologna, Modena and Reggio Emilia
Paola Grifoni (superintendent)
Elisabetta Pepe (zone officer)
Structures
ErreCi Ingegneri Associati;
G. Ragazzi, P. Catellani
Lighting designer Mario Nanni
Mechanical installations
Temoprogetti, M. Conforti,
E. Zanni
Electrical installations
Progetec, M. Ferrari
Fire prevention
A. Ansaloni
Safety coordinator in the design phase and execution A. Bonori
Consultants Carmen Del Grosso
(restoration methodology)
Franceschetti s.a.s. (survey)
Project manager R. Spagliardi.
Construction management
Restoration works
Vincenzo Corvino–
Corvino + Multari
Structural works, installations
and accounting
Alberto Zen
Construction site technical director
A. Castagnetti
Ongoing static tester
L. Bellesia
Interior layout
Coin Store Design S. Caldato,
D. Fornterrè
Functional programme
Commercial area, offices,
urban redevelopment
Chronology
2009—Design phase
2009–12—Realisation

LA CARTIERA SHOPPING AND CRAFTS CENTRE

Place Pompeii, Naples
Client Fergos s.r.l. (Coopsette Soc. Coop.), Reggio Emilia
Fingiochi s.p.a. Milan
Pompei Municipality
Architects Corvino + Multari
Structures and installations (design phase) Engco
Structures (executive project)
B. Boldrin
Interior and lighting design
Design International
Safety coordinator
P. Longobardi
Consultants
R. Marone (town planning law), L. Piemontese (urban planning), F. Federico (archaeology), In.Co.Se.t. s.r.l. C. Troisi (mobility), M. Cannaviello, N. Guadagno (installations and energy sustainability), F. Zaccarelli (fire prevention), A. Di Bartolomeo (landscape), P. Santarpia (agronomy), P. Cutino (geology), P. Longobardi (survey), S. Lubrano Lavadera, G. Schiano Lomoriello (commercial permits), I.S.A.F. s.r.l. (characterization and remediation plan)
Construction management
Alberto Zen
Artistic direction
Vincenzo Corvino–
Corvino + Multari
Direction structural works
B. Boldrin
Functional programme
Integrated centre for crafts and trade, Public Park
Chronology
2007–9—Design phase
2010–12—Realisation

2 MONUMENTAL RESTORATIONS

RESTORATION OF THE PIRELLI SKYSCRAPER

Place Milano
Client Lombardy Region
Emergency Commissioner
Roberto Formigoni
Ministry of Cultural Heritage and Activities–DARC
Pio Baldi
Scientific and technical committee Giulio Ballio, Giovanni Carbonara, Maria Antonietta Crippa, Carla Di Francesco, Adriano De Maio, Pietro Petraroia
Architects Corvino + Multari with Renato Sarno Group
Consultants
A. Migliacci, M. Acito (structural design)
G. Torraca (mosaics restoration)
Ariatta Ingegneria dei Sistemi srl (installations)
M. G. Monelli (fire prevention)
Idesi–G. M. Rossi (safety)
Tecno Future Service (survey)
A. Crotti (curtainwall)
Construction management
Giovanni Multari–
Corvino + Multari
Lots: facades, auditorium, exterior accommodation, square hill, new accesses
Building companies
La Manutenzione srl
Eleca s.p.a.
Impresa Costruzioni Grassi e Crespi s.r.l.
Marcora Costruzioni s.p.a.
ISA spa, Magatti srl, ICG. Srl, ICEMS srl
Functional programme
Offices and council room of the Regional Council of the Lombardy Region, auditorium Giorgio Gaber, exterior accommodation
Chronology
1998 Competition auditorium and belvedere
2001–2—Executive project
2003–5—Realisation

RESTORATION AND ENERGY UPGRADING OF THE CAPODIMONTE MUSEUM

Place Naples
Client Museo e Real Bosco di Capodimonte
Director
Sylvain Bellenger (2020–23)
Eike Schimdt (from 2024)
Promoting, implementing and managing entity
ENGIE Servizi spa
Director South Area
Fabrizio di Battista
Operation manager
E. Consorti, F. Forestiero, E. Fienga
Architects Corvino + Multari
HBim survey 1 a 1 Architetti
Structures RINA Consulting
Installations CLIMOSFERA
Lighting design A3S Progetti
Archaeology
Davide Ivan Pellandra
Restoration of surfaces and decorative elements
Maria Rosaria Vigorito
Acoustics C. Bortot
Safety coordinator for design phase
E. Rambaldi–RINA Consulting
Digital and multimedia services
Magister Art
Artists Mimmo Paladino (Reception Hall)
Christiane Löhr (Terrace and Belvedere)
Scientific consultants
Architectural restoration
R. Picone, G. Proto
Building physics, energy diagnosis F. Peron
Project manager
Maria Pia Cibelli–MIC
Construction management
Eva Serpe–MIC
Renata Marmo–MIC
Artistic direction
Vincenzo Corvino–
Corvino + Multari
Safety coordinator for the construction site
M. Carfora
Responsible for conducting the contract
P. Musmarra–ENGIE
Building company
Modugno Restauri
Functional programme
Exhibition areas, public reception and service areas, public park
Chronology
2020–22—Design phase
2023–25—Realisation

3 REPRESENTATION BUILDINGS

OFFICE BUILDING

Place Casoria, Naples
Client Griec a.m. Ascensori srl
Architects Corvino + Multari
Installations, safety
G. Cancello, G. Porpora
Construction management
Andrea Casillo
Artistic management
Vincenzo Corvino–
Corvino + Multari
Building companies
Celestino Pezzella, Naples;
Luxy s.r.l., Vicenza;
International Office
Concept s.p.a., Milano;
Renato Saporito, Naples
Functional programme
Offices
Chronology
2002—Design phase
2003–4—Realisation

NEW PUBLIC PROSECUTOR'S OFFICE IN THE FORMER MILITARY HOSPITAL

Place Catanzaro
Client State Property Agency
General manager
Alessandra dal Verme
Regional managers–Calabria division during the design and realisation phases
Pier Giorgio Allegroni
Dario Di Girolamo
Vittorio Vannini
User entity
Prosecutor's Office in Catanzaro
Prosecutor Nicola Gratteri
Institutional partners
Catanzaro Municipality
High supervision for Superintendence for Archaeology, Artistic Heritage and Landscape of Catanzaro and Crotone
Stefania Argenti
Francesco Vonella
Person in charge of the process
Salvatore Virgilio–State Property
Agency Calabria
Architects Corvino + Multari
Architectural restoration
Fiammetta Adriani–AS
Structures, project management
RINA Consulting
Installations DFP Engineering
Geology Donatella Pingitore
Sustainability Giorgia Lorenzi
Survey Giovanni Malara
Historical consultant
Oreste Sergi Pirrò
Safety coordinator
F. De Falco, A. Perisano–DFP
Engineering
Construction management
Fabio De Falco
Contractors
Consorzio Athanor Scarl
Impresa Giovanni Izzo Restauri
Building companies
Costruzioni Edili 2001 s.r.l.
SAMI s.r.l.
Construction site manager for the contractor
S.M. Engineering: D. Mazzarella
Artistic management
Vincenzo Corvino–
Corvino + Multari
Operational direction of restoration works
Fiammetta Adriani–AS
Operational direction of structural works
Gianluca Ciullo–RINA Consulting
Operational direction of installations works
Giovanni Russo–DFP Engineering
Functional programme
Offices of the Prosecutor's
Office in Catanzaro
Chronology
2017–18—Design phase
2019–22—Realisation

RESTORATION OF THE CASA D'ITALIA

Place Zurich
Client Ministry of Foreign Affairs
and International Cooperation
Italian Consulate
Architects Corvino + Multari
Structures and project management RINA Consulting
Installations, esteem and security
DFP Engineering
Building physics
Gartenmann Engineering AG
Restoration
Fontana & Fontana AG
Artist Francesca Pasquali
Monument preservation
Ruggero Tropeano
Landscape architecture
Raymann
Fire Prevention AFC AG
Artistic direction
Vincenzo Corvino–
Corvino + Multari
Construction management
ZPF AG Luis Looser
Building company Pizzarotti SA
Functional programme
Italian consulate,
Italian Cultural Institute
Chronology
2021–22—Design phase
2024–26—Realisation

THIRD TOWER OF THE TUSCANY REGIONAL AUTHORITY

Place Florence
Client Tuscany Region
Architects Corvino + Multari
with Daniele Lauria,
Edoardo Fanteria
Structures
Ingegneri Mannelli Associati
Installations
Tecnoengineering s.r.l.
Geology and landscape
Terra & Opera s.r.l.
Rendering Proloog
Functional programme
Offices–Public spaces
Chronology
2022—Competition

ITALIAN EMBASSY IN KENYA

Place Nairobi
Client Ministry of Foreign Affairs
and International Cooperation
Embassy of Italy, Nairobi
Ambassador Roberto Natali
Project manager Paolo Rotili
Architects Corvino + Multari
Structures and project management RINA Consulting
Installations Climosfera
Quantity surveyor CMAS
Local architect
Avanti architecture
Local service engineer
Bosch East Africa
Local structural engineer BDP
Consultants L. Boursier
(agronomy and landscape)
G. Pentella
(energy and environment)
Chronology
2021–25—Design phase
2026–28—Realisation

4 THE 'HOUSE INSIDE THE HOUSE'

RESTORATION OF THE TEMPLE–CATHEDRAL IN THE RIONE TERRA

Place Pozzuoli, Naples
Client Presidency of the Campania Region
Architects Corvino + Multari
Archaeology Bernard Andreae
Restoration Rosario Paone
Restoration methodology Carmen Del Grosso
Structures Aldo Bottini
Static reinforcement Gabriele Salvatoni
Installations Alberto Zimbelli
Urban history Teresa Colletta
Liturgist Antonio Giannotti
Restoration decorative elements Giuseppe Giordano
Scientific survey Ruggero Morichi
Functional programme Liturgical spaces, archaeological area
Chronology
2004—Competition

RESTORATION AND UPGRADING OF THE OLD CUSTOMS HOUSE

Place Avellino
Client Avellino Municipality
Project manager Filomena Smiraglia
Architects Corvino + Multari with Italo Luigi Urciuolo
Engineering SPI s.r.l.
Geology F. Giordano
Safety coordinator G. Di Giacomo
Construction management Giacomo Rizzo
Operational direction A. Mastantuoni, G. Iannaccone
Artistic direction Giovanni Multari–Corvino + Multari
Italo Luigi Urciuolo
Sergio De Felice–SPI s.r.l.
Building company MAR SAL Restauri
Functional programme Youth service centre
Chronology
2022—Design phase
2023–26—Realisation

RESTRUCTURING OF THE MUNICIPAL STADIUM

Place Florence
Client Florence Municipality
Architects Corvino + Multari with Kengo Kuma Associates, B5, Daniele Lauria, Edoardo Fanteria
Structures
RINA Consulting
Studio Ingegneri Mannelli Associati
Installations Tecnoengineering
Geology Terra e Opere
Landscape Michelangelo Pugliese
Rendering MIR
Functional programme Sports facility complying with UEFA category 4 standards
Chronology
2021—Competition first phase
2022—Competition second phase

PARISH COMPLEX MADONNA DELLE GRAZIE

Place Dresano, Milan
Client Italian Episcopal Conference Diocese of Lodi–S. Giorgio Martire Parish
Project manager Roberto Spagliardi
Architects Corvino + Multari
Structures Gabriele Salvatoni
Installations Luigi Sgobaro
Acoustics Gianpiero Majandi
Liturgist Antonio Giannotti
Artist Nino Longobardi
Construction management I. Chiesa, M. Carella, C. Rotta
Building company Eco Costruzioni s.r.l.
Functional programme Liturgical spaces, parish centre, public spaces
Chronology
2009—Competition
2010–12—Design phase
2013–17—Realisation

5 THE FUNCTIONS OF INHABITING: RESIDENCES AND SCHOOLS

PIAZZA MOLINO RESIDENTIAL AND COMMERCIAL REDEVELOPMENT

Place Cosenza
Client Molino Bruno s.p.a.
Architects Corvino + Multari
Structures G. Chiappetta, O. Quintieri
Installations E. Cesario, N. Siciliano
Geology A. Grispino
Green Building Certification System M. Settimio
Testing F. Guido
Building companies
SI.TE. Costruzioni s.r.l., Cosenza
Antonio Santelli s.r.l., Cosenza
Functional programme Residences, offices, commerce
Chronology
2002–4—Design phase
2005–8—Realisation

RESIDENTIAL BUILDINGS ON SEISMICALLY ISOLATED PLATFORMS

Place Sant'Elia 1, Gignano e Paganica 2, L'Aquila
Client Presidency of the Council of Ministers Civil Defense Department Administration and Budget Office
Architects Corvino + Multari with Gina Furia, Pasquale Guarino, Luigi Nefasto
Consultants F. A. Renna (Structures), M. Romei (mechanical installations), B. Mattia (electrical installations)
Building company D'Agostino Angelo Antonio Costruzioni Generali s.r.l.
Prefabricated structures PREFAB.I. s.r.l.
Functional programme Residences
Chronology
2009—Design phase
2009—Realisation

TWENTY-FOUR CO-OPERATIVE HOUSING DWELLINGS

Place Quarto, Naples
Client
Soc. Coop. C.E.L.T. s.r.l., Naples
Project manager
Francesco Accarino
Architects Corvino + Multari
Structures Corrado D'Alessandro, Gianfranco Di Tella
Installations, esteem and safety
Roberto de Rosa
Construction management
Vincenzo Corvino–
Corvino + Multari
Building company
CT Costruzioni, Casoria
Functional programme
Subsidized residences
Chronology
2009–10—Design phase
2013–14—Realisation

TWO SOCIAL HOUSING BUILDINGS IN LA SILA

Place Olivaro,
San Giovanni in Fiore
Client
San Giovanni in Fiore
Municipality
Calabria Region
Project manager Nicola De Luca
Architects Corvino + Multari
Consultants
C. Mascolo (Structures),
Coprat (installations,
esteem and security),
L. Boursier (landscape),
L. Lamanna (geology)
Construction management
Sergio Pagano
Building company
Edil Loria s.a.s.
Artistic direction
Giovanni Multari–
Corvino + Multari
Functional programme
Social housing
Chronology
2016–17—Design phase
2018–21—Realisation

MODULES FOR PROVISIONAL SCHOOL USE

Place L'Aquila
Client Presidency
of the Council of Ministers
Civil Defense Department
Architects Corvino + Multari
Engineering Sinergo s.p.a.
Building company
Impresa Generale
di Costruzioni Steda spa
Artistic direction
Giovanni Multari–
Corvino + Multari
Functional programme
Nursery, kindergarten,
primary and secondary school
Chronology
2009—Design phase
2009—Realisation

NEW PRIMARY SCHOOL

Place Carate Brianza
Client Carate Brianza
Municipality, ATI C.C.C.,
Malegori srl
Project manager
Giuseppe Amodeo
Architects Corvino + Multari
with Giovanni Podestà
Structures Studio Salvatoni
Installations, esteem and security
Teco+ Partners
Building company
Eco Costruzioni s.r.l.
Artistic management
Giovanni Multari–
Corvino + Multari
Functional programme
Primary school
Chronology
2011–12—Design phase
2012–14—Realisation

6 DECOMMISSIONED LOCATIONS

NEW HEADQUARTERS OF THE REVENUE AGENCY

Place Cagliari
Client Ministry of Infrastructure
and Sustainable Mobility
Interregional Superintendency
for Public Works Lazio
Abruzzo and Sardinia–Cagliari
Coordinated Headquarters
in collaboration with
State Property Agency–
Regional Direction Sardinia
Sardinia Revenue Agency
Cagliari Municipality
Proveditor Vittorio Rapisarda
Project manager Walter Quarto
Architects Corvino + Multari
with Gianluca Vosa,
Raffaella Napolano
Structures RINA Consulting
Mechanical installations
TECNOLAV Engineering
Electrical installations
DFP Engineering
Consultants
PROAP ltd, Joao Nunes
(landscape), Geolog (geology),
N. Dessi' (archaeology),
F. Varone (urban planning)
Head of procedure
in the execution phase
Silvia Murgia MIT
Safety coordinator
for the design phase
F. Barabino, RINA
Safety coordinator
for the execution phase
A. Porcu
Construction management
Alessandro Pasqualucci MIT
Operative manager–
Renovation and restoration
Artistic management
Vincenzo Corvino,
Corvino + Multari
Andrea Martis MIT
Building company
RTI. REPIN Srl / EMME4
Functional programme
Revenue agency
Chronology
2019–22—Design phase
2024–27—Realisation

CITADEL OF SECURITY

Place Miano, Naples
Client State Property Agency–Campania Regional Directorate
User entity State Police–Department of Public Safety
Project manager Luca Damagini, State Property Agency
Architects Corvino + Multari AS (bld 10–16–21–22); DFP Engineering (bld 20–23–24)
Structures and project management RINA Consulting
Installations
DFP Engineering (bld 16–21–22)
ARETHUSA (bld 13–15–19–25)
Geology D. Pingitore
Archaeology F. Avilia, I. De Luca
Sustainability
G. Lorenzi Macrodesign
Safety coordinator
F. Barabino–RINA Consulting
Urban planning F. Varone
Functional programme
Offices, forensic police laboratories, auditorium, housing, general services
Chronology
2018–25—Design phase
2026–30—Realisation

MANTOVA HUB

Place Mantua
Client Mantua Municipality
Institutional partners
Presidency of the Council of Ministers
State Property Agency
Lombardy Region
AIPo (Po Interregional Company)
Province of Mantua
Mincio Park
Mincio Territories Land Reclamation Consortium
University of Mantua Foundation
Mantua Chamber of Commerce
ASPeF (Person and Family Service Company)
Confederation of Mantua Industry
Project manager Giacomo Celona
Emiliano Giorgino from 2024
Architects Corvino + Multari
Project Management
RINA Consulting
Structures Sparacio & Partners
N. Sangiuliano
Installations Icaro–A. Puorto
Sustainability G. Lorenzi
Construction management
Alessandro Aliotta–RINA Consulting
Artistic direction
Vincenzo Corvino–Corvino + Multari
Building company
Manelli Costruzioni Generali s.r.l.
Functional programme
Mincio Educational Trail–Valsecchi Urban Park; Science Centre–New Piazza Fiera Catena; CONI Gymnasium; 'Mantegna' Higher Technical Institute; Museum of Memory; Municipal Offices Hub Lavoro; Research Centre; Offices of the ASPEF Disability Centre; Infopoint of Mantua Municipality; Redevelopment of public spaces
Chronology
2018–19—Design phase
2020–23—Realisation
ex Ceramica and Fiera Catena
2024–26—Realisation
Area San Nicolò

'AFTER US' WELFARE CENTRE

Place Messina
Client Metropolitan City of Messina–VII Directorate
Project manager Giacomo Russo
Architects Corvino + Multari
Structures and project management
RINA consulting
Mechanical installations
Arethusa
Electrical installations
DFP Engineering
Construction management
Fabio De Falco–DFP Engineering
Artistic direction
Vincenzo Corvino–Corvino + Multari
Building company
Opera s.r.l.
Functional programme
Social welfare
Chronology
2023–24—Design phase
2025–28—Realisation

POLCEVERA PARK

Place Genoa
Client Genoa Municipality
Project manager
Anna Iole Corsi (manager)
Mirco Grassi (interim manager)
Urban Lab
Architects Corvino + Multari
Landscape M. Pugliese
Agronomy L. Boursier
Sustainable architecture
L. Masella
Energy and environmental redevelopment
Studio progettazioni d'ingegneria–SPI
Geology
Studio Associato Caniparoli Geologia e Ambiente
Urban Planning E. Formato
Participatory processes
L. Fatigati
Applied economics
P. Rostirolla
Artists
Inward National Observatory on Urban Creativity (Rosk&Loste, Gomez, Truly Design, Giulio Vesprini)
Functional programme
Park and urban facilities
Chronology
2019—Competition

BIOGRAPHY

Vincenzo Corvino (1965) and Giovanni Multari (1963) founded the Corvino + Multari architecture studio in 1995, following a shared experience over a number of years as assistants to Professor Alberto Izzo in the Department of Urban Planning of the Faculty of Architecture in Naples, where they carried out teaching and research activities. As tutors, they were invited to numerous international design workshops, and they were professors at the University of Bologna Alma Mater Studiorum, the Aldo Rossi Department of Architecture in Cesena and the 2nd-Level Master's in Outstanding Design of the Historic City in Naples.
Vincenzo Corvino is a specialist in Urban Design and was invited as a critic to the Academy of Architecture in Mendrisio, Switzerland, and as an Academic of Honour to the Academy of Arts and Design Florence. Since 2023 he has been president of the Fondazione Ordine Architetti of Naples and its province.
Giovanni Multari, a Doctor of Research in Urban Design, has been an associate professor since 2019 in the Department of Architecture at the University of Naples Federico II.

After the founding of the studio, Vincenzo Corvino and Giovanni Multari participated in several international competitions, following which they realised buildings for residences and public and private offices and were responsible for the upgrading of outdoor public spaces. There are many works and projects offering evidence of an active dialogue between contemporary art and architecture: a dialogue that, in the words of the architects themselves, is 'destined to design and realise public locations in continuity with the testimonies of the historic city,' and that takes concrete shape in shared experiences with, among others, Mimmo Paladino, Nino Longobardi, Sergio Fermariello, Anna Maria Pugliese, Lello Esposito and Pierre-Yves Le Duc.
Projects and creations by the studio have found space inside solo and group exhibitions in Milan, Rome, Naples, Bolzano, Lucca, Narni, Parma, Graz, Krakow, Prague, Warsaw, Havana, Paris, Berlin, London, Barcelona, Zurich and New York, and have been published in national and international architecture magazines.

In 2000, with the redevelopment of Piazza dei Bruzi, and in 2003, with the site for the offices of Cosenza Hospital, the studio was honoured with a silver plaque in the Luigi Cosenza European Awards; they then won the 3rd Edition of the Centocittà Prize (2004), held by the Fondazione Compagnia di San Paolo, with the upgrading of the Bourbon military quarter in Casagiove.
On the occasion of the studio's tenth anniversary, the magazine *Ventre* devoted the first issue of its 'Ventre Zoom' series to the monograph *Corvino + Multari 1995-2005*. The following year, with the restoration project for the Pirelli Skyscraper in Milan, Corvino and Multari won the Special Prize for Restoration in the Gold Medal to Italian Architecture competition run by the Milan Triennale. In 2010 they realised the documentary *Corvino + Multari: Vesuvius*, directed by Gianpaolo De Siena and published on DVD by Graus of Naples: this is a publishing project that tells of the evolution of Corvino and Multari's *modus operandi* during the studio's fifteen years of activity. Embellished by the photographs of Mimmo Esposito, the documentary tells in particular of their bond with Naples and offers evidence of the active dialogue that has always existed between the studio's architectural projects and contemporary art. In 2017 the monograph *Corvino + Multari – Esperienze dell'architettura* came out, published by List Lab of Trento; in the same year, with the project for the parish complex Madonna delle Grazie in Dresano, in the diocese of Lodi, the studio was awarded the Italian 'Ceramica e Progetto' Prize.
The studio has participated in the Architecture Biennale in Venice three times, over a period of years, with projects that have become famous: for the 10th edition (2006), Corvino and Multari presented the project for the new station at Castellammare di Stabia; six years later, on the occasion of the 13th edition, they participated with the project La Cartiera–Integrated Centre for Crafts and Commerce in Pompeii, which in 2013 was awarded second prize in the ninth edition of the Grand Prix Casalgrande Padana in the section devoted to shopping centres, and, in 2016, they gained a Mention of Honour in The Plan Awards, in the Retail category. Their latest participation in the Architecture Biennale was for the 17th edition (2021), when Corvino and Multari exhibited inside the Italy Pavilion with the Mantova Hub urban regeneration project. In 2023, the studio won the In/Arch National Prize with the project for the restoration and enlargement of the former military hospital in Catanzaro, which became the new headquarters of the Public Prosecutor's Office.
Numerous recent projects are in the process of realisation in various cities in Italy and abroad, among which we may mention in particular the restoration and repurposing of the Casa d'Italia in Zurich, the new Italian Embassy in Nairobi and the project for the restoration and enlargement of the Capodimonte Museum in Naples.

STAFF 2025

Salvatore Ivo Aiello
Marika Carpiniello
Mirella Ciano
Salvatore della Corte
Teresa Crispino
Mattia Errico
Anna Esposito
Cristina Esposito
Rita Esposito
Giovanni Gagliardi
Francesco Giaquinto
Marco Gisonni
Jacopo Marino
Michele Natale
Leonardo Ossuto
Lorenzo Palladino
Marco Poerio
Veronica Russo
Jeanhdria Vaz

STAFF 1995-2024

Francesco Aletta
Mikel Angjeli
Carlo Ardone
Chiara Ascione
Marianna Assante
Carolina Bergamasco
Lucienne Bowden
Michele Buso
Leonardo Caliandro
Laura Cannarile
Manuela Cappelli
Salvatore Carleo
Rita Carosone
Valentina Casalboni
Gennaro Casillo
Gabriella Casoria
Davide Cassese
Giovanna Castaldo
Agostino Castellano
Alessandra Cavaccini
Nicola Cavaliere
Melania Cermola
Francesco Maria Cerroni
Ernesto Cesario
Gianfranco Chiappetta
Davide Cibelli
Massimo Cicala
Rossella Cincotti
Raimondo Ciocchi
Paolo Cirelli
Ascanio Colombo
Paolo Conforti
Paolo Corvino
Michele Cozzolino
Emanuela Cresta
Mario Crisci
Elisa De Crescenzo
Vito Del Gaudio
Nausicaa De Rosa
Francesco Di Caprio
Luisa Di Costanza
Matteo Di Cuonzo
Inga Dworak
Giulio Esposito
Marco Esposito
Vincenzo Esposito
Livia Falco
Manuela Ferro
Francesco Finelli
Martin Fireira Alessandri
Antonella Galassi
Matteo Galise
Ivana Galli
Ludovica Gasperini
Sarah Gentiletti
Rossana Giallonardo
Giulia Silvia Giordano
Luisa Grasso
Alessandra Guglielmo
Alessandra Iannuzzi
Gabriele Lamba
Loredana Lanteri
Riccardo Lauro
Elisa Magliarditi
Sabrina Maiorano
Simone Martino
Michela Matrisciano
Eleonora Matrone
Irene Matteini
Chiara Mazzarella
Armando Melillo
Carmine Moreni
Manuela Musto
Iole Napolitano
Daniela Nappo
Antonio Maria Nese
Anna Nunziata
Monica Ombra
Camilla Ostinato
Luana Paesano
Silvio Pagnano
Francesco Paolo Palmese
Rosario Pane
Andrea Paoletti
Maurizio Parisi
Rodrigo Pessoa
Nicola Piacquadio
Rossana Piccolo
Giovanni Podestà
Marco Polito
Ciro Priore
Mario Rea
Francesca Reale
Giuliana Rebecchi
Debora Regio
Rocco Ripoli
Federico Ruberto
Ivano Ruocco
Faisal Saleh
Sara Gina Salino
Monica Sandulli
Enrica Santaniello
Milena Savoia
Elisa Scaglione
Paolo Scarpati
Simona Schettini
Mario Settimio
Michele Silvers
Giuseppe Sorrentino
Marco Staiano
Marzia Stancati
Giovanna Tedeschi
Alessandro Telese
Giovanna Togo
Giorgio Tomasello
Alfredo Tuya
Michele Vassallo
Maria Rosaria Villani
Gianluca Vitale
Alessia Vitiello
Mino Vocaturo
Augusta Zanzillo
Malgorzata Zbroinska

ON PAGES 334 AND 335,
VINCENZO CORVINO AND GIOVANNI MULTARI ON THE CONSTRUCTION SITE OF THE SACRED TEMPIO DELLA SCORZIATA IN NAPLES (PHOTOGRAPH BY ANTONIO ACUNZO WINNER OF THE DESIGN SHOOTING NAPOLI 2024 AWARD).

GRAPHIC DESIGN AND LAYOUT
IRENE BACCHI
LEONARDO SONNOLI
- STUDIO SONNOLI –

TRANSLATIONS
LESLIE A. RAY
(FOR LANGUAGE CONSULTING CONGRESSI)
PIERRE-ALAIN CROSET (APPENDIX)

PROJECT REPORTS AND APPENDIX
CORVINO + MULTARI S.R.L.

FIRST EDITION MAY 2025

ISBN 979-12-5463-293-2
WWW.MARSILIOARTE.IT

REPRODUCTION AND PRINTING
GRAFICHE VENEZIANE S.C.R.L., VENEZIA

FOR
MARSILIO ARTE® S.R.L., VENEZIA

PHOTOGRAPHIC CREDITS
© ANTONIO ACUNZO, PP. 334-335
© PAOLO CAPPELLI & MAURIZIO CRISCUOLO - STUDIO F64, PP. 18 (ILL. 2 E 4), 28 (ILL. 12, 13 E 14), 32 (ILL. 21), 43, 44, 45, 47, 49, 50, 51, 59, 60-61, 62, 63, 87 (ILL. 26), 99, 105, 115, 117, 120 (ILL. 2), 123(ILL. 5, 6, 8), 125 (ILL. 9, 12), 132 (ILL. 20), 145, 147, 154-155, 176 (ILL. 9), 205, 207, 209, 214 (ILL. 2, 4) , 217(ILL. 6, 8), 219 (ILL. 9, 10), 231, 232, 234, 239, 240-241, 243, 244, 245, 247, 248-249, 256-257, 259, 260-261, 265
© MARCO CASCIELLO, PP. 93, 94, 96
©FEDERICO CEDRONE, PP. 108, 109
© MARIO FERRARA, PP. 32 (ILL. 19), 40 (ILL. 35, 36), 68 (ILL. 6 ON THE LEFT), 132 (ILL. 22, 23), 149, 151, 152, 153, 208, 224 (ILL. 18, 19, 20), 251, 252-253
© MARCO INTROINI, PP. 103, 276, 277, 278 (ILL. 28),276 (ILL. 19, 20, 21), 278, 280 (ILL. 26, 27), 299, 301, 302-303, 304, 305, 307
© LUCIANO ROMANO, PP. 87 (ILL. 28), 111, 112, 113, 171 (ILL. 2)
© KAI UWE SCHULTE, PP. 34 (ILL. 24, 25), 37 (ILL. 26, 27), 53, 54, 55, 56, 57

AVAILABLE THROUGH ARTBOOK | D.A.P. 75 BROAD STREET, SUITE 630
NEW YORK, NY 10004
WWW.ARTBOOK.COM